Forbidden Passages

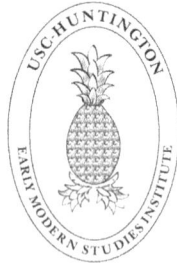

THE EARLY MODERN AMERICAS

Peter C. Mancall, Series Editor

Volumes in the series explore neglected
aspects of early modern history in the
western hemisphere. Interdisciplinary in
character, and with a special emphasis on the
Atlantic World from 1450 to 1850, the series
is published in partnership with the USC-
Huntington Early Modern Studies Institute.

Forbidden Passages

MUSLIMS AND MORISCOS IN COLONIAL
SPANISH AMERICA

Karoline P. Cook

PENN

UNIVERSITY OF PENNSYLVANIA PRESS   *Philadelphia*

ML the modern language initiative

THIS BOOK IS MADE POSSIBLE BY A COLLABORATIVE GRANT
FROM THE ANDREW W. MELLON FOUNDATION.

Published by
University of Pennsylvania Press
Philadelphia, Pennsylvania 19104-4112
www.upenn.edu/pennpress

Printed in the United States of America on
acid-free paper

10 9 8 7 6 5 4 3 2 1

A catalogue record for this book is available from the
Library of Congress.

ISBN 978-0-8122-4824-1

CONTENTS

Forbidden Passages

Map 1. The Iberian Peninsula, the North African coastline, and the Canary Islands

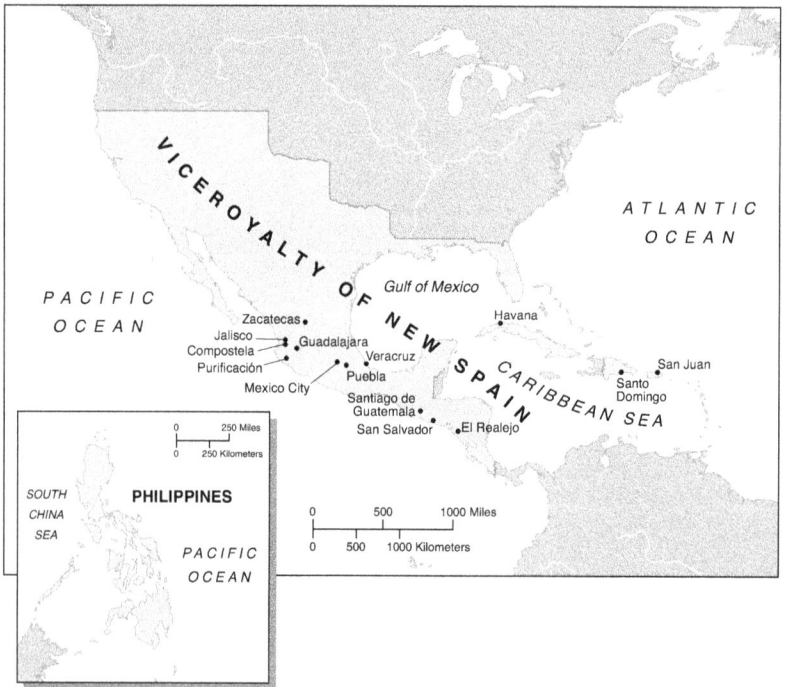

Map 2. The Viceroyalty of New Spain and the Caribbean

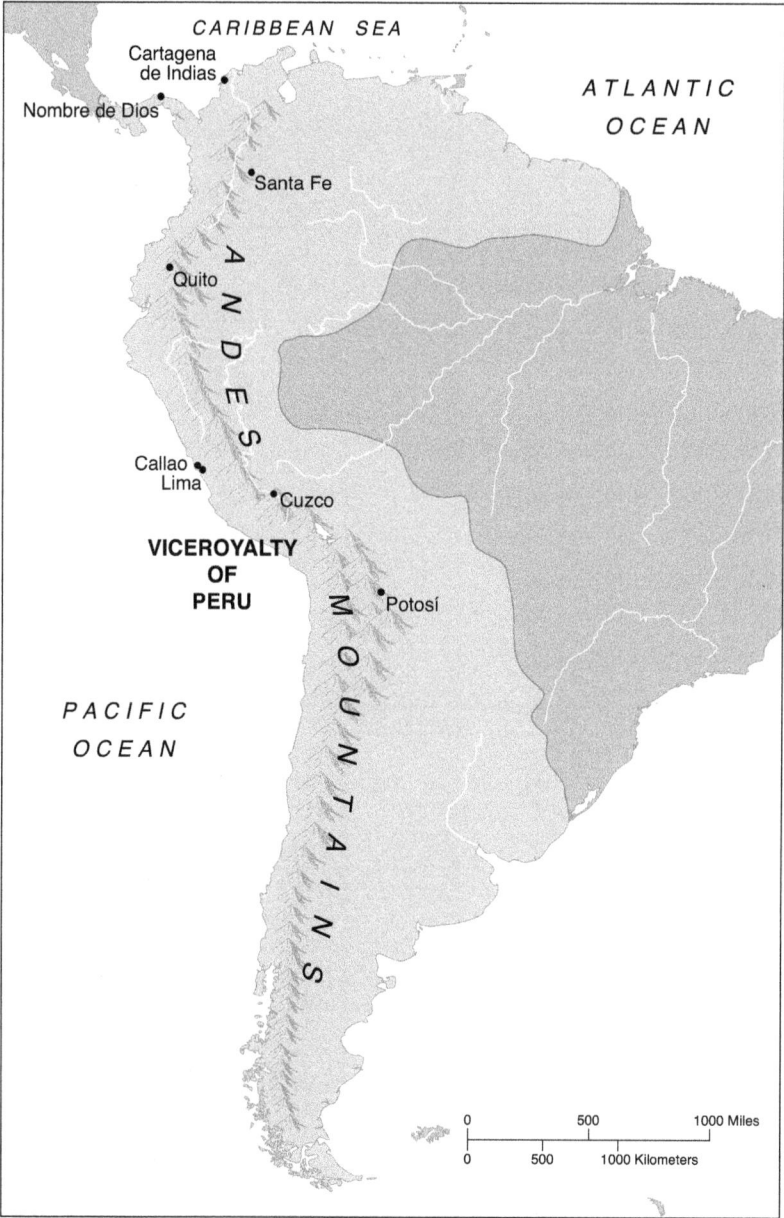

Map 3. The Viceroyalty of Peru

Introduction

During the sixteenth and seventeenth centuries, Spanish authorities restricted emigration to the Americas to long-standing Christians, individuals who could prove they descended from families that had been Catholic for at least three generations. Due to the Crown's preoccupation with maintaining religious orthodoxy across an expanding empire, frequent royal decrees prohibited Moriscos or Iberian Muslims, many of whom had been forcibly baptized at the beginning of the sixteenth century, from settling in Spanish America. But these laws, like so many others during the period, faced uneven enforcement. The extensive legislation prohibiting Morisco emigration has led many historians to assume that no or very few Moriscos settled in Spanish America. However, the rich parallel historiography concerning Spanish and Portuguese conversos in the New World, who were subject to the same legislation as Moriscos, suggests that individuals evaded the restrictions by a variety of means and settled in the forbidden territories. That the royal decrees were reissued on a regular basis also indicates that controls on emigration were not so tight in practice and that individuals discerned openings through which to slip unnoticed.

Moriscos, both free and enslaved, traveled clandestinely from Spain to Spanish America. Colonial sources reveal their mobility both geographically through the crossing of the Atlantic and socially as they forged new lives for themselves. While the numbers of Moriscos appearing in the archives are relatively low, representing only the denounced, their presence had a significant impact on colonial

Spanish American society and the everyday workings of empire. Indeed, even small numbers could induce powerful anxieties about defining nation.[1]

Understanding the attitudes projected onto Moriscos and North African Muslims by sixteenth-century Spaniards can reveal how Spaniards were coming to understand empire and their place within it. For some commentators, the presence of Muslims and Moriscos in Spanish America challenged prevailing notions that Spain was a Catholic empire whose goal and justification rested on the conversion of indigenous peoples to Christianity. Some Spanish officials were actively defining their role as members of a nation on the verge of acquiring preeminent status through conquests overseas and the incorporation of a new continent and its inhabitants into its sphere of influence. Spaniards brought with them definitions of conquest and colonization drawn from both their experiences with non-Christians on the Peninsula and in the Mediterranean, and their interpretations of Greek and Roman texts. The role that Muslims played in these understandings of "Spanish" nation and identity, and by extension empire, was crucial. In creating their global empire, Spanish authorities drafted and debated a series of policies that were informed by their interactions with peoples in various parts of the world and at home. They aimed to create a Catholic empire, and in doing so, they focused their attention on molding the religiosity and customary practices of peoples in the Americas.

Moriscos inspired extraordinary fears among many Spanish imperial authorities, who associated Muslims with rebellion and disloyalty. These officials conflated religious and political loyalty, and they viewed Moriscos as a fifth column that would ally with the Ottoman Turks or with North African corsairs. Peninsular attitudes toward Moriscos hardened by the late sixteenth century, at a moment when royal officials were also concerned with maintaining their empire and jurisdiction over Amerindians. Anxieties about native rebellions and incomplete conversions were increasingly embedded within these fears of Muslims and Moriscos. Royal authorities' restrictions on travel to the New World also tightened during this period, as they required prospective emigrants to prove their purity of blood and exemplary Christian conduct. Accordingly, depictions of Morisco and Muslim bodies became increasingly racialized, and eventually colonial officials composed treatises that projected these images onto indigenous bodies in the form of arguments advocating native groups' subjugation and enslavement.

During the sixteenth century, Muslims and Moriscos were being incorporated into colonial legal categories, and anyone suspected of being a Morisco was obliged to define themselves in relation to these categories.[2] Individuals labeled Moriscos could negotiate their status in court, by arguing in Spain that they were "good and faithful Christians," or in Spanish America, that their actions during the conquests gave them the same rights to rewards and status as any other Spaniard. In the case of Moriscos, religious identity contributed greatly to how individuals were perceived and incorporated into the emerging Spanish nation.

Much of the prevailing work on citizenship, identification, and belonging in various corners of the early modern world has focused on the eighteenth century, but a rich and growing body of scholarship addresses these questions for the earlier period.[3] My work intervenes to shed light on how these relationships operated in the lives of suspected Moriscos in sixteenth- and seventeenth-century Spanish America. For example, the ways that people described each others' public behavior and appearance, and by extension a group's religious and customary practices, had legal implications. Descriptions of individuals and of peoples informed legal identities such as Spaniard, Indian, African, the mixed-race castas, new or old Christian, noble or commoner, slave or free person. These public identities could be appropriated, manipulated, or redefined through litigation or self-presentation to establish oneself through "public and notorious" behavior to which witnesses could testify.

Printed and manuscript works such as titles of nobility, accounts of services to the Crown (*probanza de méritos y servicios*), and histories of conquest also rendered an individual's status public in a variety of legal settings. A copy of an individual's *méritos y servicios* could have many afterlives, circulating from the viceroyalties of New Spain or Peru to Spain and back again, before being transmitted to heirs who could request recognition for their ancestors' deeds during competing claims for lands or encomiendas. A conviction by an inquisitorial tribunal could similarly impact future generations through the hanging of *sanbenitos* in churches and the circulation of pamphlets naming individuals penitenced or executed in autos–da–fé. Witnesses who testified in each case, whether an individual wanted a license to emigrate, freedom from slavery, or to enslave others through claims to just warfare, or increase in status, dredged up rumors and gossip about families that carried weight in the courtroom. In this context, ideas about Muslims and Moriscos played a critical role in defining colonial relationships. Some Spanish authorities increasingly associated Moriscos with racialized qualities and invoked anxieties about converted Muslims and their descendants to justify both imperial policies and the outcome of local court cases. By studying the often-overlooked references to Muslims and Moriscos in colonial documents, we can better understand how sixteenth- and early seventeenth-century inhabitants of Spanish America conceived of their relationships to each other and of their own location within the empire.

The black North African slave Estevanico who accompanied Álvar Núñez Cabeza de Vaca on his journey across the American Southwest is one of the better-known converts from Islam. Like many Moriscos in Spanish America, traces of his presence survive in few sources. Unlike the three other survivors of the Pánfilo de Narváez expedition, Estevanico did not produce an account (probanza de méritos y servicios) describing his sufferings and heroic deeds during the expedition. Instead, he is only glimpsed in the writings of Cabeza de Vaca, Viceroy Antonio de Mendoza, and Friar Marcos de Niza, whom he later accompanied on an ill-fated expedition to the Zuni. Reputed to have been from Azemmour in the Kingdom of Morocco, and the slave of Andrés Dorantes, also a survivor of the Narváez expedition, Estevanico acted as scout and intermediary during Cabeza de Vaca's journey.[4] He was not the first Arabic speaker to be sought out to accompany an expedition in Spanish America. In fact, some officials requested Moriscos for their perceived skills as interpreters or artisans. Yet from the earliest voyages to the New World, the Spanish Crown issued decrees that restricted the overseas presence of new Christians of Muslim and Jewish descent. Throughout the sixteenth century, additional royal decrees issued by subsequent Spanish monarchs reinforced and expanded these initial measures.

Perhaps the most we know about Estevanico concerns his death at the hands of the Zuni. The surviving Spanish accounts describe him in contrasting ways, from fellow Christian and "persona de razón" to, in Francisco Vázquez de Coronado's words, the object of indigenous rage who assaulted local women and behaved like a "bad man, and not like the Christians who never kill women."[5] Were his associations as an *alárabe*, the term Cabeza de Vaca used to describe him in his *Relación*, enough to cause him to be cast as such a violent figure? Suspicions that someone was a Morisco carried with them a series of associations that surface in the denunciations housed in the inquisitorial archives. Similarly contradictory images appear in trials from the royal courts (*audiencias*) across Spanish America, as in the case of Diego Romero, an *encomendero* in New Granada who was accused of being a runaway North African slave. As will be explored in later chapters, Romero defended himself successfully as one of the privileged first conquerors of the region whose services to the Crown entitled him to retain his encomienda. Depictions of Estevanico in the Spanish sources remain consistent with contemporary perceptions of Moriscos, revealing the local contests and rivalries as individuals negotiated their status in their new surroundings. While Estevanico could not speak for himself in the colonial records, other cases like Romero's step in to suggest some of the dynamics taking place.

Estevanico's case, and the language his contemporaries used to describe him, raise the question of what model we can apply to studying Moriscos in the early modern Spanish world. The meaning of the term "Morisco" was slippery and varied depending on who was using it. It would therefore be problematic to accept the narrowest definition of Morisco, as a Muslim convert to Catholicism.[6] I move away from trying to determine who was or was not a Morisco, thereby mirroring Spanish authorities' assumptions about Moriscos, by shifting the focus to practices and attitudes that early modern Spaniards associated with Moriscos.[7] Expanding the term Morisco to include its usage in Spanish as an adjective, "Muslim-like," can also broaden and pose questions about a range of cases in which the accused may or may not have resembled what we traditionally think of as Morisco. Defining Morisco as Muslim-like would have also resonated with sixteenth- and seventeenth-century Spanish audiences. Accusations ranged from religious practices to language, dress, occupation, and racially inflected physical descriptions.[8]

I use the term Morisco in its broadest sense, in a way that would have been intelligible to Spaniards during the early modern period. The word "Morisco" had appeared in Castilian beginning in the medieval period as an adjective to refer to all things "Moorish" in material culture. By the first decade of the sixteenth century, after the first Alpujarras rebellion when Granadan Muslims rose up against violations of the surrender treaties negotiated after the 1492 conquest of that city, many were forced to choose between exile and baptism. "Morisco" began to be applied to a few of these converts from Islam, although the label "newly converted from a Muslim" (*nuevamente convertido de moro*) was more common. Nonetheless, by the mid-sixteenth century, the term Morisco gained greater currency and was being conceived of broadly as a quasi-legal category, to define converts to Catholicism from Islam. In practice, Morisco described a range of people. Some descended from voluntary converts in medieval Iberia who had gained privileges under Christian rule from their new status, including exemption from certain taxes. During the sixteenth century many of these Castilian Moriscos petitioned the Crown to be considered old Christians, having converted before the forced baptisms at the turn of the sixteenth century.[9] Others attempted to continue to practice their versions of Islam in secret, as was the case with many of the Granadan and Valencian Moriscos who were swept up in the waters of mass baptism. This was a difficult proposition, as the Granadan and Valencian Moriscos were increasingly subject to restrictions on not only their religiosity but also their cultural and regional practices. North African baptized slaves, known as *berberiscos*, were also sometimes referred to as Moriscos in contemporary documents. Prior to baptism, they were also sometimes called alárabes, as occurred with Estevanico. The derogative term "moro" (Moor) that was applied to Muslims throughout the early modern Spanish world denoted a category separate from that of Moriscos and also had legal implications.[10] For sixteenth-century Spaniards, Muslims were not subject to the same rights and privileges as Christians, and the Moriscos who rose up in protest during in the second Alpujarras rebellion in 1569–72 were labeled moros and apostates, thereby subjecting them to enslavement, something that was not permissible for Christians. In the Philippines, moro referred to members of the Muslim population of the islands who were also subject to enslavement, unlike many other indigenous groups under Spanish rule.

As a legal category, defined according to religious terms and varying geographically, Morisco could invoke some protections despite its marginal connotations. For example, Moriscos could also claim status as baptized Christians who were not subject to enslavement and who were legitimate members of the body politic. During the period leading up to the expulsion, some Castilian Morisco communities, supported by their parish priests, defended themselves as good Christians and loyal subjects against those making arguments against them. In contrast, proponents of the expulsion focused on exclusionary and protoracist imagery, defining Moriscos as Muslims and apostates who were excluded from the emerging Spanish nation. How Moriscos and old Christians understood this label and applied it to themselves and to others therefore varied greatly.

By examining Morisco as a legal category, I am concerned with the meaning that the debates over the status of Moriscos in Spain held for contemporaries and their transformation and repercussions in communities across the Atlantic. My focus is on how individuals labeled Moriscos negotiated their public reputations, both as they faced secular and religious authorities' attempts to categorize them and in daily interactions in their communities. Spanish jurists and theologians, and people on the streets, became increasingly invested in defining and describing customs and behavior, in ways that had legal implications. Descriptions of a range of peoples, from Muslims and Moriscos to Amerindians, were invoked in the realm of imperial policy at the Spanish court and universities, in the courtroom, and in published works that connected customs to groups of peoples, making arguments about their status. I am interested in how the category of Morisco was conceived of and invoked in a New World context. What did it mean to be a Morisco and to be deemed a Morisco in the Americas? How did images of and ideas about Moriscos and Muslims circulate overseas? How did they enter into daily interactions "on the ground" as Spaniards, Africans, and indigenous peoples negotiated the spatial and ethnic boundaries of a new colonial society? How did individuals conceive of and define community in the early modern Spanish world, and how were such conceptions set in motion to include and exclude people? Accusations of Morisco descent were leveled in disputes over offices and encomiendas. The legal makeup of the category Morisco, as construed by religious and cultural practice that was constituted publicly, pointed to who could enjoy certain rights or be denied others.

In the pages that follow, I trace how legislation and attitudes concerning Moriscos in Spain crossed the Atlantic, assuming new forms and meanings in Spanish America. Debates over the legal status of Moriscos in Spain that ranged from restrictions on their religious practices, to whether or not they could be enslaved, influenced Spanish policies and attitudes toward indigenous peoples. The label "Morisco" held public meaning, constituting evidence that could be brought into court and reflected the "public and notorious" nature of an individual's gestures, speech, and performance in charged settings such as during Mass. Contemporaries tied Catholic religiosity to trustworthiness in business and personal relationships and loyalty to the Crown.

Few historians have studied the ramifications of Morisco emigration to Spanish America, and to date no scholars have delved into the wealth of archival documentation on Moriscos in the Americas to produce a monograph on the subject.[11] In contrast, a rich parallel historiography on the conversos, Iberian converts from Judaism and their descendants, has surveyed their religious practices, social relationships, and transatlantic commercial networks. Historians working on this subject have examined how individuals continued to practice their faith in the face of increasing persecution and have focused on periods of intense inquisitorial repression during the union of the Spanish and Portuguese Crowns. Works on the conversos suggest how migration to the Americas brought a number of advantages to those wishing to escape increasing inquisitorial surveillance in Spain. The benefits of remaining within a familiar Iberian culture may also have attracted free Moriscos to the Americas. Moriscos and conversos did emigrate to Ottoman lands following their expulsion from the Peninsula, but they were not always welcomed by the societies where they settled.[12]

Before the 1570s, conversos who wished to live as Catholics, or to continue practicing their faith without the constant pressure of the Inquisition, could do so in territories where the tribunals in Peru and Mexico were not yet officially established.[13] Ecclesiastical authorities' complaints about the difficulties of regulating religiosity on the frontiers of the expanding Spanish Empire suggest that areas far from Lima and Mexico City provided greatest respite from inquisitorial control. An obsession with purity of blood arising from the statutes of *limpieza de sangre* and stemming from competition over offices between old and new Christians in Spain also intensified in Spanish America with the establishment of inquisitorial tribunals.[14]

The creation of empire and patterns of settlement produced an interconnected world as individuals and ideas crossed the Atlantic. Morisco emigrants, as both individuals who struggled to join a community that was increasingly restricting their activities, and as fictive entities who fueled authorities' fears and sparked denunciations, shed light on the negotiated nature of empire in the Spanish world. Yet there was no single pattern that emerged in the Americas, and the range of experiences under consideration requires close analysis of a series of case studies that reveal how Moriscos negotiated their status,

religious practices, and relationships. Through a thorough examination of colonial legislation, inquisitorial records, and court cases it
becomes possible to reconstruct individual actions and explain how
they illuminate broader imperial relationships. Such cases shed light
on issues of religious identity, honor, and local power struggles,
including the role that images of Muslims played in Spanish ideologies of conquest and in the uneven consolidations of colonial rule.
Furthermore, the presence of Moriscos in Spanish America, as well
as the circulation of knowledge about them, complicates notions of
what it meant to be a Spaniard and part of an early modern Spanish
world. Morisco presence requires us to rethink the colonial category
of Spaniard (*español*) by troubling its implication of an "old Christian" who possessed purity of blood and formed part of a unified
Catholic society. Moriscos and conversos formed part of the Republic of Spaniards, despite attempts to racialize these categories and
exclude them from membership in the emerging nation and empire.
Moriscos also appear in colonial discourses, interacting with peoples
of indigenous and African descent, pointing to more complex ways of
understanding how people negotiated status and defined belonging to
a community. The story begins in fifteenth-century Iberia, in changing relationships among Christians, Muslims, and Jews, and in the
first Spanish and Portuguese voyages to conquer the Atlantic islands
and find trading routes that put them in contact with new peoples.

CHAPTER I

Who Were the Moriscos?

Introducing a Transatlantic Story

María Ruiz was faced with a difficult decision. Born in Spain, in the town of Albolote near Granada, Ruiz found herself in Mexico City fifty years later, married to an old Christian wine merchant and pondering whether she wanted to live and die as a Muslim or as a Christian. In 1594 she denounced herself to Mexican inquisitors for having had thoughts about continuing to practice Islam when she first moved to Mexico City ten years previously.[1] Although she had attempted initially to continue to recite the prayers she was taught as a child in Granada, Ruiz now expressed the wish to be reconciled with the Catholic faith and reincorporated into the church, in order to live out the rest of her life as a good Catholic. Whatever the crisis of faith that she faced, she described her attempts in New Spain to reconstruct the prayers and practices she first observed as a child in Albolote. Her story spans the Atlantic, suggesting how individuals struggled with their beliefs and adherence to a religious community in a world that was rapidly changing. What events were occurring in Spain during her lifetime that prompted her and countless individuals to have to choose which faith they considered to be the "true" one in which they might attain salvation?[2]

Individual struggles differed from officials' concerns. For example, in Spain, a couple was denounced to the Toledo Inquisition for secretly practicing Islam following a gathering at their home in which they invited their friends to dance *zambras* and eat dishes piled high with couscous. On the other side of the Atlantic, in New Spain, a man was charged with being a relapsed Muslim because a neighbor claimed to have overheard him invoking Muhammad. Why did sixteenth-century Spanish authorities care about the presence of Muslims in their communities? What did early modern Spaniards imagine Muslims to be like, and what practices did they associate with Islam? Many of the accused were baptized Catholics, and some had been Christians for more than a generation. So how did the purported "stain" on their character and lineage continue to persist in the minds of accusers?

THE MEDIEVAL BACKGROUND IN IBERIA: *MUDÉJARES*, RECONQUISTA IDEOLOGY

The conquest of the Muslim Kingdom of Granada and the expulsion of the Jews in 1492 by Ferdinand and Isabel foreshadowed the end of what many historians argue had been a lengthy period of coexistence among Muslims, Christians, and Jews on the Iberian Peninsula. The so-called Reconquista, or Iberian Christian crusading effort to conquer and colonize Muslim territories, spanned the preceding four centuries. Ongoing struggles between armies distinguishing themselves along religious lines—Christian and Muslim—ensued. These struggles have shaped how historians have understood the history of this period that fluctuated between violence and coexistence. Following the Arab conquests in 711, the Iberian Peninsula, known as al-Andalus, became an important commercial and cultural node of the Islamic world. The Caliphate of Córdoba flourished from 929 to 1031 until internal factions began to undermine its cohesiveness. During the Caliphate, al-Andalus was incorporated into commercial networks that extended from the Mediterranean to the Indian Ocean. On the northern parts of the Peninsula, Christian forces began to unify and push south to conquer territories under Muslim control. With the fall of the Andalusi city of Toledo to Christian forces in 1085, the small Muslim kingdoms called *taifas* that had emerged with the fall of the Caliphate turned to the Almoravid dynasty, based in Marrakesh. The Almoravids were soon succeeded by the Almohads, and by the late thirteenth century they too were driven from the Peninsula by Christian forces.[3] Granada remained the last Muslim stronghold from this period onward.

Initial surrender treaties provided a contractual agreement between Christian conquerors and Muslim communities that was borrowed from the Islamic principle of the *dhimma*, the status conferred on protected religious minorities. *Dhimma* status enabled Iberian Muslims in Christian cities to maintain their religious institutions and administrative infrastructure, including an Islamic court system.[4] Conquered peoples thereby became tributaries in exchange for religious and administrative autonomy. As time passed, Muslims in thirteenth-century Catalonia and Aragon began to participate in the emerging Christian Iberian institutions and were slowly transformed into a *mudéjar* society.[5] Incompatibility between Muslim and Christian social structures such as those governing taxation forced subject Muslim populations to alter their practices somewhat and adopt Christian ones. Social changes came about not through instant Christian domination, but rather by "a bundle of changes in the administrative, judicial, fiscal, economic, linguistic, social, and cultural spheres."[6] Muslim-Christian responses to each other varied regionally, however, due to differences in the demographic and economic importance of Muslim communities. While the Muslims of the Ebro Valley in Aragon tolerated Christian rule, in Valencia, Christian conquerors faced a longer period of resistance.[7]

The uneven pace of Christian conquests and regional differences produced geographic variations within the mudéjar societies that developed throughout the fifteenth century and remained visible in the Morisco populations of the sixteenth century. This geographic diversity among mudéjar and eventual Morisco populations is important to keep in mind, as it would later have an impact on the claims Moriscos made as they negotiated their status during the period of forced expulsions. It also cautions against settling on a term like Morisco that homogenizes the experiences of individuals who fell into this category. Castile experienced some of the earliest conquests and retained some densely settled enclaves of mudéjares, although the region was predominantly Christian. Aragonese conquests had faced less violent conflict than those of Valencia a century later. Mudéjar religious and scholarly elites, or *faqihs* active in Christian-controlled lands, maintained contact with jurists in dar al-Islam in order to answer pressing questions that mudéjares faced under Christian rule. The activities of the faqihs can also be traced to the varying histories of the Iberian regions.[8]

By the end of the fifteenth century, growing tensions on the Peninsula prompted the dissolution of many of these agreements, leaving Muslim minorities with fewer political recourses in an increasingly oppressive society. The marriage of Ferdinand of Aragon and Isabel of Castile united the two Crowns. While administratively separate for generations, the union of Castile and Aragon pointed to a broader move toward national and religious unity, as would become apparent in the court chronicles.[9] They also provided growing stability that allowed the Catholic monarchs to push overseas in their competition with the Portuguese over trade routes to Asia. While these developments were neither neat nor linear, they pointed to a changing atmosphere as Iberians began to wrestle with questions of nation and identity, linked to territorial changes at home and overseas. As Spain began to establish its empire, these anxieties over nation and identity came to the forefront, in tension with regional identities within Spain and the identities of religious and ethnic minorities across the empire, from the Iberian Peninsula, to lands in the Mediterranean and northern Europe, to the Americas, to the Philippines.

In late 1491 the Catholic monarchs presented a surrender treaty to the Muslim population of Granada that granted them a number of freedoms. In exchange for the city of Granada and the Alhambra fortress, the treaty granted Granadan Muslims the right to continue to practice Islam without persecution. It stipulated that the monarchs, "and their successors, in perpetuity, allow . . . [everyone] to live according to their law, and not consent that anyone remove their mosques or their towers or their muezzins . . . nor disturb their ways and customs."[10] It provided for Granadan Muslims to maintain their courts, to be judged "by the Shari'a law that they are accustomed to following, with the opinions of their *qadis* and judges."[11] The capitulations permitted Granadan Muslims to bear arms, emigrate freely to North Africa if they desired, without danger of having their possessions confiscated by local authorities, and not be forced to pay the Crown "any tribute other than that which they were accustomed to give the Muslim kings."[12] Furthermore, prior converts from Christianity to Islam, especially women who married Muslim men (*renegadas*) and their children, could not be harassed or forced to convert back to Christianity.[13] The terms of the capitulations were soon violated.

MAKING MORISCOS

The Kingdom of Granada changed greatly in the half century preceding María Ruiz's birth. Following the conquest of Granada in 1492 by the Catholic monarchs, the local Muslim population faced increasing pressure to convert to Christianity. Archbishop Hernando

de Talavera carried out a relatively peaceful campaign to attract converts from Islam that included concessions to the new converts such as
allowing local dances and music, zambras and *leilas*, to be performed
during Mass. In contrast, Cardinal Francisco Jiménez de Cisneros's
aggressive program to Christianize Granada, which included mass
baptisms and the persecution of Christian converts to Islam, created
resentment among the Muslim population.[14] These violations of the
capitulation treaty following the fall of Granada, combined with prohibitions that ranged from carrying arms to buying land, prompted
the Granadan Muslim population to rebel in 1499. Between 1500
and 1502, Spanish authorities responded to this increasing dissent
by ordering that the mudéjares be baptized en masse. A royal decree
issued in 1502 after royal forces had suppressed this first Alpujarras
uprising, gave Granadan Muslims the choice between baptism and
expulsion.[15] The resulting mass baptisms restructured already uneasy
social relationships on the Peninsula by creating new categories by
which to define and control a population that in many cases was only
nominally Christian. The first Alpujarras uprising also had repercussions across the Iberian Peninsula and prompted mass conversions
in other regions. Due to their newly acquired legal status as Christians, this population, now known officially as Moriscos, fell under
the jurisdiction of Spanish ecclesiastical authorities and institutions
such as the Inquisition.[16]

Because their conversions had been coerced, many Catholic authorities and old Christians became suspicious that the Granadan Moriscos
were only nominally Christian. While members of the elite were more
integrated into old Christian society and were Catholic, some Moriscos continued to practice Islam in the privacy of their homes.[17] Religious and cultural practices of the Morisco population varied greatly,
not only according to social status but also with respect to geographic
location. In Aragon, Valencia, and Granada, many Moriscos continued to practice Islam. Their proximity to Muslims in the Mediterranean and the continued presence of Muslim religious leaders—faqihs
or *alfaquíes* as they were known in the Spanish documents—suggests
that they were able to maintain some of their practices.[18] By contrast,
in Castile, many Moriscos had converted to Christianity several generations previously, and some even petitioned to have their status as
old Christians legally recognized by the courts.[19]

During the first half of the sixteenth century, a number of laws were
passed that placed restrictions on Morisco dress, speech, mobility, and

a range of practices perceived as Islamic. By 1513, this growing "corpus of prohibitions" had cast suspicion on their public baths, butcheries, births, weddings and funerals, and on texts written in Arabic.[20] Maintaining these practices became an offense that could render individuals liable for inquisitorial prosecution. Inquisitors reprimanded Moriscos for dancing and singing zambras, observing Muslim dietary practices and fasts, reciting prayers, and speaking the Arabic language. While many Spanish officials and clergy recognized that the new converts' relationship with Catholicism was tenuous, they nevertheless developed a "politics of acculturation" whose goal was to completely assimilate the Morisco population within the next half century.[21] The forced conversions therefore raised a number of unsettling issues for contemporaries, deepening suspicions about the Moriscos' faithfulness, in both the term's religious and political connotations.

The conversion campaigns undertaken by religious authorities stressed the persistence of Islam in Spain. The documents they crafted made Morisco practices appear uniform, as a formulaic set of examples of "Islamismo" that they hoped to eradicate. Among these, ecclesiastical authorities stressed praying the *zala* five times a day, performing the *guadoc* or ritual ablutions, observing Fridays, and fasting during Ramadan.[22] Although many Moriscos did not speak Arabic outside of Granada and parts of Aragon, its use also became subject to persecution.[23] Inquisitors ordered that books and manuscripts in Arabic and *aljamiado* be destroyed, and those discovered hidden in homes were confiscated and burned periodically. They stigmatized the *fadas*, or naming ceremonies for Morisco children to welcome them into the community, concerned that they were purposefully washing away the baptismal oil.[24] Ecclesiastical authorities also prohibited the use of Muslim names like Hamete, Ali, Zahara, or Aixa.[25]

Religious practice often became confused with what some contemporaries argued was actually customary practice. In 1526 Charles V convened in Granada a panel of theologians, jurists, and prelates to debate policies toward the Granadan Moriscos. Doctor Lorenzo Galíndez de Carvajal's *Parecer* on this issue was fundamental and discussed both beliefs and practices. He condemned anything that varied from the old Christian ways of doing things.[26] Moriscas were forbidden to wear veils (*almalafas*), to use henna, and to carry amulets in the shape of hands, crescents, or stars. Moriscos were prohibited from becoming butchers because it was feared they would slaughter animals in the manner permitted in Islam.[27] The Inquisition of Granada was established later that year, following Galíndez de Carvajal's recommendation.[28] However, these initial measures from 1526 failed to gain much ground following negotiations between the Crown and the Moriscos, with the support of Iñigo López de Mendoza, Count of Tendilla.

The Synod of Guadix (1554) compiled a number of both religious and customary practices of the Granadan Moriscos, presenting them as signs of continued adherence to Islam. Not only abstaining from pork but also eating couscous (*alcuzcuz*) came to be considered by ecclesiastical authorities a sign of Islamismo, and the Synod recommended that ecclesiastical authorities work to eradicate these practices.[29] Finally, in 1566, the Royal Council in Madrid drafted a series of laws that were met with outrage when proclaimed publicly in Granada on 1 January 1567. These new laws proscribed a number of Morisco practices and increased the severity of the penalties for anyone who failed to obey them to imprisonment and fines.[30] In addition to many of the above measures, they decreed that the Granadan Moriscos should learn and speak only Castilian within a period of three years, banned all books in Arabic, and prohibited Moriscos from owning slaves.[31] Attempting a new round of negotiation, Francisco Núñez Muley, a member of the Granadan Morisco elite, composed a *Memorial* that he presented to the Royal Audiencia and Chancery of his city. Núñez Muley argued that wearing Morisco dress, dancing zambras, going to public baths, and conversing in Arabic was not incompatible with Catholicism. Concerning Morisco dress that included the veil for women, Núñez Muley pointed out that "it can be said that it is clothing of the kingdom and province, like in all the kingdoms of Castile."[32]

These increasing restrictions prompted the Morisco population to respond in various ways. Many among those who remained faithful to Islam developed a confrontational attitude toward Christianity, producing a peninsular polemical literature in aljamiado, or Spanish written using the Arabic script. Its contours were shaped in response to the arguments put forth most likely by missionaries and parish priests, if not also by the old Christians in their midst. Other misunderstandings were simply the result of confusion over doctrine. Some missionaries sought to bridge the gap in understanding by presenting difficult concepts such as the Trinity in the sign of the cross. For example, in his catechism for the Valencian Moriscos (1566), Martín Pérez de Ayala instructed them to recite, "In the name of the Father, and of the Son, and of the Holy Spirit, one God, Amen."[33] Missionaries active among the Moriscos hoped to reduce confusion about the Trinity by asserting the unity of God, so that the three elements of the Trinity could not be confused with three deities.

SIGNS OF ISLAMISMO: HOW INQUISITORS DEFINED ISLAM

When taken together, the extensively detailed trial records compiled during inquisitorial proceedings for Islamismo depicted Moriscos as unrepentant Muslims, thereby producing an image that Spanish jurists and theologians favoring expulsion seized upon. Much of the existing documentation concerning Moriscos, both in Spain and in Spanish America, comes from inquisitorial trials and correspondence. The terminology used to refer to Islam, as the "sect of Muhammad," the "law of the Moors," or the "law of Muhammad," reflects the biases of ecclesiastical officials regarding Islam and presents a point of view that was also widespread.[34] These records supplied images of Moriscos that individuals also drew upon when crafting accusations during local disputes. The public reading of edicts of faith listed a series of characteristics that came to essentialize Morisco-ness for an early modern Iberian audience. Yet what can we say about the religiosity of individual Moriscos and the importance Islam, Catholicism, or some combination of the two might have held in their daily lives? This question cannot be entirely dismissed, as lived religiosity was important in the lives of people across the early modern world. Preoccupation with salvation, and living and dying according to the precepts of the "true" faith, appear not only in the inquisitorial records but in a number of other sources. Individual struggles with faith surfaced during inquisitorial interrogations, often in tension with inquisitorial constructions of Moriscos.

When approaching her confessor in Mexico City with her wish to live and die as a good Catholic, María Ruiz may have known from her experiences in Granada that she might end up before inquisitors. Founded in Spain in 1478 to prosecute heresy among converts from Judaism, the Inquisition's jurisdiction expanded to include the Moriscos, in addition to anyone accused of blasphemy, heresy, bigamy, and witchcraft, among a series of other "offenses" against the sacraments.[35] The Granadan tribunal would have been active during Ruiz's childhood, and she may have had neighbors whose lives were affected by its reach. While sworn to secrecy about their experiences in the inquisitorial prisons, and during interrogations, confessants very likely shared strategies for dealing with inquisitors after their release.

In delineating its jurisdiction, the Inquisition removed from priests the power to absolve sins of heresy, requiring them to direct potential heretics to one of the tribunals. Only the Inquisition had the power to absolve sins of heresy, utilizing preoccupations with salvation to its advantage. Being caught in an ambivalent position between Islam and Catholicism, and the dilemma of choosing the "true" law that would lead to salvation, was not an infrequent anxiety voiced by converts from Islam.[36] The Inquisition exploited Morisco preoccupations with salvation by claiming to bestow absolution from sin and salvation by hearing confessions.

The punishments that the Inquisition inflicted on Moriscos for quotidian lapses in Catholic practice reveal the extent of its deployment of the image of the confessional, through its vocabulary of salvation. Spared the harsher penalties incurred by those convicted of outright political dissidence, most Moriscos received the more common sentences of "absolution" and "reconciliation." These lesser sentences often involved what inquisitors referred to as "spiritual penance" that included reciting certain prayers and receiving religious instruction. Instruction in Catholicism became a way for inquisitors to regulate and impose a self-representation on confessants, which they might not necessarily have shared.

By soliciting confessions, inquisitors were simultaneously involved in producing a body of knowledge about Muslim and Morisco practices, accounts of which they circulated to other tribunals, including those in Spanish America once they were founded in Lima (1570), Mexico City (1571), and Cartagena de Indias (1610). The questions that the tribunals asked of Moriscos reflect similar, albeit subtler, aspects of the Inquisition's aims to procure a large body of information about them. Inquisitorial inquiries in these trials extended surveillance into the home. Through inquisitors' questions, the internal space of the home became politicized as a site for potentially subversive activity, where Morisco women could teach their children about Islam and encourage their family to uphold dietary practices and observe holidays.[37]

To obtain declarations of these practices, inquisitors would demand that those testifying, "scour their memory and relieve their conscience by telling the entire truth of everything they might have done or said, or seen done or said to people, that is or might appear to be against our Holy Catholic Faith and evangelical law."[38] They would also imprison confessants and require them to return to the courtroom during the course of several days or months to continue testifying. In this way, inquisitors would be certain that they had extracted all the information that they could.

The questions inquisitors asked of suspected Moriscos paralleled their interpretation of the Five Pillars of Islam, the steps every devout Muslim was obligated to follow. The Five Pillars include the *shahada*, or profession of faith, the *salat*, or praying five times daily, *zakah*, or almsgiving, fasting during Ramadan, and making the hajj, or pilgrimage to Mecca.[39] In her study of African Muslims enslaved in the Americas, Sylviane A. Diouf demonstrates how they continued to practice their faith despite the challenges of enslavement. Diouf suggests that "despite being far outnumbered by Christians, polytheists, and animists, they preserved a distinctive lifestyle built on religious cohesiveness, cultural self-confidence, and discipline."[40] The Spanish inquisitorial records contain many references to the important prayers professing faith in Islam, as well as almsgiving and fasting. The hajj is the only Pillar that does not appear in the available inquisitorial documentation, and it was not a requirement for Muslims who were financially or otherwise unable to travel to Mecca. However, some evidence suggests that despite travel prohibitions, a few Moriscos managed to undertake the journey.[41]

When trying Moriscos, inquisitors had at their disposal a lengthy list of practices that they considered evidence of "Islamismo." This list of thirty-six points against Moriscos, compiled by the fifth Inquisitor General Alfonso Manrique, contains accusations concerning both their perceived religious beliefs and customary practices.[42] These points, echoed in the promulgations of Spanish synods and the writings of Spanish theologians depicting Moriscos and Islam, also appear in the early edicts of grace preached across Spanish American towns in the newly established inquisitorial tribunals. Several points on Manrique's list informed inquisitors' opinions on the case of Juan de Burgos, a Morisco who was tried before the Toledo tribunal after having held a party for his friends. According to Manrique, "With respect to the heretical mahometanizing Moriscos, let [Christians] be ordered to denounce the following acts and sayings: . . . If they have circumcised their sons and given them Muslim names or expressed a desire that others participate in their naming. . . . If they have sung Muslim songs and done zambras or dances, and *leilas* or songs using prohibited instruments."[43]

The trial against Juan de Burgos highlights the inquisitorial prosecution of a number of these practices. In 1538 Burgos, his wife Julia, and a number of their friends gathered together at his house for "the *zambra* where they were dancing and singing in Arabic, and there they all ate dinner together."[44] The Morisca slave Catalina's testimony reflects the course of events that night: "Around the time of the Christmas that just passed, there came to this city of Burgos Moriscos from Seville and they went to spend the night in the house of Julia. This witness, having been asleep in her bed, was called by Juan de Burgos. . . . [They] went to the house of the said Juan de Burgos . . . and there . . . [they] did the *zambra*, playing a cane like a flute, with *atabalejos*, and dancing barefoot and singing and speaking in Arabic."[45] Catalina added, "The two Moriscos called the said Julia Fatima and the said Julia called her husband Nazar . . . and this witness was called Fiasea by the said Julia and her husband, and that all these names were spoken there that night, and also they were spoken outside when they encountered each other, talking in Arabic."[46] These images of dancing zambras, conversing in Arabic, and maintaining Arabic names provide insights into the vitality of Morisco social networks. (See Figure 4.) Conflating religious and ethnic diversity with disloyalty and political dissent, Spanish authorities came to interpret social gatherings as underlying a larger subversive trend.

Peninsular officials feared that travel and movement would facilitate communication among Moriscos, allowing religious beliefs and practices to be reignited in communities across Spain, and eventually spread to Spanish America. The spaces created by these encounters could provide opportunities for individuals such as Julia and Juan de Burgos, Catalina, and their Morisco visitors to exchange ideas about religion and politics, and even engage in teaching Islam. Furthermore, slaves in an urban environment like Catalina were often mobile and participated actively in social networks. The policies that authorities put into place in Spain reflected their anxieties about the ability of Moriscos to continue to practice Islam in a variety of new settings. After the expulsion of the *alfaquíes* from Spain during the first waves of repression in the early sixteenth century, devout Morisco parents often took charge in teaching their children about Islam. Nonetheless, they faced many challenges to the cohesiveness of their families, especially following the second Alpujarras uprising when royal policies enabled the forced resettlement of Granadan Moriscos amidst old Christian communities across Spain. Many women and older

Figure 1. Morisco dance from Christoph Weiditz's *Trachtenbuch*.

children were enslaved during the rebellion, and children too young to be enslaved legally were sent to live with old Christian families until they reached the age of twenty, so that they could be reeducated.[47] This larger peninsular context would have an impact on the numbers and lives of the Morisco women who crossed the Atlantic as slaves.

Some Granadan Moriscos received instruction in Islam from their families before the second Alpujarras uprising. In 1570 Elena, an eighteen-year-old slave of the count of Chinchón captured during the uprising, testified before the Toledo inquisitorial tribunal that while living at home as a young girl she would pray daily, "until she left the law [Islam], and it was during five or six years that she was taught by her grandfather whose name was Benito, and her father." Elena further related that "her grandfather also taught her to read *algarravia*, and that she knows how to read a little bit."[48] Some of the enslaved Moriscas found themselves serving in noble households. While there is no evidence to suggest Elena ever left Spain, the fourth Count of Chinchón, Luis Jerónimo Fernández de Cabrera y Bobadilla, served as viceroy of Peru from 1628–38. His royal license to travel issued in 1628 includes the licenses and permissions for his household and servants to accompany him. Among the eighty persons allowed to set sail with the new viceroy to Peru appear the names of Joan Jerónimo and his wife Casilda, "free new Christians of the *berberisco* nation," and Ana and Antonio, two *berberisco* slaves, despite being among those prohibited to pass to the Indies.[49]

The Moriscas' testimonies also show how individuals continued to observe Islamic fasts and religious holidays in Spain, with varying degrees of commitment and participation. Elena, the slave of the count of Chinchón, declared that she "fasted during Ramadan and observed Fridays, dressing herself in a clean shirt."[50] She described the two times she had observed the holy month of Ramadan, saying that "each lasted an entire month of not eating during the entire day until the star came out at night, and that at midnight they got up . . . moistening their mouths with a little water, and then they would go to sleep."[51] Another Morisca slave, María de Andrada, also spoke of Ramadan when she informed Spanish inquisitors how her father had taught her to observe "the fasts of the Muslims . . . on the days which were customary for the Muslims, not eating during the entire day until the night when the first star appeared in the heavens. Later, at dawn, they would take a jar of water and wash themselves under their arms, and their hands and ears and feet, each of these things three times."[52]

In Mexico City, María Ruiz similarly recalled before inquisitors how, when she was a child in Albolote before the Alpujarras rebellion, her mother had taught her to fast during Ramadan. She participated in the fasts "two or three times, but she did not continue with them because, as such a young girl, she became hungry and ate. . . . Her mother carried out the said fasts with other women in the neighborhood . . . and they were cautious around her, and her mother told her not to talk about the fasts . . . because if she did they would be burned."[53] Other Morisco parents in Spain were similarly cautious, delaying their children's instruction in Islam until they were old enough to be discreet around old Christians and not rouse the suspicion of inquisitors.[54] The contrasting accounts of María Ruiz, Elena, and María de Andrada portray differing approaches and strategies taken by parents in the Alpujarras to raise their children in light of increasing inquisitorial scrutiny.

Spanish inquisitors also stigmatized certain dietary restrictions and practices, collecting numerous examples of their observance. Evidence of abstention from pork and meats not butchered in the manner licit in Islam and consuming foods such as couscous appear repeatedly in inquisitorial accusations against Moriscos in Spain. In this way, inquisitors conflated foods prepared in the halal manner with dishes like couscous that had no religious significance but that they associated with Muslims. Before the Toledo tribunal, María de Andrada also recalled that when she was living with her family prior to the Alpujarras rebellion, her father had told her, "She could not eat fowl or any other thing unless it was killed with the ceremony mandated by the law of Muhammad, for which [her father] took a knife, and she does not remember well to which part of the heavens he turned and said certain words, and cut the throats of the fowl, and she saw them butchered with this ceremony, and because she was a young girl, she does not remember the words which were said."[55] Knowledge of dietary practices was passed on clandestinely within families and communities, despite the now obligatory participation of Moriscos in Catholic feast days. Andrada described a conversation she had had with other Moriscas while attending Mass. During this encounter, which may have taken place in the back rows of the church, they lamented, "That it was their great misfortune to have come to this land where they were made to go to communion and [Andrada] said what a shame . . . and [the Moriscas] also said that the sacrament was nothing but a piece of bread. They also asked her if she ate bacon, and replying that she did not, they said that she was doing a good thing to not eat it because it was against the law of Muhammad and otherwise she would not be saved, and [they advised her] that she also not drink wine because it was against the same law, and she would not be saved. They said that they neither ate bacon nor drank wine for the same reason."[56] In the eyes of Spanish inquisitors, Moriscos who recited Islamic prayers, engaged in ritual bathing, and exchanged words in Arabic were committing subversive acts. In Toledo in 1530 a slave named Pedro testified against another slave, Isabel. Pedro accused Isabel of having spoken to him in the "Arabic language and this witness [Pedro] did not want to reply unless it was in the Castilian language, and because of this the said slave Isabel reprimanded this witness a great deal, asking him why he did not speak the Morisco language."[57] When summoned to testify and asked whether she had ever spoken in algarravia, Isabel responded that she had several times while reciting a prayer, invoking God. The testimonies of later Morisca slaves in Toledo during the 1570s, after the Alpujarras rebellion, continue to suggest the persistence of algarravia. Angela de Hernández, an eleven-year-old slave of the princess of Portugal, declared that she could speak "some algarravia," although her parents, as a precaution, had taught her Christian prayers and had taken her to church "with the other small children, and she does not know anything about the sect of the Muslims because they would not teach her."[58] Andrada presented another aspect of maintaining language through prayer. She confessed that her father "taught her to say certain words, putting her hands next to her ears, which were *es hedu alehilla la huete es hedu mohamat reculala* . . . and these same words she would say during the times in the morning when she would wash herself as she had said, and [the words] mean that God is our savior and Muhammad is very dear to Him."[59] The prayer that Andrada confessed to saying each morning was the shahada, the first Pillar of Islam. Sylviane Diouf argues that the shahada, which she transcribes as *La-ilaha ill'l-Lah Muhammadan rasul-ul-lah*, and translates as "there is not another God but God and Muhammad is His Prophet," was significant in its recitation by enslaved African Muslims in the Americas.[60] By praying the shahada in spite of a tightly controlled environment, Muslim slaves affirmed their faith daily, implicitly rejecting the conversion to Christianity many had been forced to accept after their enslavement.[61]

GROWING SUSPICION: THE SECOND ALPUJARRAS UPRISING AND ITS AFTERMATH

In 1568 a large Morisco community in the Sierra de Alpujarras in Granada responded violently to the expanding currents of repression and surveillance. During the course of these "wars of Granada," many Moriscos were captured and sold to various regions across Spain. Some enslaved Moriscos were also taken to Spanish America. Their individual displacement foreshadowed the expulsion and dispersal of Granada's Moriscos, which was decreed officially in 1571 after the Alpujarras rebellion was suppressed. Because men were more likely to be killed during rebellions, a majority of the Moriscos who were enslaved were women.[62] This second "Guerra de las Alpujarras" had a profound impact on both Moriscos and old Christians across the Iberian world.

The Alpujarras rebellion had lasting repercussions because it resulted in the first diaspora of the more orthodox Granadan Moriscos among the diverse Morisco communities in other regions of the Peninsula. Large numbers of displaced Granadan Moriscos, who were among the last forced converts in Spain, carried Islamic beliefs and practices with them to other towns and cities. The presence of small concentrations of individuals whose commitment to Catholicism was deemed less than secure created the propensity for the wider old Christian community to conflate both groups and label all Moriscos, regardless of geographic diversity, as potential Muslims and rebels. Rumors spread across various municipalities that their local Morisco populations could similarly rise up against old Christians and invite the Ottomans to invade Spain.

The accounts told by the Granadan Morisca slaves to Toledo inquisitors illuminate aspects of the Alpujarras uprising, its aftermath, and the enslavement they suffered. María Agueda stated, "Being in the place called Veneacir in the house of her parents, there came to the said place the Muslims who had risen up. . . . Afterwards they went to the Sierra with the others, where this confessant remained for about six or seven months until she was captured and taken to Córdoba to the house of a certain Captain Borja."[63] Agueda stated that she had always been a good Christian and had known nothing about Islam until the uprising. However, she claimed that Muslims in the Sierra soon taught her "things of the sect of Muhammad, telling her that the said sect was good and that in it they could serve God and be saved, and this confessant took these things to be true and believed what they told her. They showed her how to fast the fasts of the Muslims, not eating during the entire day until night, and they did the guadoc and the zala, washing their faces and entire bodies and raising and lowering their heads and hands, and prayed Muslim prayers."[64] Two other Morisca slaves also described the events that took place during the Alpujarras uprising, their testimonies emphasizing a strong Muslim presence in the province. In 1570, María, a twelve-year-old slave of the count of Chinchón, testified, "All the people whom she knew from her country were Muslims, and she knew this because they communicated with one another, and they are all in the Sierra. Others are captives, and she does not know where they are now."[65] Elena, the eighteen-year-old slave of the count of Chinchón, told inquisitors that before she was enslaved and instructed in Catholicism she practiced Islam "in her land with her parents and brothers and with the entire community, because she knew that they were all Muslims and that they communicated with one another and that the entire place rose up and climbed to the Sierra."[66]

The impact of the Alpujarras rebellion and subsequent enslavement of Granadan Moriscos was also felt across Spanish America. Some

Moriscos, especially women captured during this uprising were taken to the Americas to serve individuals with temporary travel licenses from the Casa de Contratación. Others became galley slaves and were transported to the Caribbean with the idea that they would remain on the ships and not disembark. Nonetheless, a few were able to gain their freedom. They carried with them memories of peninsular exchanges that paralleled those described in the Spanish inquisitorial sources.

DEBATES OVER EXPULSION

According to many accounts, relationships between new and old Christians deteriorated quickly on the Peninsula, between the second Alpujarras uprising and the expulsion of the Moriscos from Spain between 1609 and 1614. However, no consensus existed at the time among Spanish authorities concerning what policies to apply to the Morisco population.[67] While Philip III and his council made the ultimate decision to expel the Moriscos, it was by no means clear from the outset that expulsion would be the outcome of the deliberations over Morisco policies. There was no generalized or popular clamor to expel the Moriscos but rather a series of ill-conceived policy decisions pushed by a small number of vocal proponents at court.[68] Growing evidence suggests that not all communities felt threatened by their Morisco neighbors, who became integrated into local activities, and informally there may have been many exchanges between old and new Christians.[69] During the final decades of the sixteenth century, however, ecclesiastical and secular authorities debated measures that they could apply to the Moriscos. Connected to these debates over policy were heated discussions about who the Moriscos really were—faithful Christian subjects or disloyal crypto-Muslims and apostates.

Persistent rumors that the Moriscos would ally with foreign powers, whether Ottoman, French, or British, led some old Christians to regard them with suspicion.[70] Those in favor of expulsion were convinced the Valencian Moriscos posed a real threat to Spain, in light of war with France and growing tensions with the Ottoman Empire, and were likely to ally with foreign powers. Stephen Haliczer charts the problematic placement of the concept of loyalty in sixteenth-century Spanish ideology, demonstrating that it permeated accusations leveled against the Moriscos. By the beginning of the seventeenth century "religious conformity had become synonymous with political loyalty in the Catholic states of Europe. In this process, the Moriscos were the earliest but by no means the only victims."[71] Perceived by many authorities as being unassimilated, Moriscos were cast as subversives in official discourses about the Spanish nation. Increasing paranoia during the second half of the sixteenth century, fed by not entirely unsubstantiated rumors that Moriscos were involved in plots to join the Turks or the French as a "fifth column" to invade Spain, prompted even tighter controls. In Seville in 1580, rumors abounded that the large resettled Granadan Morisco population was on the verge of rebellion.[72] Officials obtained confessions through torture of the accused Moriscos that they were planning a revolt and moved swiftly to restrict the movement of the Moriscos. This situation increased the severity of the rumors, as many of Seville's inhabitants told stories about acts of violence committed by their Morisco neighbors.[73] While evidence exists that a few individuals were in early stages of plotting insurrection, the broader Morisco community that had nothing to do with this bore the brunt of the suspicions and reprisals.[74] Rumors of rebellion persisted in communities across Spain, and the Inquisition assumed the position of collecting information about Moriscos' activities, tailoring questions to varying degrees of perceived political threat. For example, the Zaragoza tribunal prepared a questionnaire "designed specifically to test the loyalty of the Moriscos and find out if they were preparing for revolt."[75]

Debates over whether the Moriscos could remain in Spain wrestled with questions concerning the legitimacy of their baptism, their lineage, their actions as Christians, and ultimately how these issues contributed to or detracted from their membership in the emerging Spanish nation. Valencian Archbishop Juan de Ribera's frustrated attempts to minister to the old Christian population in his diocese and improve the Catholic instruction of the Morisco population led him to become an ardent proponent of expulsion.[76] In 1602, Ribera addressed a petition to Philip III in which he cast the Moriscos as traitors. Invoking a number of racialized accusations, Ribera depicted the Moriscos as bandits, "avaricious" hoarders of gold, and unrepentant Muslims who were "wizened trees, full of knots of heresy."[77] Ribera's arguments pushed Philip III to move away from previous royal policies supporting the evangelization campaigns and to carry out the expulsion at a time when he was reorienting his foreign policy away from northern Europe and toward the Mediterranean.[78]

Catholic Apologists envisioned the expulsion as the culmination of centuries of Reconquest, and they crafted histories to fit this notion. They cast Philip III as "Emperor of the Last Days," drawing on strains of millennial prophecy that were circulating in Spain during the late sixteenth century, in order to formulate arguments justifying the excision of the Moriscos from the body politic.[79] In light of writers such as the Humanist Pedro de Valencia who emphasized the injustice of the expulsion and the harm that would come to the king's conscience in carrying out such a deed, Catholic Apologists worked hard to legitimize expulsion. In these histories, writers such as Jaime Bleda and Pedro Aznar Cardona presented Spain as the "foremost Christian nation" and Spaniards as a new Chosen People, a line of thinking that was also linked to discourses to justify conquest and Spain's title to the New World.[80]

The authors of treatises debating whether it was justified to expel the Moriscos applied racializing arguments to them. The treatises illustrate how Moriscos were perceived by jurists and theologians at the level of imperial policy in ways that had repercussions on the ground across the Spanish world. Writers on both sides invoked Divine Providence in assessing the Spanish Empire and used medical imagery to describe the Moriscos, albeit to very different ends.[81] A vehement apologist for the expulsion, Pedro Aznar Cardona wrote that many well-educated men esteem "a bitter purgative to expel bad humors, from which valued health follows, even while they loathe the bitterness of the medium."[82] He cast Christ as a "celestial doctor" who could cure the "pestilential Mohammedan sect" with the sacraments, which the Moriscos refused due to their obstinate nature.[83] Aznar Cardona proclaimed, "What cannot be cured by delicate unguents, oils, or softness, should be cured by a rigorous cauterization by fire."[84] As a result, Philip III issued an order that would "tear from their roots and extricate such fruitless weeds of bitter and mortal effects, unworthy of . . . occupying such a holy and fruitful land."[85] In contrast, Pedro de Valencia advocated in his treatise the "mixture" (*permixtion*) or intermarriage between Moriscos and old Christians in order to fully assimilate them. Writing to advise Philip III against expelling the Moriscos, Valencia proposed a series of measures to incorporate them into Spanish Christian society and thereby decrease their threat to the Spanish Empire. Valencia wrote that Spain should be very worried about Moriscos acting as spies for the Turks because they were enemies of Christians as a result of their "lineage and nation that has professed . . . genuine hatred from Ishmael . . . toward all the children of Sara."[86] Following the biblical narrative, contemporary jurists and theologians traced Morisco genealogies to Ishmael, Abraham's first son who was cast out of his father's house alongside his mother Hagar, Sarah's slave. In a twist on the standard account of Abraham's wife Sarah's jealousy, which reveals how writers could recast biblical narratives for their own purposes, Aznar Cardona claimed Ishmael's expulsion from his father's home was due to his idolatrous practices. This led Aznar Cardona to specifically list and label Ishmael's descendants, including Muhammad, as inherently "idolatrous."[87] In contrast, Valencia argued that Morisco assimilation was nevertheless possible if they were permitted entry into honorable public and ecclesiastical offices because they had lived in Spain for nine hundred years: "With respect to their natural complexion, and by consequence their wit, condition, and spirit, they are Spaniards like the rest."[88] If resettled in communities across Spain, adequately catechized, and married into old Christian families, the Moriscos would become Spaniards, and "their lineage would be lost with their name."[89] Otherwise, if Spanish families continued to be "stained by *razas*, they would never lose the label and name of Moriscos . . . There would be no more old Christians."[90] To Valencia, customs and education were more important than blood: "Thus, when you take away . . . infamy, we should not be afraid that Spanish blood is infected by mixture with that of the Muslims; many have had this since ancient times, and it does not harm them . . . The popular opinion to the contrary is ridiculous and very damaging."[91] However, many jurists failed to share Valencia's view.

In 1609 the Consejo de Estado moved to expel the Valencian Moriscos, summoning the Italian galleys to Mallorca and sending galleons to patrol the North African coastline to prevent resistance or attempts to aid the Moriscos.[92] The expulsion decree for the Valencian Moriscos, made public on 22 September 1609, presented their exile as a merciful alternative to the punishment of what was ruled to be the Moriscos' collective *lèse majesté* (*lesa Magestad diuina y humana*) due to their persistence as "heretical apostates."[93] This decree also provided exemptions for some Moriscos to remain in Spain. Those protected from expulsion included children under four years of age and their parents or guardians, children under six years of age if their father was an old Christian, and Moriscos who had been living "for a considerable amount of time" among old Christians, without returning to their aljamas, and who had obtained a license from their local prelate confirming that they were receiving the sacraments.[94]

The period of expulsion lasted approximately five years, from 1609–14, as Moriscos from communities across Spain were assembled at port cities and forced onto ships. Parents fought separation from their children, who were to be raised by old Christian families if they were under the age of seven.[95] Some Moriscos applied for exemption from exile on the basis of marriage to an old Christian, or having filed a petition for old Christian status.[96] The expulsion decrees were publicized at various points during this period, as an increasingly restricted group of Moriscos remained immune while new categories were deemed subject to expulsion.[97] Reports of abuses and violence against the departing Moriscos also reached Philip III, but he did not intervene.[98]

EXILES AND EMIGRATION TO NORTH AFRICA:
PATTERNS ON A SPANISH FRONTIER

Why did some Moriscos emigrate to the Americas, rather than to North Africa? Some answers can be found by examining Moriscos' varying responses to the expulsion decrees. Some embraced exile in the Maghreb while others made every attempt possible to remain in or return to Spain.[99] Some Moriscos traveled to France briefly, before recrossing the Pyrenees and hiding out in Spanish mountain towns. Rising suspicion among the French who perceived them to be potentially treacherous Spaniards, led Moriscos in France also to attempt to move to Italy or settle among communities of Spanish Morisco exiles in the Maghreb.[100] Evidence that a number of individuals labeled Moriscos practiced Christianity and considered themselves Spaniards suggests that they may have hoped to forge new lives for themselves across the Atlantic, where there was less surveillance, rather than emigrate to North Africa both before and after the expulsion. In the Americas, they could continue to try to identify themselves as Spaniards, by claiming old Christian status, and if they gained honors or encomiendas, they could establish themselves among the local elite. In North Africa, the Morisco exiles received mixed reception. Even those who considered themselves to be good Muslims were perceived by many across the Gibraltar straits as lacking orthodoxy and in need of immediate instruction in Islam. Moriscos formed their own communities in Morocco, Tunisia, and Salé, which became a corsairing republic, and were also encouraged by Ottoman bureaucrats to settle in Ottoman lands to counterbalance more rebellious and malcontent local populations.[101] Writings of Morisco exiles in North Africa reflected their regionally divergent experiences. Aragonese Moriscos expressed a desire for religious hybridity, blending Christianity with Islam, whereas many Granadans who had already experienced waves of expulsion and resettlement on the Peninsula reasserted their faith in Islam and retained resentment toward Spain.[102] These differences in experience are also reflected in cases of Moriscos in Spanish America following the expulsion.

In 1623 inquisitors in the Spanish American port city of Cartagena de Indias encountered a Morisco slave in the galleys whose case suggests the diversity of Moriscos' attitudes toward belonging to a community following the expulsion. Francisco Martínez presented himself voluntarily before the Cartagena tribunal, claiming he had been born in Murcia and was a baptized Catholic before he and his parents had been expelled with other Moriscos to North Africa. He described how "upon entering the sea they declared themselves Muslims, and they treated him as such. Within two months of their arrival in Algiers, they made him get circumcised, and although he was a grown boy of sixteen or seventeen years of age, he did not dare to resist. They tried to teach him the *suras* and the *zala*, and they made him do them many times, but he was always so firm in the faith, that they did not make him renounce it. He considered the sect of Muhammad as coarse and cruel, and every time he could, he interacted with Christians. After three or four years he left as a corsair with the intention of arriving in the land of the Christians."[103] Martínez claimed he was captured near the Portuguese coast where he tried to appeal unsuccessfully to the Inquisition to allow him to return to Spain and to Christianity but did not have time to make his case. He thus waited to denounce himself until after his arrival in Cartagena de Indias. Inquisitors ruled that he should receive instruction in a local monastery because "it seemed that he spoke from his heart and told the truth in all things."[104]

In a contrasting case, on 30 March 1625 the inquisitor Doctor Agustín de Ugarte Saravia addressed a letter to the Supreme Council of the Inquisition in Madrid. In it, he described how "six or seven Moriscos, of those who had been expelled from Castile" had reached the port of Cartagena de Indias in the galleys.[105] They had been captured by the Spanish during a corsairing raid off the North African coast and enslaved on a galley force that was headed for the Caribbean. Ugarte Saravia expressed confusion about the Inquisition's jurisdiction over them because they had been expelled when they were "young men who were sixteen and eighteen years old. They were circumcised in Berbería, and today they live on the said galleys in the sect of Muhammad and its belief, confessing that they are Muslims and not Christians."[106] Muslims were not subject to the Inquisition, whereas Moriscos—as converts to Christianity from Islam—could be tried as apostates if they were suspected of practicing Islam. Ugarte Saravia wrote that he presumed they had been baptized as children in Spain and should therefore be considered renegades. His argument was complicated by the fact that they were royal slaves, and their removal from the galleys would present a loss to the king. He therefore requested a ruling from higher authorities in Spain. The inquisitors in Cartagena received the Suprema's reply in 1630, ordering them not to proceed against "the Moriscos who, having been expelled from the Catholic kingdoms of his majesty, were captured as corsairs or who in any other way come to them as slaves or [who] are in his majesty's galleys professing to be Muslims."[107]

* * *

Whether reaching the Americas as the servants of powerful Spaniards, as galley slaves, or as free but clandestine emigrants, Moriscos settled in the New World despite travel restrictions. Many were caught or denounced, but others like María Ruiz appeared voluntarily before the Inquisition for a variety of reasons. They were concerned about their religious identity and social standing, as were Spanish authorities.

In their policies toward Moriscos, Spanish ecclesiastical authorities framed their debates in terms of essentialized notions of what it meant to be a Morisco. Inquisitors, bishops, missionaries, and local parish priests collected information about the Moriscos residing under their jurisdiction in order to better carry out campaigns to convert and Christianize them. Their visions of Moriscos became polarized, presenting them as either potential converts to Catholicism who needed proper instruction, echoing the program of Tridentine reforms that called for well-trained priests and the creation of institutions to administer to the new Christian population, as well as improve instruction of the old Christian population. Another more sinister vision of Moriscos, one that eventually gave way to expulsion, cast them as unrepentant Muslims whose cultural and religious differences would render them traitors to Spain and prompt them to ally with the Ottoman Turks.

Ecclesiastical authorities carried out similar programs in the far reaches of the Spanish Empire, as they encountered new peoples and attempted to bring them into the folds of the Catholic faith. Beyond official discourses, the reach and impact of these policies on the ground, on both sides of the Atlantic, as applied to Moriscos, Africans, and indigenous peoples, had vastly ranging consequences. Early modern Spaniards grappled with how to incorporate new categories of people into their emerging empire. At the same time, individuals labeled Morisco attempted to wrestle with the images applied to them, in their own attempts to secure status across the Iberian world.

CHAPTER 2

Into the Atlantic

Justifying Title and Establishing Dominion

Upon returning from his first voyage westward across the Atlantic, Christopher Columbus penned a statement to the Spanish monarchs Ferdinand and Isabel as prologue to his *Diary of the First Voyage* that covered the events of 1492–93. While the original copies of his journals and logbook were lost, his account survives in a copy transcribed by Friar Bartolomé de Las Casas. In the first entry of the diary, Columbus articulated a powerful and enduring association between the conquest of Granada, Christian expansion, and Castilian possession over lands encountered. He wrote, "After Your Highnesses ended the war against the Muslims who ruled in Europe, and having ended that war in the very great city of Granada, where this year [1492] . . . by force of arms I saw the royal flags of Your Highnesses in the towers of the Alhambra, the fortress of that city, and I saw the Muslim king emerge from the gates of that city and kiss the royal hands of Your Highnesses." Later that month, "by the information I gave to Your Highnesses of the lands of India and of a Prince called the Great Khan . . . of how many times he and his predecessors requested that Rome send doctors in our holy faith so that they could be taught it." When the calls for Christian missionaries went unanswered, "so many peoples were lost, falling into idolatries . . . and Your Highnesses, like Catholic Christians and princes who love the holy Christian faith, and increase it and are enemies of the sect of Muhammad and of all idolatries and heresies, you thought to send me, Christopher Columbus, on the said voyages to India to see the said princes and peoples and lands and the disposition of them and of everything, and the manner which should be had for their conversion to our holy faith."[1] This idea was echoed in the papal bulls granting the Spanish dominion over the Americas and upheld by the official policies of subsequent monarchs and the Council of the Indies.

Associations between conquering lands under Muslim rule and spreading Christianity overseas were also echoed in the papal bulls of donation and resurfaced in subsequent Spanish claims to empire and dominion in the New World. As imperial claims became intimately linked to the evangelization of native communities, it became imperative for the Crown to restrict the movement of peoples and ideas to the Americas to devout Catholics. As definitions of Spanishness became increasingly linked to exclusionary attitudes based on genealogy and religious identity, restrictions on overseas emigration also became more and more connected to emerging notions of "race"—to individuals who could prove their lineages were of "pure" old Christian ancestry.

Like the Portuguese, the Spanish presented a "world on the move."[2] Following the conquest of Ceuta in 1415, Portuguese ships in search of African gold and slaves began to make voyages into the southern Atlantic. During the fifteenth century, the Portuguese established trading posts and colonies in the Canary Islands, Madeira, the Cape Verde Islands, and the Azores.[3] In competition with the Portuguese, the Castilians also staked their claim to the Canary Islands, raiding and enslaving the native *guanche* population. With growing competition over access to maritime trade routes, Isabel of Castile and Ferdinand of Aragon had to negotiate treaties with Afonso V of Portugal. In 1479 they signed the Treaty of Alcáçovas in which Portugal recognized Castilian sovereignty in the Canary Islands and Castile acknowledged Portuguese claims to the other Atlantic islands and the African coast south of Cape Bojador. Following Columbus's return from his first voyage to the Caribbean islands, Ferdinand and Isabel became concerned the Portuguese would attempt to claim them under the Treaty of Alcáçovas.[4] They immediately appealed to Alexander VI to grant them title to these islands and any subsequent "discoveries," which the pope conceded in the bulls of donation.[5]

Spanish authorities' interest in restricting new Christian presence in the Americas was in many ways shaped by the terms of the papal bull *Inter Caetera* (1493). In this bull, Alexander VI granted dominion to the Catholic monarchs Ferdinand and Isabel to oversee the conversion of peoples encountered in the new territories, effectively rendering the Spanish Crown's title to the Americas contingent upon the successful evangelization of indigenous peoples.[6] The bull highlighted the role played by Ferdinand and Isabel in the conquest of the Muslim Kingdom of Granada in 1492. It buttressed their claim to being Catholic monarchs who, because of their actions in Granada, presented themselves as the most suitable rulers in Europe to oversee the expansion of the church in the new territories.[7] The language and terms of *Inter Caetera* infiltrated subsequent legal decisions and debates concerning the legality of Spanish conquest and colonization. Other legal documents and protocols tied to conquest, such as the *Requerimiento*, attested to the continued importance that spreading Catholicism held for the colonial enterprise.[8]

For decades to come, jurists and theologians at the Spanish court debated the legality and morality of Spanish dominion and just title to the Americas. Initial juridical arguments drew upon Christian-Muslim relations in the medieval period that recognized the pope's jurisdiction over lands belonging to non-Christians. Precedents for European claims over non-Christian peoples generally involved lands deemed "vacant" or societies labeled "primitive," such as the guanches in the Canary Islands. The Spanish Crown needed to establish clearly the legitimacy of its claims to the Americas before an international audience.[9] Numerous lawyers, theologians, and royal officials convened in Salamanca to debate the lawfulness of the conquests, their arguments grounded in Castilian legal culture.

Bartolomé de las Casas, whose writings questioned the extent of Spanish dominion and cited horrific abuses of indigenous peoples as its consequence, was not alone in his critiques.[10] In 1565, Franciscan friar Alonso de Maldonado also petitioned the king to protect indigenous peoples, claiming the Crown lacked legitimate title to the Americas. At court, Friar Diego de Chaves responded that Maldonado's propositions would allow other monarchs to assert claims over the Indies and deemed Maldonado's failure to recognize the papal grant "scandalous and seditious."[11] In 1568, with the encouragement of the Jesuits, Pope Pius V created a commission to examine the Catholic missions in the Spanish Americas.[12] Those who participated in the commission submitted a report to Philip II concerning the good treatment and conversion of indigenous peoples. Echoing Tridentine reforms, their report reiterated that the papal donation stipulated true conversion of the Amerindians, and it recommended that well-educated priests carry out this enormous task with the financial support of the encomenderos.[13] Encomenderos therefore were responsible for upholding the religious instruction of indigenous peoples under their supervision, and in some cases they became vulnerable to accusations that they were new Christians who were ill suited to this role. While the Crown did not heed the papal briefs in their entirety or the commission's instructions, growing criticism of both the encomienda system and royal policies toward Amerindians produced a flurry of reforming activity.[14]

What was at stake? Critics across Europe also actively disputed Spain's claim to the Americas. With the Reformation, Protestant rulers had little regard for the papal bulls granting dominion to Spain. Even Catholic monarchs such as Henry VII of England and Francis I of France held differing opinions from those of the Spanish Crown about the role of papal intervention in secular matters of state.[15] They argued that papal authority did not extend to granting the Americas to Spain, and they financed their own voyages under John Cabot and Jacques Cartier to explore the lands north of the territories settled by Spain. Spanish jurists soon found themselves having to defend papal authority against the wave of disturbing images in manuscripts and printed books surging across Europe.[16] Theodor de Bry produced vivid engravings of Amerindians and Protestants ravaged by Spanish soldiers and the Inquisition in his 1594 and 1596 editions of Girolamo Benzoni's *Historia del Mondo Nuovo* (1565).[17] Other polemical images critical of Spanish dominion conflated Spaniards with cannibals in their Eucharistic devotion, fanning rival nations' expansionist claims and aiming to challenge Spain's moral title to the Americas.[18] As late as the seventeenth century, Spanish jurist Juan de Solórzano y Pereira continued to defend the Crown's title to the Americas. He argued that indigenous peoples possessed humanity and a right to *dominium*, and only papal support for their conversion to Christianity to ensure their salvation justified Spanish rule.[19] The English and Dutch built up fleets to challenge Spanish dominance in the Caribbean, yet Spanish defenders of papal power, as late as Solórzano, hoped their bid for the "spiritual welfare" of indigenous peoples would stave off English, French, and Dutch interference with their activities, by articulating a legal basis for conquest.[20]

The Spanish sovereigns' determination to present themselves as Catholic monarchs, who complied with the papal bulls that established their title to the Americas, had a profound impact on their imperial policies. These included religious restrictions on settlement and emigration. Official policies issued by the Crown in royal decrees were often met with differing attitudes and projects on the ground. As a result, they issued restrictions on the emigration of recent converts to Christianity—Moriscos and conversos. Emigrants also had to prove their upstanding behavior and pious comportment. Because it was a matter of faith, church and state both defended these exclusions, through institutions such as the Inquisition and the ecclesiastical courts, and even the Casa de Contratación. Individuals such as Estevanico in the early and still fluid period of exploration had an opening to the Americas, yet they were always vulnerable to accusation. As valuable as he had been to Cabeza de Vaca and Friar Marcos de Niza, the vivid description of his downfall by Francisco Vázquez de Coronado tells a more complicated story.

ARABIC SPEAKING INTERMEDIARIES IN THE EARLY ATLANTIC VOYAGES

A number of Europeans, including Magellan and Columbus, recruited or captured Arabic speakers to act as interpreters in the lands they traded in or conquered, due to their perceived linguistic skills.[21] They followed patterns well established by the Portuguese, who left individuals behind to learn local languages and then picked them up again for future voyages. In the case of many of the Arabic speakers, the Spanish and Portuguese also used captives from North Africa or Asia to act as interpreters in their first meetings with local rulers to establish trading relationships. For example, in his first voyage to the Antilles, Columbus brought as interpreter Luis de Torres, who was familiar with several languages, including Hebrew and some Arabic.[22] Portuguese chronicler and historian João de Barros described how Pedro Álvares Cabral used speakers of Arabic and West African languages to try to communicate with the peoples of coastal Brazil. When Cabral realized indigenous peoples did not understand these languages, he switched strategies to leave a group of criminal exiles (*degradados*) behind to learn the local languages.[23] Bringing Arabic speakers on initial voyages must have seemed an obvious choice to the Portuguese who were familiar with seizing Berbers during their attempts to conquer parts of North Africa, then carrying these men and women south as interpreters to sub-Saharan African ports.[24] On Vasco da Gama's voyage to India, Arabic speakers facilitated trade with Muslim merchants in Mozambique and acted as interpreters during both his and Cabral's encounters with the Muslim ruler of Calicut.[25] Estevanico's home city of Azemmour, a Portuguese protectorate in the Kingdom of Morocco from 1508 to 1540, was described by Leo Africanus as attracting Portuguese merchants in the 1520s who had been trading in Africa since the conquest of Ceuta.[26]

Estevanico's involvement in the Pánfilo de Narváez and Friar Marcos de Niza expeditions demonstrates the precarious turns his role as interpreter could take. Following several years of wandering what is today the American Southwest, in 1536, Estevanico and Cabeza de Vaca finally stumbled across a group of "Christians," including Captain Diego de Alcaraz who had participated in Nuño de Guzmán's 1530–31 conquest of Nueva Galicia. Having learned the local trade language that enabled him to communicate with the peoples of northern Mexico, Estevanico returned with indigenous escorts. They guided the remaining two survivors of the Narváez expedition, Andrés Dorantes and Alonso del Castillo, and a group of six hundred indigenous peoples from Sonora and Sinaloa, back to join the Spaniards in San Miguel.[27] The reaction of some Spaniards, according to Cabeza de Vaca, was to try to enslave them, and Estevanico had to persuade the Indians that they were not like the other Spaniards. Although many Spaniards in the first *entradas* into "hostile" frontier regions hoped to enslave Amerindians, others acknowledged the Crown's emphasis on evangelization and limiting enslavement and personal service, so they spoke out.

In 1537 Viceroy Antonio de Mendoza purchased Estevanico from Andrés Dorantes to act as a guide, being a "persona de razón" who had prior knowledge of northwestern New Spain.[28] In 1539 Estevanico joined the expedition of Friar Marcos de Niza. The friar describes him as having perished alongside three hundred Indian allies near the legendary city of Cíbola, amidst the Zuni pueblos, although they most likely never made it beyond northern Sonora.[29] A more contradictory and negative portrayal is provided by the 1540 report of Francisco Vázquez de Coronado. He had written to Viceroy Mendoza that Estevanico was killed because "the Indians of Chichiltcale said that he was a bad man, and not like the Christians who never kill women, and he killed them, and because he assaulted their women, whom the Indians love better than themselves."[30]

Estevanico's contradictory characterization as both a good Christian and "person of reason," and as a violent and unpredictable man, lie in his liminal status in the colonial documentation as being labeled a *negro alárabe*. Alárabe was a loaded term in the period, which was associated with Islam and used by sixteenth-century writers to refer to the seminomadic peoples inhabiting North Africa.[31] Regardless of Estevanico's actual background, the mere association with alárabes would have raised concerns among his contemporaries. Estevanico and his supporters would have had to constantly justify his position and his behavior as a good Christian. For example, when Baltasar Dorantes de Carranza requested that the king grant encomiendas to the first conquerors of New Spain, and by extension their direct descendants, he portrayed his father's slave Estevanico as a Christian martyr who was "shot through with arrows like a Saint Sebastian, in the service of His Majesty."[32]

Estevanico is perhaps the best-known interpreter among this group of Arabic speakers in New Spain. Yet other enslaved North Africans and Moriscos learned indigenous languages upon their arrival in the Americas.[33] Knowledge about captivity in the Muslim world played a role in everyday interactions between Spaniards and indigenous peoples in the so-called frontier regions of Spanish America. During the 1530s, Spaniards brought interpreters to northern New Spain, and there were some who were Moriscos or North African Muslims conversant in Arabic dialects. Their perceived facility with languages made these individuals attractive candidates for becoming *naguatatos*, or translators of Nahuatl, the language spoken in much of central Mexico.[34]

Records from the earliest entradas into northern New Spain during the 1530s reveal the growing need for interpreters to translate between Spaniards and their Nahuatl speaking allies, and the new indigenous linguistic groups they encountered.[35] Spanish incursions to conquer and subjugate the seminomadic peoples inhabiting Nueva Galicia dragged on for decades. These events took place during the term of Viceroy Antonio de Mendoza, a member of the influential Mendoza noble family from Granada. He traced his lineage to ancestors who fought in battles of the so-called Reconquista, and his father, Iñigo López de Mendoza, Count of Tendilla, acted as captain-general of the Christian forces conquering Granada. Historical memory of these earlier battles continued to hold meaning for elite Spanish families and continued to be mentioned in histories and genealogies composed on both sides of the Atlantic. Viceroy Mendoza's brother, Diego Hurtado de Mendoza, composed the *Guerra de Granada*, one of the more detailed and well-known accounts of the Alpujarras uprising.[36]

As can be seen through the Mendoza family, Christian-Muslim inter-actions on the Iberian Peninsula and in the Mediterranean influenced many Spaniards who made their way to the Americas and guided their responses to the "new" lands. Imperial and local policies, per-ceptions of others, and strategies for self-fashioning were all bound up in peninsular interactions that were transformed during the course of new encounters and experiences in the Americas.

Antonio Tello's *Libro segundo de la cronica miscelanea en que se trata de la conquista espiritual y temporal de la Santa Provincia de Xalisco* recounts the history of Jalisco to 1653. Tello's depiction of the conquests of New Spain and Nueva Galicia develops gendered parallels between Spanish interactions with North African Muslims and Turks in the Mediterranean and with indigenous peoples in the Americas. Describing Cortés's participation in a Spanish campaign to Algiers in 1541, Tello emphasized Cortés's masculinity and the authority he gained from direct experience in the conquest of Mex-ico, in light of peninsular Spaniards' skepticism: In Algiers, Cortés "served his majesty, and had some disagreements when he gave coun-sel concerning the winning of that city, because they told him that he thought that that war was with the naked Indians of New Spain. To this he replied, 'It only takes one of those Indians to fight with six clothed Spaniards'."[37] Through Tello's eyes we can envision how his readers might have imagined these parallels that were already being inscribed onto early accounts of conquest. Describing Spaniards bat-tling indigenous groups in northern New Spain, Tello notes, "When they fight, they yelp and cry out like Muslims."[38] Nuño de Guzmán's forces engaged peoples in feathered dress in Chiametla, whose bows were "so big they appeared Turkish."[39]

As in Spain, St. James or Santiago reputedly assisted the conquer-ors during his "first apparition" in New Galicia. A shrine was built in his honor on the mountain ridge (*cerro*), and the adjacent settlement added Santiago to its name, becoming Santiago de Tonalán, thereby transforming the landscape to reflect Spanish devotions to Recon-quest saints.[40] After the fall of Granada, St. James, or Santiago Mat-amoros, had gained currency as the patron saint of Spain, as myths depicted his early arrival on the Peninsula, making it the first Euro-pean nation to learn about Christ, thus bestowing preeminent status on Spain. Santiago had been invoked during Christian battles against Muslims in medieval Iberia, and he continued to be called upon dur-ing conquests in the Americas. Depictions of Santiago had become

more prevalent in the changing political climate in Spain, especially
as the Catholic monarchs' personal devotions to him seeped into their
political decisions.[41] These images inhabited the mental worlds of the
Spaniards as Estevanico was making his way with Cabeza de Vaca
and Friar Marcos de Niza as interpreter and as later generations reinterpreted these events in their written histories of the early conquests.

In 1535 Viceroy Mendoza sailed to New Spain to assume his
fifteen-year post, which involved establishing Spanish control and
jurisdiction over the recently explored and conquered territories of
the viceroyalty, extending from La Florida and the Caribbean, to the
area that is now the southwestern United States and Baja California.
In Nueva Galicia, Spanish settlers were met with strong indigenous
resistance in 1540, when native leaders formed alliances to oust the
early settlements established under Nuño de Guzmán. Viceroy Mendoza quickly sent Spanish forces to suppress the mostly Cazcan-
speaking "rebels" in the Juchipila Valley, in a two-year struggle that
became known as the Mixton War.[42] However, conflicts between
Spaniards and indigenous groups in Nueva Galicia never completely died down after the Mixton War, setting the stage for the
Guerra Chichimeca that broke out nearly ten years later in 1550.[43]
The Spaniards had left a profoundly transformed society in their
wake, in both the emerging towns of Guadalajara, Purificación, San
Miguel de Culiacán, and Compostela, and in settlements such as
Jalisco, Etzatlan, and Juchipila, which had previously belonged to
indigenous communities. In Nueva Galicia, the demographic bal-
ance shifted after the Mixton War to comprise a multiethnic society
of Spaniards, Africans, and mixed-race peoples, as well as the native
peoples whose population was dwindling due to the ravages of war
and disease.[44]

By the 1541 Spanish campaigns against the peoples whom they
labeled "Chichimeca," Viceroy Mendoza had working for him a
group of interpreters who were reputed to be Moriscos.[45] The 1546–
47 tour of inspection or *visita* that Francisco Tello de Sandoval carried out against Viceroy Mendoza and the Audiencia of Mexico
provides ample information about the activities of these Morisco
naguatatos.[46] Through denunciations and complaints tying these men
to Mendoza, it is also possible to glimpse attitudes toward Moriscos
that would surface in later disputes over offices and encomiendas. It
is hard to gain a sense of who these men were from the visita records,
but read alongside other documents, it reveals the importance in early

expeditions of Morisco interpreters, the need for them to fill certain niches in the emerging viceroyalties, and the opportunities for gaining status available to those who participated in the first generations of conquest.

Francisco de Triana, Marcos Romero, and Alonso Ortiz de Zúñiga were all described during the visita as sons of Moriscos. Their cases were bound to an investigation of Antonio Ortiz, interpreter for Viceroy Mendoza in the Guerra de Jalisco, and they were all affected by the charges against him for extortion, illegally selling "indios jaliscos" as slaves, and cheating the people for whom he was interpreting. Licenciado Lorenzo de Tejada, judge of the Audiencia of Mexico, presented charges against these men as part of his ongoing enmity with Antonio Ortiz, whom he accused of bribing them to ruin his credibility as *visitador*. Tejada's accusations reveal insights into the lives the interpreters forged for themselves in New Spain, as well as Spanish conceptions of honor and anxieties about intermixture between Amerindians and Muslims. They cast Ortiz de Zúñiga, Triana, and his cousin Romero as men who "live more like Muslims than like Christians."[47] They had achieved some degree of authority in colonial society due to their role as interpreters, which may have made other Spaniards uncomfortable or envious, given their reputedly lower status. Tejada described Triana as a Morisco slave whose parents were also "newly converted" Muslim slaves in the household of the Marqués de Tarifa in Seville. In New Spain, Triana had found work as a gardener (*hortelano*) for the Marqués del Valle Hernán Cortés before being removed from his post for unseemly behavior. Triana's cousin Marcos Romero was also portrayed as a "Morisco, son of newly converted Moriscos."[48] Finally, Alonso Ortiz de Zúñiga, who acted as tutor and guardian to a young woman from a prominent family, was labeled a "bad Christian . . . the bastard son of the Morisca slave of Doña María, wife of the señor de Ginés."[49]

A recurrent concern in the accusations against the interpreters was their contact with indigenous women. Triana lived "among Indians" and had in his house a tavern where he sold pulque to Indians and Africans. Spanish authorities remained anxious about indigenous drinking throughout the colonial period, as consumption of fermented beverages like pulque in New Spain or chicha in the Andes had enduring religious and ceremonial significance that ecclesiastical authorities deemed contrary to Christian baptism.[50] Triana's "conversation and dwelling has always been with Indians and among Indians, eating with them on the floor and doing their dances and ceremonies (*mitotes*)."[51] Furthermore, although married to a Spanish woman in Castile, Triana was "cohabiting (*amancebado*) with many Indian women, living more according to the law of Muhammad than as a Christian."[52] In Cuernavaca, Triana also allegedly stole from Alonso Pérez Tamayo a female slave and a free indigenous woman, both of whom he held "captive and hidden for many days, being a drunk, a thief, and an amancebado, and having other dirty and low vices."[53] Similarly, Marcos Romero had resided "among Indians and outside the *traza* of the Spaniards," before the Royal Audiencia ordered him to leave his house and live with Spaniards under pain of one hundred lashes "for the damage and evils he does to [the Indians]."[54] Romero was "blasphemous and amancebado with many Indian and mestiza women. He lives more like a gentile and according to the law of Muhammad than as a Christian, and his business and conversation was and is with Indians."[55]

Although Spanish authorities attempted to keep the "Republic of Spaniards" and the "Republic of Indians" physically and jurisdictionally separate, recent studies have demonstrated that a great deal of interaction did occur. Royal officials developed and implemented urban spatial models such as the *congregación*, in which native communities were to be organized and settled under the care of priests who would see to their religious instruction. This idealized spatial arrangement was intended to keep indigenous peoples separate from the feared "vagabonds" and persons of mixed ancestry who were known as *castas* and generally deemed disorderly.[56] In both viceroyalties of New Spain and Peru, members of religious orders strived to create segregated settlements that would facilitate their efforts to evangelize indigenous peoples, establishing missionary village parishes (*doctrinas*). Viceroys such as Francisco de Toledo in Peru carried out programs of resettlement (*reducción*) to move indigenous peoples into small towns and villages on a Spanish model that would be easier to administer and control.[57] However, by the 1550s in New Spain, this sometimes controversial project to maintain two separate republics was already being undermined by the movement of castas into indigenous settlements.[58]

The design of the new Spanish settlements echoed idealized images of Roman city plans, in the form of the traza, or grid pattern, that surrounded a central plaza, in ways that also followed the contours of early modern Spanish ideas about what constituted good government (*buen gobierno, policia*).[59] In Nueva Galicia, the Spanish towns were also likely founded according to this orderly municipal model, with the *cabildo* (town council), church, public works, and governor's house given their own blocks (*cuadras*) along neatly organized streets radiating from the main plaza. Residents, or *vecinos,* were assigned spaces for their homes, four to a block.[60] The surrounding indigenous pueblos were then granted by the governor to the men who had participated in the conquest as encomiendas, or labor grants, to be exploited.[61] The grid pattern layout of Spanish American settlements stood in sharp contrast to the Iberian towns and cities such as Granada, Córdoba, and Seville, their winding narrow streets mirroring the medinas across North Africa. Marcos Romero's life "outside the traza" cast him as disorderly and unwilling to live a lifestyle associated with proper Spanish and Catholic mores. The traza established a deliberate spatial distinction from Muslim cities, a rupture from the Islamic past in a "New World," as Spaniards increasingly looked back to ancient Rome for a model of imperial expansion, conquest, and settlement. Romero's dwelling also put him in too-close proximity to the indigenous peoples whom authorities hoped to Hispanize and assimilate into colonial society, while still keeping them legally separate.

The question of trustworthiness also arises frequently in witnesses' testimonies. A perceived lack of proper Christian comportment, or anything that would cast doubt on an individual's piety, could call into question that individual's credibility or loyalty in business ventures, especially in their role as interpreters. In the early Portuguese accounts by João de Barros and Eanes Gomes de Zurara, members of these expeditions expressed concern that a translator who was a Muslim captive would defect once among other Muslims, or translate in ways that would benefit his or her own precarious position.[62] Go-betweens could assume the role of arbitrator, someone whose allegiance was crucial to the success of colonial projects, yet who ultimately ended up favoring a certain side in the encounter, or whose actions were aimed to benefit only themselves. Intermediaries were often shrouded with suspicion, due to their ability to speak multiple languages and inhabit two or more worlds.[63] While members of these early Atlantic expeditions may have relied on Arabic speakers as cultural brokers, they did not entirely trust them.

In this context, labeling someone a Morisco and noting they did not attend Mass was sensitive in its connection with the Crown's projects to evangelize indigenous peoples and professed concern to limit their exploitation by Spanish settlers. In their role as interme- diaries, interpreters could easily fall under suspicion of manipulating translations for personal gain. This anxiety is reflected in Licenciado Lorenzo de Tejada's charges against the interpreters accused of being Moriscos. The judge of the Audiencia of Mexico took aim at Triana's trustworthiness, in what must have been an attempt to cast doubt on his reliability as an interpreter: Triana was "such a liar that he never, or only by mistake, tells the truth, and a very bad Christian who never enters any church, nor has anyone seen him confess."[64] Tejada claimed Marcos Romero took advantage of his role as translator in order to trick and mistreat the Indians. Romero's frequent drunken- ness also led him to lie and hurl insults, rendering him as dubious a figure as his cousin Triana.

Each of these charges amounted to an attack on the interpret- ers' personal honor. The full list of charges presented by Tejada as he summoned witnesses against Triana noted that because he lived among Indians, took part in their dances, and "serve[d] them for pay and as watchman of their fields, which is the greatest coward- ice, vileness and dishonor that a Spaniard can do in this land."[65] Triana also "eats with them [the Indians] on the ground" and is "so full of vices and bad customs that in these parts there is not known a man so vile . . . of so little honor and such a bad Christian."[66] Marcos Romero was also a "very poor man of vile roots (*raiz*) without honor or shame."[67] Clearly outraged, Tejada exclaimed, "even if one looked, I wager that there would not be found in all of New Spain or in any of the Indies three persons so vile, without honor, and bad Christians, so lacking in truthfulness and shame, nor in whom coincide so many ugly and enormous vices as in the said . . . naguatatos."[68]

As seen in the denunciations against Triana, Romero, and Ortiz de Zúñiga, perceived new Christian presence added to already exist- ing anxieties about the catechization of indigenous peoples and the infiltration into the Republic of Indians of non-Catholic beliefs and unorthodox behavior. Spanish authorities increasingly restricted Spaniards' and Africans' access to indigenous communities, and the recent converts from Islam fell in between these two categories. Some Moriscos did make their way to Spanish America during the early years of colonization, before greater attempts were made to enforce the royal decrees restricting emigration. In a few cases local authorities requested their participation in local projects, as interpreters or as artisans, occupations traditionally associated with Moriscos. A number also arrived as slaves.

MORISCO SLAVES

Many of the Moriscos arriving in Spanish America during this earlier period were slaves who accompanied their masters' households as dependents. The royal licenses granted for them to emigrate placed strict limits on the length of their presence in Spanish America. However, a number of these Morisco men and women remained in Spanish America, either because their masters looked the other way, or because they were able to run away and forge new lives for themselves, in communities where they would presumably, although not always, go unrecognized. Traces of these individuals can be found in the records of the Casa de Contratación in Seville, which kept track of the length of time Morisco and North African slaves remained in the Americas. The license that Bartolomé de Anaya y Villanueva obtained for his *berberisca* slave María in 1624 to accompany him to New Spain, where he was to assume his post as secretary of the Consejo de Guerra, shows the process whereby slaveholders proved their slaves were qualified to enter the Indies. Anaya summoned witnesses who signed statements that María was commonly held to be "a Christian, because they see her go to Mass and pray, and she does Christian works."[69] The final portion of the document was her official royal license to emigrate without restrictions, "despite being of the berberisca nation," and like most official licenses, it listed her identifying markers: María was "twenty-four years old, white, fat, branded on the chin and forehead."[70] While no limits were placed on María's term in this license, earlier ones show that individuals of lesser status were subject to restrictions on the number of years their slaves could spend in the Indies, and could be prosecuted if they did not comply. For example, in 1578 the Crown issued a royal decree to the officials of the Casa de Contratación, to ensure that Ruy Díaz de Mendoza return the two Morisca slaves he brought to New Spain for a limited period of four years, and if he did not comply, that he would be punished.[71]

In 1512 Hernando de Peralta was granted a license to bring to the island of San Juan two *esclavas blancas,* or "white slaves," a term often applied to Moriscas, so long as they were baptized Christians.

They were to be brought for the service of his wife and household, which he was transplanting to San Juan.[72] Another license was granted in 1537 to Licenciado Iñigo López de Cervantes who was traveling to Santo Domingo as judge (*oidor*) of the audiencia, to bring two esclavas blancas in addition to four African slaves. The two slaves were Christians, "raised in his household," and they were granted royal licenses so long as López de Cervantes could prove they had been Christians since before the age of twelve.[73] The license stipulated that the women "be brought to the island of Hispaniola . . . for the service of his household. He cannot take them from the said island to any other place other than to return them to these kingdoms [Spain]."[74]

Many of the enslaved Moriscos were women, and some of them were eventually freed. They gained status through marriage to Spaniards, thereby joining prominent or upwardly mobile families in the Peruvian viceroyalty.[75] In 1968 James Lockhart proposed that Morisca slaves "did not have a broad spectrum of roles," acting only as concubines for Spanish male conquistadors. They then "disappeared from view" during the 1530s with the arrival of Spanish old Christian women who were the preferred companions.[76] However, their supposed disappearance was likely related to the *cédulas* restricting Morisco immigration, which were issued during this period. Such restrictions and brushes with authority may have driven individuals to be more careful when transporting slaves, or when emigrating to the Americas themselves. In this sense, Joanne Rappaport's idea of the "disappearing mestizo" is useful in describing the active choices individuals made to present themselves before their communities. This goes beyond racial "passing" by encompassing attempts to hide one's lineage or religious identity while making claims to status in colonial society.[77]

Testimonies describing the slave market in Lima in one riveting case mention the notable presence of Moriscas in Peru. In 1543, Juana, a "white slave" and a Morisca from Tunis, petitioned for her freedom before the Royal Audiencia and Chancery of Panama. She had been the slave of Hernando de Zevallos in Peru before she was sold to cover a debt that he owed the royal treasury. Juana's new master Juan de Cáceres freed her and her infant daughter Ynés, but Zevallos wanted them back, citing the nullity of their sale to Cáceres, under an illegitimate judge appointed by Diego de Almagro the Younger's tyrannical government, formed after the assassination of Francisco Pizarro. Zevallos also claimed that his debt to the royal treasury was unfairly leveled against him by another "tyranically" appointed *alcalde* and should now be forgiven.[78] Juana gave Luis Suárez, the father of her daughter, power of attorney. He was to appeal in her name to the Royal Chancery in Panama the order that the governor of Peru, Licentiate Cristóbal Vaca de Castro (1541–44), had issued in favor of Zevallos that he keep Juana and Ynés as his slaves. Juana and Luis Suárez presented the freedom papers (*carta de libertad*) given to her by Cáceres and emphasized that "in conformity with the law, her freedom should be favored being as she is a free person possessing a title. . . . It should never have been ordered that she return to servitude and captivity."[79] They expressed concern that Zevallos was planning on labeling Juana and her daughter physically as his property, by "marking them with a brand or a sign so that they appear to be subjected to servitude, being as they are free persons. . . . [This mark would be] injurious and an affront."[80] Witnesses testified that Juana had conceived Ynés with Luis Suárez who was an "honorable and rich" Lima merchant and whose responsibility it should be to free the girl, especially as Juana became pregnant after having been manumitted by Cáceres.[81] A number of witnesses also discussed the average price of Morisca slaves auctioned in Lima, as Zevallos was attempting to determine the value of Juana and her daughter. Alonso de Huete testified in Suárez's favor, saying that he knew Juana and that she and her daughter were worth no more than 300 or 350 pesos because he "had seen other Morisca slaves sold in Peru for less, who were as beautiful or more so than the said Juana."[82] Two other witnesses for Suárez testified to similar practices in Lima, including Jerónimo de Aliaga.[83] Aliaga stated, "According to what he had seen, there have been sold in Peru Morisca slaves of Juana's quality for [300] and [400] pesos, some for more and others for less."[84] Miguel Vendrés added, "According to the experience and knowledge I have concerning slaves, especially Moriscas, Juana as a slave and her daughter could be worth up to 400 pesos of gold, in the places and provinces of Peru."[85] The Council of the Indies finally ruled in 1547 that Zevallos drop his cases against Juana Morisca and Luis Suárez, and cover the cost of the trials. Juana and her daughter were now presumably free either to live with Suárez who had remained by their side during the years that the trial unfolded, or to forge their own lives altogether.[86] In 1547 she is mentioned in the final documents of the case as a resident of the city of Nombre de Dios in Panama, and Suárez had assumed the post on the city council of Nombre de Dios previously held by his brother. By this time, Suárez and his extended family represented merchants in Seville and Panama, and they ran one of the most lucrative firms in Peru.[87] Juana's case is echoed in others of Moriscas in Peru who associated themselves with prominent families.

REQUESTS FOR MORISCOS DENIED

Local authorities in Spanish America on a number of occasions requested that the Crown send Moriscos to help settle and build colonial towns and fortifications. Reputed to be skilled artisans in Spain, Moriscos were sought to start silk-raising production in New Spain and to build fortifications in Havana and along the northern coast of South America in the area that is today Venezuela. These requests were eventually denied by the Crown, and Moriscos were not officially granted licenses to pass to the Americas to carry out these activities. However, as the cases of interpreters show, their perceived usefulness enabled some to make the journey anyway, supported by powerful Spaniards in need of their services.

During the early years of Spanish colonization of the Caribbean islands and mainland, the granting of licenses and the enforcement of emigration restrictions was more fluid. Officials of the town councils and royal courts composed a stream of letters to the Council of the Indies, lamenting the small Spanish population and requesting that more emigrants be recruited to populate and settle the new towns.[88] From the late 1550s to 1575, African slaves were transported to Havana to construct the fort of La Fuerza, and approximately two hundred slaves continued to work on urban military constructions into the seventeenth century. According to Alejandro de la Fuente, in 1596, some of the forty-five forced laborers on Havana's forts were Muslim and Turkish slaves.[89] These Havana slaves also included the Mandinga and Wolof peoples of the Senegal Valley, deemed Muslims and potentially rebellious. In the seventeenth century the neighboring Fulo, also thought to be Muslims, joined the Mandinga and Wolof as slaves in Spanish America.[90] The Spanish Crown placed some restrictions on their importation to the Americas, but a number nevertheless were also forcibly taken across the Atlantic. In Havana, local officials were aware of the presence of Muslims laboring as royal slaves, and in the 1650s ordered slave owners to declare their Muslim and North African slaves.[91]

Demands were similar along the northern coast of South America, in the defense of the coastline of what is today Venezuela. By 1600 fears

of Dutch incursions along the Caribbean basin led local officials to petition the Crown for assistance in defending their towns and islands. In
1604 the engineer of the Cartagena fortifications Juan Bautista Antoneli
examined the salt pans of Araya, a haven for Dutch smugglers. Antoneli
determined that the salt mines should be inundated via canals linking the
ocean with the low-lying salt-producing areas, in order to discourage the
Dutch who had been actively loading their ships with salt. Approaching
the eve of the expulsion of the Moriscos from Spain, Antoneli requested
that the Junta de Guerra de Indias allow between five and six hundred
Moriscos from southern Spain to travel to Araya to construct the canals
that he hoped would drench the salt pans, rendering them useless to the
Dutch.[92] While gaining initial support from the Junta de Guerra, Antoneli's project was soon abandoned due to lack of funds.

Moriscos were noted for their skills as artisans in Spain, and some
local colonial officials considered bringing them to Spanish America to work on a number of projects. This was in sharp contrast to
Crown policies. In 1537 the bishop of Mexico Friar Juan de Zumárraga requested that a group of married Moriscos be allowed to travel
to New Spain to teach indigenous peoples the delicate art of raising
silkworms and producing silk. Zumárraga hoped sericulture would
provide both a civilizing activity and a source of income for the indigenous peoples congregated in the newly founded mission communities.[93] However, the Crown rejected his request to grant Granadan
Moriscos licenses. The intricate wooden ceiling and door carvings on
churches in the new city parishes and countryside doctrinas also suggest the work of Morisco carpenters and artisans in Spain. However,
recent art historians have found evidence that Amerindians trained by
Spanish artisans and clerics, not Moriscos, participated in their construction in the Americas.[94] If Moriscos ever did labor on these, they
most likely would not have been officially listed as Moriscos in the
records, after requests like those of Zumárraga were turned down by
the Crown. The churches of the doctrinas were well inland, in close
proximity to indigenous dwellings, unlike the fortifications that drew
galley slaves who were bound by royal decrees to return to their ships
in the more cosmopolitan ports such as Havana, Callao, or Veracruz.

* * *

Due to the concerns over title and dominion, the Spanish Crown sought
to control and limit access to indigenous peoples to only devout Catholics

who could prove good social standing, pious behavior, and eventually trace their lineage back several generations to old Christian families. While there was some demand for Moriscos and North Africans to labor in the Americas, primarily as slaves, but also as interpreters and artisans, due to their perceived linguistic abilities or skills as carpenters or silk workers in Spain, the Crown's concerns with evangelization took precedence. Throughout the sixteenth century, Spanish monarchs issued a number of royal decrees restricting emigration. However, enforcement wavered during the early conquests, and free emigrants obtained false licenses or crossed the Atlantic in a variety of clandestine ways.

Unfree emigration accounted for the presence of many Moriscos in Spanish America, and the status of slaves plays into the discussions over the social standing of suspected Morisco encomenderos and wealthy office holders. This is a very different dynamic from the one that conversos faced. Although Jews in medieval Iberia could in theory be enslaved under similar conditions as Muslims, no such cases in sixteenth- and seventeenth-century Spain or Spanish America were uncovered during my research. As potentially enslaveable, Moriscos faced a very specific set of circumstances that defined their social status. Actions, dress, customs, and appearance mattered, and descriptions of individuals in the courts emphasized some elements over others in determining if someone had been a slave, whether someone could be enslaved, or whether they could possess honor and the accompanying benefits.

CHAPTER 3

Forbidden Crossings

Emigration Legislation
and Morisco Responses

In 1577, Diego Herrador, a shoemaker residing in Mexico City, stood before inquisitors, charged with passing to New Spain with a false license. Inquisitor Licentiate Francisco Santos García accused Herrador that he, "being of the caste and lineage of Moriscos and the grandson of a *quemado* on his mother's side, made a false report that he is an old Christian of pure blood and ancestry, and that no one of his lineage has been punished by the Holy Office."[1] During his trial, the shoemaker described how he obtained his false license. Herrador's case was eventually dismissed because inquisitors learned that they no longer had the jurisdiction to prosecute cases of false licenses and had to restrict themselves to matters of the faith. It is unclear what happened to Herrador after this ruling, yet it reveals the openings in the legislation that allowed "new Christians" to reach the Americas despite prohibitions. Knowledge of the strategies that prospective emigrants could use to cross the Atlantic spread not only among those searching for false licenses but also across various sectors of colonial society, as royal decrees were read publicly and officials aired their complaints. The anxieties created by the frequent breaches of the restrictions on Morisco emigration paved the road for future conflicts over status in colonial society.

Initially, the royal decrees were enforced only sporadically, as practical concerns with populating the islands and mainland of the Americas took precedence over religious imperatives. However, the situation changed by the end of the sixteenth century with the rising Spanish presence. Royal decrees demanding the policing of interior regions and the establishment of inquisitorial tribunals created a vigilant atmosphere that individuals could exploit in their competition over offices and encomiendas, as new generations of Iberians emigrated to the Americas and came into conflict with the self-styled first conquerors and settlers. Individuals banned from settling in the New World employed various strategies to evade the restrictions. There is ample evidence that despite prohibitions, Moriscos did have the means to travel freely to Spanish America, in the event that they or powerful sponsors desired to do so.

Official policies, based on ideals that were couched in millenarian language, were difficult to carry out. Vast distances between both Spain and the Americas, and within the rapidly expanding empire, delayed the application of colonial policies. Competing jurisdictional claims also slowed the process, allowing individuals to slip through the cracks. The Spanish legal system was porous and diffuse, lacking a codified series of laws, especially before the *Recopilación de Leyes de Indias* (1681). Authorities constantly consulted one another and debated policies, providing many openings for individual action. Much if not most of Spanish civil and criminal law was applicable to the Indies, but there was also the question of its relationship to Amerindian customary practices. Expansion of the empire brought with it a host of new administrative questions. In theory, regulations for governing stemmed from the king, but in practice the royal councils reviewed the issues and made recommendations for the monarch to either reject or issue the appropriate decrees. Although the laws derived from the king and royal council, they were often initiated in response to local problems, resulting in legislation that was based on reactions to particular cases that could be applied to others and subsequently cited in new contexts. Royal decrees supporting and creating new laws proliferated, and officials on the ground would determine how and if to respond. In this sense, the formulaic acknowledgment of *obedezco pero no cumplo* (I obey, but I do not carry out the order) could allow for a degree of flexibility in colonial settings, so that peoples' actions, lawsuits, and sense of identity became situational and fluid to adapt to the circumstances.[2] Debates concerning one part of the Spanish world could have empire-wide repercussions, as they were cited in debates at court to define and restrict peoples living under Spanish rule. The cases of Moriscos in the Americas provide one such lens through which to examine the relationship between the formulation of legal identities through everyday negotiations and the debates at court to produce policies. The concurrent descriptions

of seminomadic indigenous groups such as the Chichimeca, Chiriguanos, or Araucanos with those concerning alárabes and Moriscos following the Alpujarras uprising reveal how Spanish jurists and
theologians were defining customary practices with policies in mind.
Arguments about whether it was licit to enslave either Moriscos or
Amerindians drew heavily from ethnographic descriptions.[3]

Due to the gap between expected and real enforcement of the legislation, Morisco emigrants crossed the Atlantic and played a role in
colonial society. Both enslaved and free Moriscos found in the openings in the legislation a way to pass clandestinely. But for Spanish
authorities, even the possibility of their presence raised concerns and
fears that were already inflamed by a preoccupation with justifying
imperial rule and establishing a model Catholic republic. Bishops
and inquisitors complained about the difficulty of policing frontier
regions and invoked the specter of new Christian settlement at the
edges of empire. They issued edicts stigmatizing Morisco practices
that were preached publicly, conveying a broader sense of urgency to
the local population. These fears entered denunciations arising from
feuds over position in the colonial hierarchy, as the consequences of
possessing a Morisco lineage involved material losses and could affect
a family for generations. In a system that encouraged heated disputes
over encomiendas, due to their nonhereditary nature, families had
powerful incentives to exclude their rivals.[4]

LEGISLATING EMIGRATION, A POROUS WEB: 1492–1548

During the sixteenth century, anxieties over legitimate title crept
into the royal decrees or cédulas that regulated emigration to Spanish America. According to even the earliest of these laws, settlement
of the Spanish colonies was in theory limited to old Christians. These
attempts to restrict the presence of new Christians of Muslim and Jewish descent stemmed from concerns that they would undermine Spanish missionary efforts and introduce heterodoxy into a land where
Spanish missionaries and theologians hoped to impose Catholicism
easily. Spanish authorities' fears became heightened in response to
the Reformation. The Crown's internal policies toward the Moriscos
played a role in the articulation and enforcement of laws concerning
emigration. In Spain, legislation restricting the Moriscos and appre-
hension surrounding their presence increased during the sixteenth
century. This dynamic also possessed a transatlantic dimension.

The earliest decrees regulating emigration to the Spanish Americas issued by the Crown in 1501 were included in the instructions given to Friar Nicolás de Ovando, who was appointed first governor of Hispaniola. These instructions stipulated, "As we with great care have to carry out the conversion of the Indians to our holy Catholic faith: if you find persons suspect in matters of the faith present during the said conversion, it could create an impediment. Do not consent or allow Muslims or Jews, heretics, or anyone reconciled by the Inquisition, or persons newly converted to our Faith to go there, unless they are black slaves . . . who were born in the power of Christians, our subjects and native inhabitants."[5] These restrictions were echoed in the cédulas that regulated the colonization and settlement of the new Spanish territories. In 1508 King Ferdinand ordered the Casa de Contratación not to permit either the "children and grandchildren of the converts of Jews and Muslims, or the children of those executed or reconciled by the Inquisition" to travel to or trade in Hispaniola.[6] Orders for the settlement of Florida and Bimini, issued by Queen Juana in 1514, specified that "new Christians [who are descendants] of Muslims and Jews can neither populate nor reside in the said islands under penalty of the loss of their property and of our favor."[7] Despite complaints about the shortage of Spanish settlers in the newly conquered regions and specific requests for Morisco or North African labor, the Crown maintained officially that only old Christians could settle in the Western Hemisphere.

It is unclear how enforceable these decrees against Morisco migration to the Americas were. Prior to the adoption of the statutes of limpieza de sangre in 1548, religious interests were less important than policies that would benefit imperial expansion and the Royal Treasury. Royal licenses and *habilitaciones* provided loopholes in the contradictory royal decrees restricting emigration. For example, in 1509 King Ferdinand issued a general license to Castilian converso communities paying the *composición*.[8] Some local officials in the Caribbean and in New Spain initially favored projects involving Morisco artisans and laborers. Following the arrival of these early new Christian emigrants, competition in the recently established colonial settlements placed pressures on their presence. Growing resentments tested the limits of religious tolerance as conversos and Moriscos, due to their legal status as prohibited persons, became increasingly vulnerable to denunciation.

Local authorities in the Caribbean islands lodged complaints about new Christians that resulted in renewed decrees to restrict their presence. In 1539 Charles V ordered officials to address "what has been seen by experience: the great damage and disadvantage that results from transporting to our Indies the children of burned and reconciled Jews and Muslims and those who are newly converted."[9] This decree, upon its public proclamation from the steps of Seville's cathedral, ordered that none of these individuals could pass to Spanish America "in any manner."[10] Yet it also provided an exception for purchasing a royal license, so that some could travel without penalties.[11] This permitted slaveholders to purchase licenses for their Morisco and North African slaves to accompany them to Spanish America, with the provision that they be returned to Spain after a specified number of years. Members of the Granadan Morisco nobility were also exempt from most legislation regulating Moriscos, and they could bear arms and wear silk in accordance with their high status. Some may have legally purchased licenses to cross the Atlantic.[12]

During the first half of the sixteenth century, royal policies toward the broader Morisco population in Spain were also less stringent. This may have had repercussions on their ability to cross the Atlantic. Following their initial forced baptism in 1499–1501 the Granadan Moriscos were granted a "period of grace" exempting them from full inquisitorial scrutiny, so that they could be fully instructed in Catholicism. In 1526 Charles V granted them the right, like the conversos, to pay a tax in exchange for certain privileges and allowed them to continue some of their practices for a forty-year period.[13] Nonetheless, ecclesiastical authorities issued periodic prohibitions of Morisco customs that included food, dress, language, and dance, and the terms of this agreement had to be renegotiated continuously. Even in 1526, during Charles V's stay in Granada, a panel of theologians in the royal chapel of that city banned Morisco practices and ordered the activation of an inquisitorial tribunal.[14] Yet inquisitorial prosecution of Morisco cases did not gain momentum until after Philip II's reign began in 1556.[15] During this early period, bishops oversaw the conversion of the Moriscos in their dioceses, and missionaries such as the Jesuits and Franciscans also actively proselytized among the Moriscos in Granada.[16]

LEGISLATING EMIGRATION, THE NET TIGHTENS: 1548–1621

During the reigns of Philip II and Philip III, policies restricting the movement of Moriscos intensified across the Spanish world. This was tied to changing peninsular dynamics, from Counter-Reformation politics, to the adoption of the purity of blood statutes, to growing suspicion of the loyalty of the Moriscos. This larger political context played a role in policies affecting emigration to Spanish America and also in how Spaniards were defining their nation and empire.

While the purity of blood statutes appeared in Spain in the late fifteenth century, they gained ground during Philip II's reign. They required that anyone applying to hold a prestigious post, or to attend university, provide documents testifying to their old Christian ancestry. Applicants for these positions had to prove their limpieza de sangre—that none of their ancestors descended from Muslims or Jews. These statutes delimited the official boundaries of who could hold power and status in the Spanish world. The resulting prevalence of limpieza discourses also produced and reinforced a link between concepts like heresy and faithfulness, and their physical transmission to future generations through bodily fluids.[17]

The political climate toward the Moriscos in Spain was shifting, and they appeared increasingly in protonationalistic discourses about loyalty and fears concerning the vulnerability of Spain's Catholic empire. By the mid-sixteenth century some Spanish authorities had become frustrated with the slow progress of the assimilation of the Morisco population. By this time, the growth of the Ottoman Empire, Berber incursions on Spanish outposts in North Africa, and worries that the Moriscos would ally with either North Africans or French Protestants who were active in the Mediterranean, prompted some Spaniards to fear increasingly that Moriscos would become a fifth column in Spain.[18] The Crown and local authorities issued further restrictions and enforced them more rigorously. In Valencia anxieties had already taken hold in the 1540s as peace with the Ottomans failed and North African corsairs conducted raids along the coast. Valencian authorities issued laws distinguishing between local Moriscos and those born in Granada, Aragon, and North Africa.[19] In 1560 a royal decree barred Moriscos from owning African slaves. In addition, any African slaves who had previously belonged to Moriscos were prohibited from being taken to the Americas.[20] In Granada, increasing restrictions on the Morisco population contributed to the second Alpujarras uprising of 1569–72. News of the revolt spread across the Spanish world, and fears of Morisco presence extended with it. Once the rebellion had been suppressed and the remaining Moriscos were expelled from Granada and resettled across Castile, suspicion extended to Morisco communities across Spain. Moriscos were now conflated increasingly with the Granadans and cast as rebels and apostates.[21]

By the mid-sixteenth century the Crown continued to express concern over the arrival of converts from Islam and their descendants in the Spanish Americas and intensified its efforts. Charles V issued a series of decrees during the 1550s that illustrate the difficulties of enforcing royal policies toward emigration. It is evident from these cédulas that Moriscos and North African Muslims had been able to evade the controls on emigration and disappear across the vast continent. The decrees also reflected ongoing official concerns with the religiosity of indigenous peoples, as they expressed preoccupation with their status as neophytes to the Catholic faith. In 1550 Charles V addressed a royal provision to the judges of the audiencias in the Americas. Drawing from a previous cédula that he issued in 1543 following a meeting of the Council of the Indies to discuss the subject of Muslim presence in the Spanish territories, Charles V further emphasized the need to expel North African slaves from the Americas: "We are informed that there have passed and pass daily to these parts some North African slave men and women as well as free persons newly converted from Islam and their children, although it is prohibited by us. They should in no way pass because of the many inconveniences that have followed . . . [and] because in such a new land as this in which the faith is freshly planted it is expedient that all opportunity [to pass] should be removed so that there cannot be sown or made public in it the sect of Muhammad or any other . . . that undermines our holy Catholic faith."[22] By the mid-sixteenth century, shortly after the adoption of the purity of blood statutes, religious restrictions on emigration were increasingly enforced. Ordinances for the Casa de Contratación issued in 1552 specified that no new converts from Judaism or Islam could travel to the Americas without a royal license. Furthermore, anyone convicted by the Inquisition was also barred from emigrating.[23] These new regulations required prospective emigrants like the shoemaker Diego Herrador to provide documentation proving their limpieza de sangre or old Christian status in order to obtain a license.

Subsequent royal decrees reveal that the clandestine movement of people continued. In 1559, a new cédula addressed to the bishops and archbishops in the Spanish American dioceses further emphasized the Crown's need to restrict emigration to the Americas: "Because . . . the Devil is so solicitous to sow heresies in Christendom, some Lutherans and others who are of the caste of Muslims and Jews who want to live in observance of their law and ceremonies have come to these parts.

It is expedient that where our Catholic faith is now newly planted there be great vigilance so that no heresy can be sown. . . . If any is found it should be extirpated, undone and punished with rigor."[24] In this decree Philip II urged the bishops and archbishops to investigate whether any suspected Muslims, Jews, Protestants, or heretics had settled in their dioceses, and to mete out exemplary punishment to those they found. He also ordered the viceroys, governors, and judges of the audiencias to aid the bishops and archbishops in their search for heretics. Because this decree was issued before the establishment of the Holy Office's tribunals in the Indies, the king ordered that any Muslims, Jews, or Protestants who were found be sent for trial to the Supreme Council of the Inquisition in Spain.[25]

In 1565, Philip II reissued to the judges of New Spain and the governor of Guatemala a 1511 decree of Queen Juana, that children and grandchildren of quemados and *reconciliados* could not hold offices in the Americas.[26] The 1511 cédula extended the restrictions on officeholding that were current in the Spanish kingdoms to the newly claimed territories in the Caribbean. Philip II did not refer to local specificities—he only reissued the cédula—but Juana's decree stated that she was informed of new Christians on Hispaniola, and the Crown wanted to ensure that the laws restricting officeholding in the Spanish kingdoms also applied to them. During the early sixteenth century, some conversos and Moriscos had gained positions of authority in the Caribbean islands and in New Spain, as recorded in the earlier cases of the Morisco interpreters.[27] By the time of Philip II's decree, conversos and Moriscos continued to represent competition for those without prestigious public offices, and officials moved forcefully to condemn their presence.

The establishment of inquisitorial tribunals in Spanish America illustrates how authorities responded to this perceived threat, as they in theory buttressed the Crown's policy on emigration. The earliest inquisitorial tribunals in the New World were created in Lima (1570) and in Mexico City (1571).[28] Previously, local bishops had the authority to prosecute religious offenses that were not remitted to the Supreme Council of the Inquisition in Spain.[29] Once the tribunals were formally set up, inquisitors claimed the sole right to publish edicts of faith, thereby instigating jurisdictional disputes with local bishops who wished to maintain their previous levels of control over prosecuting religious offenses in their dioceses, a practice that granted bishops power within their communities that were already experiencing conflicts between secular and ecclesiastical authorities. In 1570 Philip II issued a provision ordering the American audiencias to aid the newly appointed inquisitors in their activities. The provision stressed vehemently the need for preserving Catholicism in Spanish America: "Considering the augmentation . . . to our holy Catholic faith as a result of the discovery and conquest and new population of these provinces and that by Divine Providence and grace the native inhabitants of these . . . have been illuminated to learn the true path of the evangelical doctrine, . . . it is very necessary to take special care and vigilance in the preservation of the devotion, and the good name, reputation and fame of its settlers . . . as faithful and Catholic Christians, and natural-born and true Spaniards."[30] Invoking Spain's title to the Americas, Philip II excoriated heretics who tried to pervert the "faithful and devout Christians" who lived in the "provinces that God has entrusted to [the Spanish Crown]."[31] He argued that in punishing heretics, "by divine clemency and grace our Kingdoms and lands have been cleansed of all error, and this pestilence and contagion has been avoided. It is hoped that by divine mercy [our lands] will be preserved from now on to avoid and act so that such great offense to the Faith and Christian religion does not pass to these parts."[32] By expelling heretics, Philip II argued, "so much notice and infamy to our subjects would be avoided, and to their fealty and loyalty, and the native inhabitants of those parts would not be perverted and separated from the guild of the holy Church."[33] Philip II's decree was influenced by the idea of the *corpus mysticum*, or body politic, that was current in sixteenth-century Spanish understandings of community. This theory defined members of a group as belonging to the same body and stressed the interdependence of the various members.[34] The corpus mysticum referred originally to the conception of the church in medieval Europe as a mystical body in which Christ was the head.[35] Eventually, "the commonwealth was conceived of as a living organism and thus systematically compared with the human body."[36] This image had begun to be incorporated and codified in laws as early as the *Siete Partidas* of Alfonso X in the thirteenth century.[37] The corpus mysticum suffused contemporary political theory. During the sixteenth and seventeenth centuries, Spanish jurists and theologians conceived of the state as the collective body of the prince, parallel to the church as the body of Christ. Sermons and treatises frequently invoked the image of the corpus mysticum when speaking of heresy as illness and advocating the physical exclusion or expulsion of perceived heretics from the body politic. For example, authors such as Pedro Aznar Cardona, who condoned the expulsion of the Moriscos from Spain, used medical imagery to cast them as "the venom, the poison, the abscess and the pestilent corruption that our Catholic Galen of Galens has purged from the mystical body of the Spanish Christian republic."[38]

Once the inquisitorial tribunals were established in Spanish America, they issued a number of edicts of faith that were designed to encourage denunciations of heresy and unorthodox practices. The edicts were preached publicly, and those listening were urged to denounce suspected Muslims, Jews, Protestants, and heretics in their communities. Some of the edicts provided detailed descriptions of the practices inquisitors sought to eradicate. For example, an edict read in Cuzco in 1575, and again in 1578, prohibited anyone from performing "Morisco ceremonies" that included dietary restrictions.[39] Another edict read in 1583 in Comayagua and Valladolid, Nicaragua, described practices attributed to Muslims and Moriscos such as praying five times a day (zala), performing ritual ablutions (guadoc), observing Ramadan, and specific burial practices.[40]

In Mexico City, Inquisitors Alonso Hernández de Bonilla and Alonso Granero de Avalos wrote in 1578 to the Supreme Council of the Inquisition in Spain. They related their concern that the mere public reading of the edicts of faith would encourage indigenous peoples to adopt forbidden practices if they heard about them too often. Bonilla and Avalos cautioned that although they read the edict of faith as they were ordered to do every year during Lent in the parishes and monasteries during their visita, they had "some doubt as to whether they should do it in a land so new, for the large number of ceremonies of the law of Moses and the sect of Muhammad, the errors of Luther and the alumbrados that are expressed therein in such detail that even in Spain there are fears that through that venue some would learn them, and even more so in a land so new and among people who, although Spaniards, were born here. . . . They did not have knowledge [of these practices] and those who were born in Spain have by now forgotten them. In this way, it appears a greater inconvenience to remind them of [the practices because] . . . some things might even infect the Indians."[41]

PUSHING BOUNDARIES: CLANDESTINE PASSAGES
TO THE SPANISH AMERICAS

Geographical distance and the competing jurisdictional claims of ecclesiastical and secular authorities made control over clandestine emigrants difficult. In a letter from Nombre de Dios, Panama, on 26 June 1569, the newly appointed prosecutor for the Inquisition in Lima, Licentiate Juan Alcedo de la Rocha, expressed concern over the presence of a Portuguese Jew in Panama who had fled Seville's inquisitorial prison. Alcedo requested that the Supreme Council of the Inquisition "order that an account be sent to us whenever prisoners of the inquisitions in Spain flee, so that we can look for them here." He added, "I do not think that this one was the first, because people can pass here without license and there is much fraud and evildoing among the shipmasters, and little or no punishment."[42] The issues of deceit and illegal passage arose frequently in Spanish officials' complaints about the challenges of regulating emigration.

In order to travel legally to the Americas, emigrants needed both a royal license issued at the Casa de Contratación and, after 1552, papers proving limpieza de sangre. In addition to falsifying documents, it was not uncommon for individuals to obtain licenses legally and then sell them to prospective emigrants. Travelers often made private agreements with shipmasters to conceal them during the voyage, or they stowed away altogether. Sailors and soldiers were cited for jumping ship once they reached the coast. Finally, emigrants attempting to evade controls in Seville frequently sailed from ports in Portugal or the Canary Islands.[43] Witnesses were commonly paid to testify to a family's old Christian lineage.

Diego Herrador, the shoemaker whose case was presented at the beginning of this chapter, illustrates the ways in which individuals passed to the Spanish Americas. On 23 May 1576, Herrador was summoned before Mexican inquisitors. The inquisitors first asked Herrador about his name, a question that was informed by the practice of naming and changing names in early modern Spain, especially as individuals attempted to conceal suspect lineages. After Herrador responded to the routine request to provide his genealogy, inquisitors asked him how he came by his surname, when it had belonged to neither of his parents, whose last names were Hernández and Céspedes. Herrador replied that he had adopted the surname of his paternal grandfather, Francisco Herrador.[44] He was then asked why his father had chosen the last name Hernández, and not Herrador. Herrador testified that although he did not know why his father had chosen this last name, he had heard people from his birthplace in Mérida, Extremadura, saying that "they were Moriscos, and his parents descended from the caste of Moriscos from Hornachos where his father and mother had their origin and *naturaleza*."[45] Likewise, Herrador stated that he had not chosen the last name Céspedes because it was not from his father's side, although he was aware that it was rumored publicly in Mérida that his maternal grandfather, Joan de Céspedes, had been executed by the Inquisition of Llerena, so he did not pick this last name either.[46]

Herrador's testimony is suggestive of other cases—the ease with which witnesses could be marshaled to vouch for an individual's social standing and lineage. Herrador was able to obtain papers in Mérida to prove limpieza de sangre by summoning false witnesses. He described how he had acquired the *información*, which he showed to inquisitors at their request. He had obtained the sixteen-page document on 7 February 1572, in the presence of several witnesses, and the public notaries of Mérida, Joan Ortiz, Alonso Ortiz, and Cristóbal de Silva.[47] Inquisitors pressed Herrador as to why he had sworn to not have been among the prohibited, when he was a Morisco and a descendant of Joan de Céspedes, a quemado. He replied, "Miguel Rodríguez, his brother-in-law, made the petition and solicited the information, and presented the witnesses, and given that they swore a lie, he truly does not know how it was done, nor does he know them, nor does he know if they knew him." Herrador insisted that it was his brother-in-law who "did everything, and he secured the license from His Majesty."[48] Each of the four witnesses presented by Rodríguez and Herrador provided identical reassurance that they knew the family, their parents, and grandparents, and that all were legitimate children. They provided a physical description of the two men, as well as their wives, María de Vargas and Ysabel Rodríguez, and Miguel Rodríguez's son, Francisco. They also attested to the purity of their lineage and their status as old Christians who were "calm and peaceful, of good lifestyle and reputation."[49] For licenses to the Indies, it was important that witnesses describe prospective emigrants' behavior within their communities and provide evidence of their civility. These descriptions became increasingly important, confirming their legal status as peaceful and trustworthy, as faithful citizens and subjects of the Spanish Crown. As opposed to the Portuguese or the British, Spanish officials required evidence of good conduct for emigration to the Americas. Good conduct, in turn, was tied closely to religious standing and framed in a vocabulary that associated Christianity with civility and loyalty.

Herrador eventually admitted that instead of processing his papers at the Casa de Contratación in Seville, he sailed first to the Canary

Islands from the port of Lisbon. On the island of Palma, Herrador was able to board a ship as a passenger sailing with the priest Joan de Sant Pedro and embark for New Spain.[50] The route from Lisbon to the Canary Islands was well traveled among non-Spaniards wishing to avoid controls when engaging in trade in Spanish America.[51] A royal decree issued by Charles V in 1540 described the strategies that foreigners, especially the Portuguese, used in loading their ships with unregistered merchandise and sailing for the Indies. According to this decree, they "pretend to load their ships for the Canary Islands, and go secretly to Hispaniola, and other parts of our Indies."[52] In 1558 another decree mentioned ships departing from Portuguese ports that carried prohibited passengers and unregistered goods: "They pretend to be going to Brazil, but that due to a storm, they docked in these parts."[53] In a 1560 cédula ordering the deportation of illegal settlers, Philip II outlined some of the strategies used by travelers to circumvent the law:

> They pass to our Indies secretly, some as sailors, others as soldiers, and others pretending to be merchants or their agents. Others go through the Canary Islands, and find other routes and ways to pass. Under these guises men pass who are thugs and of sinful life and poor example, and prohibited persons . . . some people leave from ports that are outside of these kingdoms, in foreign and domestic ships, so that they go to some parts of the kingdom where they depart and pretend that with bad weather they docked in the Indies . . . With this deceit they pass . . . [and] acquire goods and estates and they come with it to these kingdoms or send them to the Casa de Contratación in Seville . . . and there they give it to their heirs.[54]

In drafting these laws, Philip II and the Council of the Indies may have had in mind individuals such as Diego Romero, an encomendero from New Granada who was accused in 1558 of being an escaped slave from North Africa and who accumulated wealth and status due to his participation in the early conquests.[55] A letter from Seville's inquisitors to the Suprema on 24 March 1562 requesting the establishment of an inquisitorial tribunal in the Canary Islands reiterated the difficulty of controlling emigration from the islands' ports. Licentiates Andrés Gasco, Miguel de Carpio and Francisco de Soto argued that the establishment of an Inquisition there "would be a useful thing because those islands are the port and throughway for all commerce with the east and west Indies, and they are also close to North Africa."[56] In this way they could "guard and oversee so that infected persons do not pass to the Indies."[57] Again, authorities invoked the image of the body politic by insisting that emigration should only be permissible for Spaniards who had not been "infected" with heresy. In Las Palmas, Herrador was required to show his license to a judge at the port in order to be allowed to sail. He had obtained it after proffering the false testimony from Mérida, in which he claimed to be an old Christian.

While the prosecutor of the Inquisition, Doctor Bartolomé Lobo Guerrero, requested full punishment for Herrador so that "others do not dare to make similar false *informaciones*," his case was dismissed.[58] Inquisitor Bonilla and prosecutor Licentiate Santos García ruled on 1 June 1583 that because the most recent edicts sent by the Suprema had removed passing to the Indies with a false license from the list of crimes subject to inquisitorial prosecution, they could not proceed any further with the case against Herrador. Herrador's case illustrates the complexities and contradictions involved in authorities' attempts to control emigration to the Americas while interpreting the law in a legally pluralistic setting. The court at the Casa de Contratación in Seville ultimately had jurisdiction over cases of clandestine emigration.

In another example, in 1569, Cristóbal Ribero was accused of traveling to the Americas without a license, as a foreigner and a Morisco. He had set sail from Cádiz to Florida earlier that year in the ship Nuestra Señora de la Consolación. The ship was full of foreigners— the Portuguese—who were forced to return to the bay of Cádiz following a powerful storm. In order to transport foreigners to Spanish America "in the guise of sailors," shipmasters Blas Donys and Sebastián Álvarez found witnesses to testify under oath during the official inspection of the ship that they were all vecinos (legal residents) of Ayamonte, near Seville and the Portuguese border.[59] Ribero was charged with having boarded the ship knowingly, despite royal prohibitions and having found witnesses to swear on his behalf that he was not a foreigner. Ribero, who was Portuguese, was reputedly the "son of a newly converted Morisco."[60] The judge in Cádiz, Juan de Avalia, sentenced him to one hundred lashes and exile from the Spanish kingdoms for ten years, which was eventually reduced to a maximum of five years of exile.[61]

Newly appointed officials embarking to occupy their posts in the Americas sometimes eased the passage of travelers who would otherwise have been prohibited. Almost all officials were allotted spaces for servants and dependents to accompany them. The number was flexible and was contingent largely on the status of the appointment with viceroys receiving the largest number of allotments. Sometimes, these included Morisco servants and slaves, who were issued licenses usually with restrictions on the amount of time they could remain in the Americas. At other times, these spaces were sold illegally. In 1561, Alonso Ortiz de Elgueta was tried by the court of the Casa de Contratación for selling licenses to small farmers (*labradores*) to accompany the newly appointed governor Diego de Vargas to Nicaragua and Río de Amazonas. According to witnesses, Ortiz and Vargas passed through the Andalusian municipalities of Córdoba, Úbeda, Baeza, and Osuna, on their way to Seville, beating drums and carrying a flag that they set up in the inns where they spent the night. One witness stated that Vargas "had put up a public banner like a captain who had orders from the king to recruit people."[62] The men claimed to be looking for small farmers to settle and work the lands they were about to embark for, and they requested up to thirty ducats in payment for each license. According to witness Francisco Mexía, "they have spread unrest . . . in that land especially in the town of Osuna and have made some small farmers sell their estates to give and lend them money."[63] Another witness described their disregard for the restrictions on who could travel to the Americas, although he primarily alluded to the limitations on married persons and members of religious orders, who supposedly had obligations in Spain. Miguel Ruiz, a witness from Córdoba, testified that he had heard that Vargas had ordered it proclaimed publicly that "all persons, married and single, widows, priests, friars and nuns and *beatas* of whatever quality who want to can pass to the Indies . . . if they spoke to Diego de Vargas, he would take them."[64]

Interestingly, Ortiz's response to these charges focused primarily on his desire to take only honorable old Christians to the Americas. Aware of the prohibitions on new Christian emigration, Ortiz turned this knowledge to his advantage. He argued that he needed to borrow money from the rich labradores to pay for the poor ones he was forced to bring with him. The king had granted him licenses for small farmers who would sustain settlement in the lands he and Vargas were to administer because "the roots of a settlement are the labradores."[65] Ortiz argued that he only "named people who were qualified (*abiles*) and not of the prohibited."[66] According to Ortiz, he included people who "although they are poor they are honorable and of good caste . . . so that it is possible to found and make the settlement . . . I was very careful and vigilant in doing this so that if the land had to be populated with labradores, that they be honorable people, and this is why I brought the poor at my expense and accepted help from the others . . . In looking into and considering this, I was serving God and his majesty."[67]

Royal decrees reveal that even enlisted soldiers and sailors had a reputation for jumping ship. Absenteeism provided a cheap means of emigrating, as individuals could bypass the extensive bureaucracy and fees charged for each step involved in obtaining an official license. Alejandro de la Fuente has noted how officials in Havana discussed these frequent desertions, in light of a 1576 decree that escaped sailors be imprisoned and sent to the galleys as punishment. Contemporaries commented on the international nature of the ships' crews, and deserters remaining in Havana might have originally been from Genoa, Greece, Venice, England, or France.[68]

Enlisting as soldiers or sailors could thus enable periodic escape to Spanish America. On 27 April 1593 Philip II granted Pedro de Vascuñán license to take Ginés Jorquera from Cartagena de Indias to Nombre de Dios, and on to Seville to face charges at the court of the Casa de Contratación. The Audiencia of Panama had sentenced Jorquera to exile to Spain, "for being a Morisco and of those prohibited to pass to the Indies."[69] On 23 June 1595 Jorquera testified before judges at the Casa de Contratación. He stated that about sixteen years previously he had sailed to the Americas from the port of Sanlúcar de Barrameda, in the fleet to Tierra Firme. He claimed to have boarded the ship with others. They spoke with the ship's master who informed them that they lacked people for the voyage, and because of this, Jorquera joined the ship's crew. Once he arrived in Nombre de Dios, he fell ill after having worked to unload the ship. Jorquera claimed he was hospitalized for three months and was thus left behind in Nombre de Dios.

The prosecutor in the Casa de Contratación, Doctor Arias de Borja, demanded exemplary punishment for Jorquera who, he argued, was actually a runaway slave. Arias de Borja charged him with "being a slave and subject to servitude and a Morisco, who with little fear of justice and against the laws of this [Casa de Contratación], the cédulas and *provisiones* of his majesty, passed without order or license . . . to the Indies where he remained for a long time."[70] In his response to the prosecutor, Jorquera denied wrongdoing. He stated that he "was and is free and the slave of no one, not subject to servitude, and he was raised from birth in the city of Cartagena" in Spain before going to the Puerto de Santa María and Sanlúcar.[71] Jorquera insisted that "I entered to serve on a ship, to travel on it, and return, serving, being as I was . . . a poor and needy boy who had nothing to eat. And as a boy I neither understood nor knew that Moriscos could not pass to the Indies. Even if I had known this, it was not my intention to go to the Indies in order to stay there, but only to serve so that they would give me food. If I stayed in the Indies it was because those on the ship left me sick in a hospital where they cured me for the love of God. The whole time I was in the Indies I served in the field, taking care of livestock, until they ordered me to come to Spain. I am a good Christian and a free man."[72] Jorquera emphasized his service and hard work, casting himself as industrious and in this way a good Christian. He stressed his experience beginning life at sea as a young and poor boy, not yet of age, who followed the paths of many cabin boys in port cities who aspired to escape a life of destitution in Spain.

Contemporaries debated the value between achieving status through actions considered honorable, as opposed to genealogy or descent from noble families. Perceived membership in the Catholic community followed similar lines, as recent converts emphasized their donations to churches and monasteries, and their pious works, over their descent from old Christian families.[73] Others, often in the context of local disputes, claimed it was impossible for individuals to truly convert if they even possessed a drop of new Christian blood. These debates over status became increasingly racialized, as physical attributes deemed inherent were applied to individuals to prevent them from rising in social standing. Similar debates were also taking place within the church, as frustrated priests asserted that conversion was impossible even after a generation, discourses that also surfaced during repressions of indigenous religiosity such as the idolatry extirpation campaigns in the Andes.

Toward the end of the sixteenth century, following the Alpujarras rebellion, the language of the decrees prohibiting Muslims and Moriscos in the Americas became more forceful. On 20 May 1578 Philip II wrote a letter to the Audiencia of Mexico in which he increased restrictions on Morisco slaves. In addition to not allowing North African slaves, Philip II added, "until now there have passed some Moriscos of the Kingdom of Granada, with our license, with whom there are the same inconveniences as with the North Africans, and it is expedient that from now on they should not pass."[74] He ordered that no more licenses be granted to

Morisco slaves and that local officials in the Americas send to Spain all enslaved and free North Africans and Granadan Moriscos, "so that in no way there should remain any of them, nor their children . . . regardless of any of our cédulas or licenses that you would have for them . . . and do the same concerning the Moriscos."[75]

Unfortunately for Jorquera, Rodrigo Gallego, in the name of his wife Juana de Ayala and his sister-in-law Ana Jorquera, was at the same time actively petitioning the Casa de Contratación for the return of their North African slave, Ginés Jorquera. As heirs of their deceased father, Captain Francisco de Jorquera, the two women had inherited his slaves, including a North African who had escaped several years previously. Gallego presented the court with Captain Jorquera's will and the order to execute it, issued in Gibraltar, that stated that "Ginés, a North African slave of approximately twenty years of age, was brought exiled from the Indies to the jail of this court for having fled from the control of my father-in-law."[76] He requested that Jorquera be returned to them in Gibraltar. In their power of attorney to Gallego to oversee the business in Seville, the two sisters described how their slave Ginés had run away ten years previously, and they requested the profits from his sale in Seville.[77]

One clause of Captain Jorquera's will stood out. Drafted on 3 September 1588, it mentioned a "white North African slave, born in Mostaganem, called Ginés who, four years ago, had left and absented himself from my service. . . . [He] is now in Cartagena de Indias with Pedro Jorquera my brother. I order the said slave be collected [whom] I declare my property."[78] The sisters presented their father's will in Gibraltar, claiming to have received news that Ginés Jorquera had returned in the fleet of Vascuñán. They also presented a different account of his flight. They claimed he had run away from the Puerto de Santa María where he had been serving Captain Jorquera on one of the galleys.[79] One witness presented by Gallego at the court of the Casa de Contratación, priest Licentiate Juan Frutuoso de Carvajal, testified that he knew that Captain Jorquera was looking for Ginés in the Americas, and that Ginés had previously run away to Italy before he was captured and sent back to Spain.[80] In the end, the case turned against Gallego who was charged by Arias de Borja with allowing his slave to pass to the Americas without a license. Next, Borja sentenced Ginés Jorquera to be confiscated for the Royal Treasury. Despite his statement that he was a free man, Jorquera was sold into slavery at an auction at the Casa de Contratación.[81]

UNCONTROLLED SPACES AND JURISDICTIONAL CONCERNS

As seen in the dismissal of Diego Herrador's case before the Mexican Inquisition, because false licenses were no longer under its purview, changing laws and jurisdictions created openings through which individuals like Herrador could slip. As local authorities in Spanish America competed with each other over a variety of interests, the Crown's official policies toward Muslims and Moriscos assumed new contours and dimensions. Throughout the sixteenth century, secular authorities, bishops, and inquisitors lamented the effects of excessive distances on controlling the regions at the edges of empire. These areas comprised ineffectively regulated spaces that were not secured by any empire or group that had their designs on them and as a result provoked concerns over their proper use and administration. Anxieties over lands at the edges of empire surfaced in the colonial documentation, in the letters of viceroys and bishops, and in everyday conversations in the *pulquerías* or on street corners. These liminal lands, inhabited by vagabonds and "barbarous" peoples, haunted the imaginations of soldiers charged with pacifying them and of families provisioned for settling them.[82]

Jurisdictional disputes further undermined secular and ecclesiastical authorities' abilities to enforce the royal decrees. Taking Tridentine reforms a step further, bishops and inquisitors linked the impact of the "inconveniences" hindering indigenous evangelization—excessive distances and jurisdictional conflicts—to their inability to regulate a qualified clergy who would instruct indigenous peoples. They also voiced concern over their inability to adequately uphold restrictions on the presence of prohibited persons in the Crown's newly acquired territories. Spanish authorities' attempts to control spaces on the edges of empire produced an image of these regions as uncultivated and unsettled landscapes that escaped imperial projects and provided a potential haven for roaming peoples, vagrants, and new Christians to settle and interact with the indigenous groups that missionaries hoped to reduce. Given the great distances spanning the Spanish Empire and the challenges of enforcement, to what extent did local officials take seriously the repeated royal demands to curb new Christian emigration?

Spanish authorities did attempt to respond to orders from the Crown to restrict the movement of Moriscos and Muslims into the viceregal towns and settlements. Although enforcement was difficult,

evidence exists that the royal decrees were taken seriously by at least
some secular authorities. On 27 August 1567 Francisco Bahamonde
de Lugo, the governor in San Juan, Puerto Rico, wrote to Philip II
complaining of the difficulties in following his instructions to expel
prohibited persons. One of the royal cédulas ordered the governor
to pay attention that the passengers on the ships did not arrive "by
other means" (por otra parte). The king further ordered that every
passenger be registered in a special book and that those who had
arrived without a license be returned to Spain. Bahamonde de Lugo
pointed out that "there is much difficulty in this," and he elaborated
on how ships bound for the Indies would advertise publicly and load
passengers in Lisbon: "Because they come unregistered and without
license, the pilots and masters on this island, which is the first land
populated with Indians, underhandedly cast them out in remote ports
where once on land they find out that they will have to be returned
to Castile. With this fear they hide and disperse across the land and
its haciendas and farms."[83] Bahamonde de Lugo's complaint echoed
Jorquera's predicament: "They do not come to a settlement unless
they are infirm and sick, so it is necessary to be merciful with them
and cure them because they are Christians. If some are convalescing,
sometimes ships are lacking to send them, because it happens that
there are none bound for Spain in this port for six or seven months.
Indeed, to keep them imprisoned all this time, since they are poor, it
would be necessary to give them food and sustain them."[84]

In a letter to Philip II in 1597, Mexican Viceroy Gaspar de Zúñiga
y Acevedo, Count of Monterrey, also responded to the royal cédulas
restricting emigration. Zúñiga y Acevedo agreed to locate and expel
Moriscos and foreigners from New Spain. The viceroy wrote that he
would be "especially careful" not to allow any "foreigners" to disembark without a royal license.[85] He added that, "with respect to
Moriscos both free and enslaved, I have made many inquiries through
letters in all of this kingdom and the neighboring ones, and I will
begin collecting the warnings in order to procure their imprisonment
in time for the next fleet to send them in. I understand that there are
very few here."[86]

Difficulties in securing frontier regions as the empire was expanding both created spaces where individuals could hide and increased
authorities' anxieties that these regions were slipping from their control. Overlapping jurisdictions played a particular role as local officials contested their authority. In their correspondence and reports,

officials in Spanish America voiced dismay over the expanse of territory that often escaped their control. According to their accounts, such regions proved an especially fruitful place for clandestine activities and ideal for persons evading inquisitorial surveillance to settle. The Audiencia of Nueva Galicia was created in 1548 in order to govern the expanding northern frontier of New Spain, to ease the burden from the Audiencia of Mexico in Mexico City.[87] In a letter reporting his inspection of Nueva Galicia on 10 September 1554 Licentiate Lebrón de Quiñones expressed concern with the excessive distances between settlements on the northern frontier. The inspector stressed the need for an audiencia to control it. In response to critics of transferring the audiencia from its location in Compostela to the city of Guadalajara, Lebrón de Quiñones stated, "It is true that that kingdom can in no way be reigned or governed by this Audiencia of Mexico."[88] He continued, "I beg that an Audiencia be placed there because other provinces have one closer, and with fewer people and less business, and they cannot be governed nor is Justice administered there as fully as would be expedient."[89] Lebrón de Quiñones later added that "every resident of this land needs an audiencia. To say that it be governed by the Audiencia of Mexico is nonsense, although the residents of that kingdom would love to be like Moors without a king as they had been before there was an audiencia."[90] This pejorative expression "like Moors without a king," surfaces frequently in early modern Spanish descriptions of lawlessness. Spanish authorities in the Americas became increasingly concerned with recording and regulating behavior and customs. These fears became heightened in New Spain, as authorities envisioned disorderly individuals inhabiting regions beyond the reaches of their control. They also used language describing Muslims and Moriscos, and comparisons of imagined behaviors, to discredit their adversaries.

Concerns about the negative influence of new Christians and heterodox beliefs on indigenous peoples extended beyond colonial centers into frontier regions, as correspondence between local bishops and the inquisitorial tribunal in Mexico City suggests. During an inspection of the province of Tabasco in 1573 Francisco López Vivero wrote to the Mexican inquisitor general Don Pedro Moya de Contreras to inform him that there were complaints that a Dominican friar from Chontalpa was advocating the "law of Muhammad." López Vivero accused Friar Pedro Lorenzo of preaching a sermon to an audience of Spaniards and indigenous peoples in which "the said religious, speaking with the said Indians, stated that if some among those who were present [the Spaniards] wanted to offend them in their persons or lands, they should defend themselves with sticks or stones or whatever they had available."[91] In his letter López Vivero indicated that he believed the priest was accused unjustly by local Spaniards because he was denouncing their offenses against the Indians. Yet López Vivero also warned Mexican inquisitors that, "because of the scandal among the Indians who heard it, and because they are new people [to the faith], of light judgment, it is necessary to . . . treat them with much caution."[92] The spread of new religious currents and unorthodox political ideas among indigenous peoples remained a concern for Spanish ecclesiastical authorities well into the seventeenth century. It continued to be a source of concern at court, as Solórzano drafted his work in defense of Spain's title to the Americas.

On 4 March 1569 four members of the Audiencia of Guadalajara wrote a complaint to Philip II about Francisco de Ibarra, the first governor of Nueva Vizcaya, following his residencia. The judges complained that Ibarra would bypass the Audiencia of Guadalajara and send individuals directly to Mexico City to be prosecuted for various offenses despite a royal decree to the contrary. The judges argued that this prevented litigants from pursuing their cases further. Ibarra's actions also rendered the Audiencia ineffective in carrying out royal orders to look for persons married in Spain and foreigners to send back to Castile: "Because [the Audiencia of Mexico] is an outside jurisdiction they flee there . . . as do other delinquents and evildoers. As a result their crimes remain unpunished."[93]

Inquisitors in the Spanish American tribunals also voiced concern in letters to the Suprema over the difficulty of policing excessive distances. On 23 September 1575 Mexican inquisitors Avalos and Bonilla expressed differing opinions on how to address the issue of individuals who changed their names and tweaked their genealogies in order to conceal a new Christian background. This exchange took place just before Diego Herrador's trial in 1576. Bonilla disagreed with Avalos that Spanish models functioned in the American context, precisely because of the difficulty of gathering accurate genealogical information on emigrants from so many different parts of Spain, and who were at times living in communities where no one had known them prior to their settlement in the Americas. Bonilla asserted that with the exception of individuals sentenced locally by the Mexican tribunal, it was "impossible" to investigate genealogies "in places so remote and of newly arrived people."[94] Inquisitors in Spanish America lacked the detailed records available in Spain, where tracing lineages "can be done properly . . . in old inquisitions which have their books of genealogies where one can compare the old names with the newly assumed ones."[95] Bonilla complained their only recourse was to "remit to Spain the said denunciations of hearsay and vain beliefs. . . . This is such a long and prolix thing, of much noise and no less scandal to him who realizes that in Spain the Inquisition had the names and bones of his ancestors."[96]

Ship inspections were also hindered by the vast distances separating the Americas from the Peninsula. On 13 January 1626 Licentiate Diego Gutiérrez de Molina, a priest and *comisario* of the Mexican Inquisition based in the port of Realejo, in Nicaragua, composed a letter to inquisitors. He noted that although he was charged with overseeing the inspections of ships in his bishopric, and of searching them for prohibited books, images, and clandestine passengers sailing from Nicaragua and Costa Rica to ports in Tierra Firme and the viceroyalty of Peru, he was unable to work effectively. Gutiérrez de Molina requested assistance in carrying out the inspections, lamenting that "in the event that I have to take care of other things relating to my work as comisario I cannot personally attend to all the ports in this said bishopric because they are so distant from one another."[97]

Whether ecclesiastical authorities were even qualified presented another obstacle to enforcing restrictions on new Christian settlement. On 15 March 1570 Doctor Francisco de Alarcón, a judge of the Audiencia of Guadalajara, wrote to Philip II calling attention to the poor preparation of the local clergy. He noted that they were not examined properly, and he urged that when ordained by their dioceses, priests be qualified (*abiles*) and well educated (*buenos latinos*). Alarcón lamented that not only had uneducated priests been ordained, who could not even read the vernacular, but that young men (*mozos*) were ordained, "without examining whether they are Christians or Muslims or Jews or of any other lineage. Just a few days later, they say Mass, which results in great indecency from such a high authority."[98] By the end of the sixteenth century, concerns over the qualifications and religious status of ecclesiastical officials entered into accusations that they descended from Moriscos and conversos.

Once inquisitorial tribunals were formally established in the Americas, inquisitors frequently voiced their concern over the scarcity of qualified officials, including familiars and commissioners considered essential for policing heterodoxy in remote regions. On 8 April 1580 Lima inquisitors Licentiate Antonio de Arpide y Ulloa and Licentiate Cerezuela wrote to the Suprema that they needed more inquisitorial officials in their district. They noted that although they had alcaldes and judges, "it is notorious" that they lacked qualifications. Furthermore, inquisitors "do not know who [the alcaldes and judges] are, and because no one asks, we consider it to be inconvenient to ask them or compel them to provide a report [of their limpieza] as your grace orders. Especially because few old Christians arrive here, either as *letrados* or other people. We suspect that he who does not ask for these things must not benefit from them."[99]

Inquisitorial officials soon responded to local conditions by granting privileges denied to those possessing new Christian ancestry. Unlike marriage to Moriscas, being married to a woman of indigenous descent did not necessarily pose a significant obstacle for applicants to become familiars for the inquisitorial tribunal in Cartagena de Indias. In a letter to the Suprema dated 14 July 1612 inquisitors Licentiate Juan de Mañozca and Licentiate Pedro Mathe de Salcedo requested that Spaniards married to mestizas and *quarteronas* not have to apply for special permission to become familiars but that the Suprema consider them to possess limpieza and confirm their admission. They wrote that "in this land about half the Spaniards are married to . . . daughters and granddaughters of indigenous women, many of whom want to become familiars and we do not see any reason why they should not be admitted since their limpieza is well known and because it is so common that honorable men marry them it means that it is not an affront."[100] Easing the bureaucratic hurdles for those married to mestizas could also mitigate the shortage of inquisitorial officials. It is illustrative that on 4 July 1611 inquisitors in Cartagena requested a license from the Suprema to allow a Genoese man, Cipion Faia, to become a familiar in the city of Mariquita in New Granada. The inquisitors noted that although he was a foreigner, he had claimed to have already worked for the Mexican Inquisition. They pointed out that, "because this land is so lacking in ministers, there are hardly any, at least in the said city of Mariquita."[101]

Jurisdictional conflicts also mounted between inquisitors and local bishops who, before the formal establishment of inquisitorial tribunals in the Americas, had exercised greater authority in policing religiosity in their bishoprics. Bishops complained that the inquisitors increasingly excluded them. Local squabbles could at times compromise the effectiveness of one group of officials or the other, making it easier for individuals to escape notice. In 1577 Mexican inquisitors Bonilla and Avalos issued an edict to the residents of the bishopric of Nicaragua that prohibited other ecclesiastical officials from prosecuting cases of heresy. They ordered that only inquisitors could proceed in matters pertaining to heresy. Inquisitors Bonilla and Avalos issued their edict in response to the decrees against Protestants, Moriscos, and conversos that were read by the ecclesiastical judge (*juez ordinario eclesiástico*) during his inspection of the province of Nicaragua in 1576. According to Bonilla and Avalos, the ecclesiastical judge's actions contravened recent royal decrees that granted inquisitors the sole authority to try cases of heresy. Bonilla and Avalos ordered all ecclesiastical officials, under pain of excommunication and a fine of 1,000 ducats, "neither to interfere, nor collect information about them [Protestants, Moriscos and conversos], nor carry out inspections, nor publish edicts, but rather that in whatever way they come into their hands, to remit them to our commissioners."[102] In 1578 Bonilla and Avalos issued a similar edict concerning the confessors appointed by the Bull of the Santa Cruzada. In it they cited the papal brief issued by Gregory XIII in Rome, on 22 September 1576, that "confessors elected by virtue of the Bull of the Santa Cruzada in no way [had] the faculty to absolve heresy. Such a sin that is greater than the rest is worthy of special punishment."[103] Inquisitors noted that some confessors, "counter to the force of the said privileges, and more with subtle and curious than true interpretation, have tried to have the faculty and authority to . . . absolve the crime of heresy."[104]

Other bishops in the viceroyalty of New Spain were similarly reluctant to relinquish their authority with the advent of the Inquisition. The bishop of Guadalajara, Friar Domingo de Alzola, voiced a series of complaints to Philip II in 1584 while carrying out his visita of Nueva Galicia. In his letter, Alzola railed about how the governor (corregidor) in Zacatecas prevented him from undertaking his inspection, in a town full of "public vices" where souls were damned and officials cheated the Royal Treasury. Alzola complained that the corregidor, upon hearing he would conduct the visita, found alguaciles to try fifty persons of "evil life" (*mal vivir*), to prevent them from falling under Alzola's jurisdiction, and refused to extend to him the resources of the secular arm for carrying out punishments. The corregidor had apparently demanded that Alzola provide evidence to substantiate each denunciation, "as if I were him and he were me."[105]

As a result, complained Alzola, he left "much of this town full of people of evil life, with there having been presented more than eighty denunciations, and all this is because there is no other government here than that of a corregidor who proceeds as he wishes."[106]

This disagreement over local authority was not the only one involving Bishop Alzola that year. On 18 February 1584, the commissioner for the Inquisition in Guadalajara, Licentiate Francisco Núñez de Segura, wrote a letter to Mexican inquisitors. He complained, "In an edict that he read, the bishop of this city . . . included cases of heresies and of Muslims and their ceremonies and of prohibited books. I warned him about this, to order it to be removed. If any declaration came of such things he should send it to me, so that the said denunciation would be received before me. Even though he received it with some resentment, saying that he was *inquisidor ordinario* so he could do it himself . . . eventually he gave in and decided he would do it."[107] Complaints about Alzola continued to surface many years later. Don Francisco de Segura Tinoco, the commissioner of Guadalajara, wrote a letter on 14 May 1611 condemning the bishop for proclaiming publicly that he would "extirpate the vices of the Republic."[108] Sitting in the choir on the Feast of the Assumption, Segura witnessed how Alzola, while "reading the edict, began to discuss heresies and sects. I told the bishop this cannot be read because these cases are reserved for the tribunal of the Holy Office, as I had already informed your grace. He again replied with much anger and resentment that he had done it, and he could do it, because he was also an *inquisidor ordinario*."[109]

* * *

From the beginning of the sixteenth century, royal decrees and instructions to settlers imposed restrictions on the presence of new Christians of Muslim and Jewish descent in the new territories overseas. Spanish authorities feared they would undermine missionary attempts to convert indigenous peoples and introduce knowledge about Muslim and Jewish practices. Beginning with the bull *Inter Caetera* and reflected in subsequent legal documents, the title to conquer and colonize the Americas stipulated that indigenous peoples be brought to the Catholic faith. As a result, one of the primary legal justifications and basis for Spanish conquest rested on the religious control of peoples residing within the boundaries of these territories.

As both the legislation and court cases show, prohibitions on the emigration of new Christians to the Americas were difficult to enforce. Approved openings such as the purchase of royal licenses enabled some to travel legally for brief periods of time. By the mid-sixteenth century, greater restrictions on religiosity and increasing persecution of the Spanish Morisco population were reflected in the legislation. A number of strategies for passing clandestinely existed as well. Falsifying papers, escaping as soldiers or sailors, and paying for space to accompany officials to the Americas, all provided some of the means by which individuals slipped unnoticed to the New World. Once in the Americas, clandestine emigrants faced authorities who found it challenging to oversee who was settling in the new viceroyalties, even as they were mapping out jurisdictions and attempting to follow up on the royal decrees. These ineffectively regulated spaces, whether by distances or gaps in administration, provided opportunities for new Christians to attempt to forge new lives in the Spanish Americas, as they could not in Spain, where peninsular controls were tighter.

Suspicions of Moriscos and North African Muslims in Spain also found their way to Spanish America. Settlers were well aware of authorities' fears and the religious restrictions on emigration. The publication of the royal decrees and inquisitorial edicts raised the question of whether Moriscos were in their midst. These fears soon entered disputes over positions in colonial administration and society, as accusations of Morisco descent were leveled against officeholders and encomenderos.

CHAPTER 4

"These Hidden Heretics"

The Politics of Morisco Religiosity

While free Morisco emigrants to Spanish America may have sought to escape the increasing tensions with old Christians in Spain, peninsular attitudes and suspicions also crossed the Atlantic, taking on new dimensions in the Americas. Although they were removed geographically from peninsular fears that they would aid the Ottoman sultan in invading Spain, negative images of Moriscos and Muslims circulated in the Americas and contributed to their perception as disloyal subjects. As Spanish authorities increasingly linked political loyalty to confessional identity, Morisco presence in the New World was seen as a threat to the creation of a model Catholic community, thereby undermining the Crown's justification for conquest, even as other parts of the world were "lost" to Protestants or the Ottoman Empire.[1]

Individuals continued to face accusations of Islamismo before the inquisitorial tribunals in Mexico City, Lima, and Cartagena de Indias. Being a North African, a descendant of Granadan Moriscos, or even having traveled beyond the Catholic lands in the Mediterranean, cast suspicion on an individual's piety. Perceptions of suspect religious identity affected an individual's standing within the community, leaving them vulnerable to slander. Those desiring encomiendas or titles of nobility had to cultivate their honor publicly, through actions and possessions, because what was "public and notorious" became an index of social standing. In their petitions to the Crown, encomenderos such as the Morisco Diego Romero from New Granada emphasized exemplary behavior and religiosity, because encomenderos were legally responsible for overseeing the religious indoctrination of indigenous peoples under their jurisdiction. This made religious identity an important point of contention. What constituted contemporary ideas about religiosity and its relationship to customary practice? Why did descriptions of customs and other forms of public behavior matter, and how did they affect status in colonial society? What it meant to be labeled a Muslim or Morisco varied during the course of these disputes. To answer these questions, it is important to address the tension between the range of beliefs in Islam that individual Moriscos might have held and the broader ideas circulating in society about what it meant to be a Muslim or Morisco. By understanding this relationship between individual piety and ascribed identity it becomes possible to appreciate the range of attitudes that resulted in the denunciation of Morisco practices.

The religiosity of individual Moriscos in the Americas was as varied as it was geographically in Spain. Morisco emigrants' experiences in Spanish America reflected the diversity of the Morisco population on the Peninsula. They represented a spectrum of beliefs and practices that ranged from adherence to Islam to considering themselves "good" Catholics. The Morisco population in the Americas was similarly diverse, ranging from North African slaves baptized in Spain, to artisans, to members of the Granadan Morisco elite who tweaked their lineages to insert themselves into the peninsular nobility. Cultural practices and belief systems associated with Moriscos in Spain were also present in Spanish America and incurred similar persecution. This provides a more complicated and diverse picture of the "Republic of Spaniards," of which Moriscos formed a part. The idealized segregation of New World settlements into the Republic of Spaniards and the Republic of Indians failed in practical terms. While Spaniards were supposed to act as exemplary Christians in the presence of indigenous peoples, this was rarely the case, and the legislation governing spatial arrangements was just as contradictory and imperfect as that restricting trade and emigration.

THE POLITICS OF MORISCO DEVOTIONS

In 1594, María Ruiz, a Granadan Morisca, denounced herself before Mexican inquisitors. She did so at the insistence of her confessor, who was required to remit cases of heresy to the Inquisition.[2] During her trial, she provided an account of her life that included descriptions of her religious practices in both Spain and Mexico. Many of the devotions that Ruiz described during her trial parallel those in the inquisitorial testimonies of Moriscos in Spain. These included praying in Arabic and invoking Muhammad.

Like many Moriscos who had been expelled from Granada following the second Alpujarras uprising in 1569, María Ruiz became a potential target of inquisitorial persecution in the parts of Spain where they were resettled.[3] Regional and customary practices among the Moriscos that included dress, food, and music could lead to individuals being labeled Muslims (moros), regardless of their actual religious beliefs. Yet a discussion of religious beliefs is important in understanding how these were perceived in relation to customary practice and came to infuse legal categories. The private meaning they held for some, especially concerning the importance of salvation, should also be considered, as these were not empty categories. Before moving into a discussion of denunciations of suspected Moriscos, it is imperative to stress the importance that personal expressions of faith held for some. Early modern Spaniards cared deeply about issues such as the nature of the Trinity or the virginity of Mary. They discussed these matters in their homes, in taverns, and on the streets. Conversations about religiosity could go awry and result in denunciations for a range of people across the Iberian world, yet through these interactions it becomes clear that religious beliefs and salvation mattered to those involved.

Regarded with suspicion, some Moriscos like Ruiz may have continued to practice Islam in the privacy of their homes, even as they traversed the viceroyalties of New Spain and Peru. It is useful to consider the concept of *taqiyya* that was associated with many peninsular Moriscos' secret observance of Islam. Meaning precaution in Arabic, taqiyya referred to the permission for Muslims living under adverse conditions to perform the exterior acts of the religion being imposed on them, so long as they remained faithful to Islam in their hearts.[4] Yet knowledge about taqiyya also allowed old Christians to become suspicious of Moriscos and to question how genuinely Catholic they were. A fatwa issued in 1504 to the Moriscos of Granada by the Mufti of Oran, Ahmad ben Yuma'a, addressed the question of how they could remain good Muslims in a repressive society. Some of the prescriptions contained in the fatwa included the maintenance of prayer "even if you do it by means of signs."[5] To comply with the ritual of purification, ben Yuma'a advised Granadan Moriscos to "bathe in the sea or in a river, and if this has been prohibited, do it at night, and it will work as if it had been done during the day."[6]

María Ruiz described how her family, due to fears of discovery by their old Christian neighbors in Albolote, was cautious about observing their religious practices. By the mid-sixteenth century, Moriscos in many parts of Spain who remained Muslims no longer spoke Arabic, and there is evidence that, because they were so actively persecuted by the Inquisition, the alfaquíes, or religious leaders, were no longer able to carry out official teachings in Qur'anic schools.[7] At the time of the expulsion of the Moriscos from Spain, some North African Muslim writers commented on the ignorance of the Moriscos about Islam. They began a campaign to teach the new arrivals a more orthodox version of the faith.

Ruiz had some knowledge of Islam before arriving in New Spain. Although cautious not to reveal too much, Ruiz's mother taught her daughter a few prayers in Arabic, so that, "until about three years ago, when she had come to this land [Mexico], she had always practiced Islam and believed in it although she did not conduct the ceremonies that her mother engaged in . . . because as she had said, her parents were cautious around her and feared she might expose them."[8] When asked by inquisitors how she prayed, Ruiz said she always "commended herself to God in heaven, and she did not say prayers, other than when she got out of bed, and before going to bed, [she said] 'Halamay' . . . which she saw her parents do, and when she needed something from God and found herself in trouble she commended herself to God in heaven, saying the said word, 'Halamay.'"[9] Upon being asked whether she "excluded the persons of the Son and Holy Spirit" when praying to God, Ruiz replied, "Yes, she excluded them because she understood that there was only one God, and she did not believe in the Son or the Holy Spirit because she thought they were things of the air, and there was nothing to them."[10] The Trinity held a prominent place in Christian-Muslim theological disputations in Spain, thereby assuming importance in inquisitorial inquiries and Morisco responses. To Ruiz, the unitary nature of God was undermined by the presence of the Son and the Holy Spirit. Some Moriscos in Spain even asserted that Christians venerated three people rather than one God, or that God had both a mother and a son.[11]

Disagreements surfaced between Moriscos and old Christians over a number of issues such as the Trinity, the nature of Christ, the virginity of Mary, the church, and the papacy. Both the Virgin and Christ appear in the sacred texts of both Christians and Muslims, yet in Spain members of each community at times attached their own sets of meanings to these figures. In the Qur'an, Jesus appears as a messenger of God who foretells the birth of Muhammad. Learned Moriscos who were familiar with the Qur'an referred to Jesus as the "spirit of God" and a prophet, although they disagreed with Christians that he possessed a divine nature. The Qur'an also praises Mary for her virginity. Nonetheless, the charged environment and increasing inquisitorial persecution positioned these as critical differences in belief and as dangerous. Some Morisco authors of polemical texts ignored this portrayal of Mary in the Qur'an, writing instead against the notion of her virginity. Verbal exchanges between Moriscos and old Christians appear in the inquisitorial records, in which Moriscos were accused of denying vehemently the virginity of Mary.[12] They also allegedly claimed that their God was different from the God of the Christians.[13] This response recurs in much of the inquisitorial documentation and betrays not atheism, but rather a distinction between the trinitarian notion of God in Christianity and the unified nature of God in Islam, which some Spanish Moriscos began to refer to as two different deities. Counter-Reformation politics also set the tone, as Catholic authorities sought to defend the role of the papacy and regulate liturgical issues concerning the use of images in churches and the Eucharist.

The Trinity became one of the most contested subjects in this polemic. For some Moriscos, the question of Christ's divinity undermined the unitary nature of God. Catholic missionaries emphasized in their teachings the divine nature of Christ. Muslims, by contrast, considered this a contradiction of one of the basic tenets of their faith, the First Pillar of Islam, concerning the unity of God, set out in the Qur'an and repeated in the shahada: "there is no God but God."[14] While many learned Morisco authors produced accounts in aljamiado engaging with these polemics, the members of the broader Morisco population claimed things not always supported in the Qur'an. Knowledge of Catholic doctrine, instilled through missionary teachings, gave many Moriscos familiarity with the main points in Christianity that they may have alternately ridiculed or condemned as heretical, as reflected in the accusations and subsequent inquisitorial investigations.[15]

Ruiz told inquisitors that for the past three years she had not had doubts about Catholicism, but that previously when she had believed in Islam "she had doubts many times" about whether Islam or Christianity was the true faith, although she continued to practice Islam.[16]

During the ten years she lived in New Spain, Ruiz had only taken communion "four times, and this she did to comply with her husband who told her to go and confess and take communion, and in all the confessions she made, she confessed all her sins except this one of her belief in Muhammad."[17] Later in her trial, Ruiz remembered a fifth time when she took communion, when she was "very sick in the Hospital de Nuestra Señora in this city of Mexico, soon after she had arrived from Castile."[18] Ruiz said that because she was so ill, she was told to take communion if she had confessed, to which she replied, "Yes she had confessed, and thus they brought her the holiest sacrament, and she received it, not believing in it, nor that in it was the body of our redeemer Jesus Christ, because she did it to comply and not be detected."[19]

María Ruiz provides a compelling example of a woman who, for a time, continued to practice Islam while married to an old Christian and living far from her family in Spain. Does this mean there were others, and was she in touch with a network of people with whom she could maintain the religious practices of her childhood? It is unclear from her testimony. Perhaps she did wish to live and die as a Catholic and formalize her position through the Inquisition, as countless individuals had done through its tribunals in the Mediterranean.[20] If she believed Catholicism was the true religion, she could ensure her salvation by being formally reconciled in the faith. Or she may have been testifying as a precaution, fearing denunciation from someone else and trying to protect herself and anyone she knew who remained a practicing Muslim. It is impossible to tell, although having spent years in New Spain far from those she grew up with may have meant she desired some closure. How many others were like her, torn between two belief systems deemed by Catholic authorities to be mutually exclusive?[21]

The Inquisition sought increasingly to penetrate the private spaces of interior piety in order to identify heresies that could be damaging to the body politic. By reading edicts of faith publicly and requiring confessors to direct the absolution of heresy to them, inquisitors encouraged denunciations and created an atmosphere of heightened vigilance. Were there others practicing alongside María Ruiz? Inquisitors wanted to know and ordered that she be reconciled in private so that other Moriscos would not be discouraged from stepping forth to denounce themselves. However, it appears from the records that no others did at the time. More often, some individuals accused others of invoking Muhammad and praying in Arabic.

Exchanges in Spanish America concerning religious doctrine and the differences between Christianity and Islam could also lead to denunciations, regardless of whether those engaging in the conversation were ultimately labeled Moriscos. Local and imperial politics influenced attitudes toward the confessional, and practices of confession and denunciation, on both sides of the Atlantic. The long history of interaction between Christians and Muslims across the Mediterranean further shaped everyday exchanges, and Spanish authorities began to interpret opinions professed in favor of Islam as an expression of political disloyalty to the Crown.

In 1605 a man named Zárate (*fulano de* Zárate) was accused of having stated that on Judgment Day, Muhammad would sit at Christ's feet and revoke sentences he deemed unjust.[22] When those listening reprimanded him, Zárate reputedly became angry and exclaimed that he "knew very well what he said, because he was neither a horse, nor an ignorant man."[23] According to Bachiller Francisco de Arteaga, on the Sunday that he had been playing cards with other men in the house of Lorenzo de Espinossa, the "so-and-so Zárate" was present. Arteaga did not know Zárate's first name, although he provided a physical description of him and said he was a weaver who lived in Mexico City, near the church of Our Lady of Montserrat. The men began to discuss that morning's sermon on the Last Judgment, and Zárate chimed in, "They say that on that day God will sit upon a chair and with Muhammad at his feet, and if Muhammad considers the sentence that God pronounces not to be well given, he would revoke it."[24] Hearing this, the men became scandalized, causing Zárate to reply defensively that "it was true what he said, and he knew very well what he was saying, and that he was not a barbarian."[25] According to the witnesses, Zárate claimed he had encountered this in a book entitled *Viage de Hierusalem*.[26] Espinossa, a silk spinner, was next to testify. He claimed that the conversation began when Zárate said, "He does not know with what purpose, that the Muslims call Muhammad Allah, and that this was their God." It was then, amidst Arteaga's objections, that Zárate made his statement about Judgment Day.[27] The silk producer Pedro de Palencia, also present during this exchange, testified that the talk about Allah began when Espinossa asked, "'Who was Allah?' and the said fulano de Zárate responded that the Muslims called God Allah."[28]

An aljamiado manuscript that circulated among Moriscos in Aragon presents the story of the Last Judgment that bears striking parallels to Zárate's account. The miscellany of which it is a part covers numerous doctrinal points on ways that Muslims living under Christian rule could continue to observe Islam. It also described Morisco legends and prophecies.[29] In "El rrekontamiyento del díya del juiçiyo," as the world ends, the angel Jibril (Gabriel) shows Muhammad the open doors of paradise. He assumes the vestments and crown of honor (*korona de la onrra*) brought to him by the angel, and asks about his community of believers (*allumma*). As the dead are raised and shown the fires of hell (*jahanama*), they seek unsuccessfully the aid of Adam, Noah, Abraham, Moses, and Jesus to plead for their souls. Finally, Jesus leads them to Muhammad, who he says has the authority to plead for them, and the souls beg Muhammad to ask God to send them where they belong, whether it be paradise or hell.[30] Muhammad takes the souls to God's throne, where he is told by God, "ask, and your demand will be granted, plead, and your plea will be heard."[31] When Muhammad witnesses the souls of the faithful who, because of their sins, were being burnt by the fires of hell, he falls down alongside Jibril and cries, begging God for mercy. God tells Muhammad to "look into the fire and take out anyone who carries in their heart an atom of belief . . . anyone who said once *la ilaha illa Allah Muhammad rraçulu Allah* in their heart."[32] The saved souls are then "taken to a fountain which is at the door of paradise, which is called the Fountain of Life; they will be bathed in it; they will leave it like the full moon, the fourteenth night; they will leave with this written on their foreheads, 'here are those whom God freed from the fire of hell.'"[33]

Other images of the Last Judgment and Paradise surface in the testimonies of individuals summoned before the Mexican Inquisition. In 1614 in the mining district of Pachuca in New Spain, a fisherman named Diego was denounced for praising Muhammad. Francisco Gonzáles testified before the *calificador* of the Inquisition at Pachuca about an event that occurred while he was playing cards in the pueblo of Alvarado one day with two fishermen he worked with, one who was named Diego. When Diego began to lose at the card game, he "said in a clear and distinct voice . . . great will be Muhammad's paradise, and those who believe in him. I believe in him."[34] Upon being rebuked by Gonzáles, Diego repeated that "he believed in Muhammad's paradise."[35]

These exchanges shed light on how, in everyday conversations, knowledge about Islam traveled in Spanish America. They present an image of difference, influenced by the Christian-Muslim polemics in Spain. Some individuals had firsthand familiarity with texts circulating in Spain during this period, which, although banned by the Inquisition, managed to survive. Ideas about Islam, as articulated in written texts and in daily conversations, also influenced how individuals perceived Muslims and Moriscos in Spanish America.

Through denunciations before the inquisitorial and ecclesiastical courts, one can glimpse common assumptions about Moriscos. These assumptions produced a sometimes contradictory set of images of Muslims and Moriscos that circulated in the Spanish world, undermined or upheld in daily interactions. Who actually fell under the category of Morisco was remarkably diverse. In 1583 Francisco López Africano, a merchant born in North Africa and residing in the mining district of Copala in northern New Spain, was denounced for speaking in the "Morisco language" and praying in Arabic (algarabía). According to one of his accusers, Juan de Santiago, it was known publicly that, "while praying in his house . . . [López] invokes the name of Muhammad, crossing his arms before his breast, saying 'oh Muhammad, oh Muhammad' two and three times."[36] Another resident of the mining district, Juan Núñez de Saavedra, overheard López speaking in Arabic: "He spoke for a long time as if praying, and finally he ended by saying two or three times Allah and Muhammad, and when he said this, his arms were crossed."[37] When he asked López what language he was speaking in, he replied that it was "the Morisco language, and that it was nothing other than that in his land they spoke that language, and when this witness asked him how far his land was from that of the Muslims, Francisco López replied that it was one or two leagues away from the land of the Muslims."[38] A witness against him, Guiomar, the slave of Pedro de Torres Arçe, told Mexican inquisitors what she had heard from an indigenous woman named Ynés, a servant in the same household and López's concubine. Ynés had told Guiomar, "Francisco López is not like the other Christians because at midnight he gets up to pray and then he kneels before the images and prays in another language unlike the one that the Christians pray in."[39] Ynés stressed that "although I can speak Castilian I cannot understand it and therefore I do not know what he says."[40]

Tensions formed between individual experiences of religiosity, and the broader community's perception of the individual's actions. When read publicly, inquisitorial edicts of faith labeled certain actions as

Morisco, condemning these before a large audience. Behavior and customary practice became associated with a person's place in Catholic society and therefore with their legal status. How someone dressed, whether in 'Moorish,' indigenous, or Spanish clothing (*hábito de moro, indio,* or *español*) represented not only the community's perceptions of an individual, but also an assumed position in the social hierarchy. The right to bear arms, wear silk, own slaves, or participate in the local economy was structured according to these assumed identities. A European Christian who had been spotted wearing a fez in North Africa would have faced close examination by the Inquisition.[41] These preoccupations with clothing and gestures also appear in Spanish America, where they too displayed and implied publicly an individual's caste, religious affiliation, social status, and gender. Whether invoked to gain privileges, or by envious accusers who wished to discredit their more successful neighbors, clothes and customs acted as statements that rendered "public and notorious" an individual's position in society.

INQUISITORIAL POWER AND RELIGIOUS POLEMICS IN NEW SPAIN

In 1621, Friar Juan de Sotomayor, the guardian of the monastery of San Francisco in Etzatlán, near Jalisco, addressed a letter to Mexican inquisitors in which he discussed a matter that he said he was obligated to respond to as it was "public, scandalous and damaging to the Republic."[42] He related that he had learned that Catalina de Ibiza and her seven grown children, who on their father's side "descended from the Moriscos of Granada . . . were people whose customs do not appear to be Christian and at times they do not allow the holy offices to be celebrated, nor the sacraments to be administered, nor the word of God to be preached, this defect being very old and customary in the said people. It stems from their father (may God forgive him)."[43]

Sotomayor's accusation revealed a shocking moment when, as he arrived at the altar to say Mass, Catalina de Ibiza and her children were so disruptive that it was impossible to continue. The outraged friar complained that they had "raised such a loud ruckus of curses, that not only could I not preach, but I could not even finish the Mass without having had to come down from the altar and send for some people at the door of the sacristy to make them shut up."[44] He lamented, "I did not dare to preach anymore to excuse such an outburst, that the bad reputation (*mala fama*) of their ancestry and the dissonance of their customs, being so ancient and customary and never before seen in that town, only in the said people, who carry within them a deformity so scandalous that the remedy of this holy tribunal [of the Inquisition] is necessary."[45] Sotomayor also included a notarized statement detailing the actions that took place during Mass, in which he further accused their relative by marriage, Lucas de Villatoro, of interfering with a religious procession in Etzatlán. At the end of his statement Sotomayor concluded that the family set "a very bad example to indigenous peoples, who believe that what they do is what is good and right, and as a result good customs are corrupted."[46]

To Sotomayor, the public nature of their outbursts during Mass was worrying "because they are many and they live among Indians and other miserable people. Anything they want they usurp and they confuse everything so that they equate liberties and vices with virtue."[47] Sotomayor noted repeatedly that "the Indians of Etzatlán are always present during [the Ibiza family's] disruption of the Word of God," and could bear witness to them if necessary, even if they could not testify to the family's Muslim lineage.[48]

Sotomayor intended his complaints to resonate with Spanish authorities who were deeply concerned with ensuring religious orthodoxy in the Americas. His mention of indigenous witnesses to Catalina de Ibiza's "blasphemous and heretical words . . . before the entire town in the church while Mass was being said" was strategic.[49] It played into Spanish authorities' concerns with indigenous religiosity and forming a model Catholic community in the Americas. Sotomayor's letter to inquisitors also highlighted the importance that ideas about customary practices held for Spanish ecclesiastical authorities. In Spain, inquisitors collected information about local beliefs and practices, in an attempt to identify signs of relapse from the recent converts. Not only religious beliefs but also what Moriscos such as Francisco Núñez Muley argued to be regional customs were stigmatized increasingly on both sides of the Atlantic.

That the disruptions of Mass by Ibiza and her children were so public, and could therefore potentially influence indigenous peoples into committing open acts of defiance against the church, was of special concern to Sotomayor. A person's public actions, how they and their families were perceived within their communities, provided the groundwork for their social standing. In this way, public places such as churches and religious processions became contested spaces where people could be identified before the community as not performing their expected religious obligations. This was also the case in Spain, where Moriscos were accused frequently of acting with irreverence during Mass, toward the images in the churches, or while taking communion.[50]

Following the second Alpujarras rebellion, accounts of Moriscos destroying Catholic images circulated in Spain, especially among advocates of their expulsion. Accounts of the rebellion by Luis del Mármol Carvajal, Justino Antolínez de Burgos and Francisco Bermúdez de Pedraza stressed the damages to churches and the sacraments reputedly carried out by Moriscos. Memory of the rebellion lingered into the seventeenth century, as seen in the *Actas de Ugíjar* of 1668–69. Composed under the supervision of Granadan archbishop Diego Escolano, the *Actas de Ugíjar* promoted an ethos of martyrdom among the Christian resettlers of Granada.[51] They continued to stress how the Moriscos "committed the most grave sacrilege, profaning the churches, burning the holy images in them as well as their edifice."[52] In his official inspection of the Alpujarras in 1669, to collect information about the martyrs, Doctor Juan de Leyba recorded how the residents of Ugíjar showed him the images damaged during the uprising. In front of the gathered townspeople, Leyba and his notary examined a stone cross bearing images of a Santo Cristo Crucificado and Nuestra Señora de las Angustias. He lamented how they had been "damaged and their faces and arms broken from the bullets and blows that the Moriscos, during their uprising, gave them out of contempt of the Christian religion, which they loathed."[53] Leyba also noted the charred walls of a church where Christians reputedly sought refuge from the Moriscos who had set fire to it. These events gained currency throughout the Alpujarras towns, both through storytelling and with the circulation of engravings, sermons, and pamphlets.[54] During the seventeenth century, individuals incorporated martyrs into their family histories, coats of arms, and genealogies as an argument for their insertion into the local nobility.[55]

Moriscos had their own responses to the events taking place in the Alpujarras, and although they are difficult to reconstruct through the inquisitorial testimonies, these documents do provide glimpses of some possible attitudes. María Ruiz described the actions taken by her brothers in Spain during the uprising. Her testimony echoes the accusations leveled against Catalina de Ibiza and her family for mocking Catholic liturgical rites. During Catholic processions,

Ruiz had heard her brothers Diego and Miguel Hernández exclaim, "Look at who these Christian animals worship—pieces of wood."[56] Ruiz recalled that her brother Diego said "that when the Kingdom of Granada rose up and the Moriscos went to the sierra [to fight] he and others smashed the images they found into pieces."[57] She also remembered how her other brother, Miguel, would often "call the consecrated host 'little tortilla' (tortillita) in Arabic while making fun of it."[58] Were accusations of iconoclasm merely a specter raised by paranoid communities to identify outsiders in their midst and supported by the imperatives of inquisitors and powerful institutions? While difficult to determine in every case, satire and iconoclasm could present powerful critiques of the validity of Catholic sacred objects and were occurring in various parts of Europe with religious conflicts during the Reformation.

Accusations of iconoclasm were also leveled against a Morisco who accompanied French pirates plundering the Yucatan coast. Cloaked in an argument of religious polemic, the Morisco and his "Lutheran" companions were accused before the Mexican Inquisition in 1571 of sacking churches, wearing garments made from cloth stripped from altars, drinking out of stolen chalices, and destroying religious images in front of indigenous witnesses. The testimony of Pedro de la Maçuca, a Spaniard captured by the French pirates on his way to Cuba, provided ample details about a Morisco who was killed during one of the raids. Maçuca did not speak French, so many of the corsairs' words were translated for him by the pilot of the ship, the *levantisco* Bernardo de Burdeos who had been married in Seville and spoke Castilian. However, Maçuca claimed he was able to communicate in Spanish with some of the indigenous men he met as a captive, and he related how they were impressed by how the French learned their language, telling them that they would free them from the Spanish so each could live according to "the law they desired."[59] Religious issues resonated as Maçuca's French captors urged him to "sail for the new religion."[60]

Maçuca claimed to have spoken with local indigenous people who recounted how, "when they had news of the said French they removed the images from [the church of] San Miguel and from many other churches, and ornaments, and all these they would hide in the mountains."[61] This theme of hiding sacred images during periods of confessional conflict echoes the accounts of actions taken by Christians during the long Reconquista and during the more recent Alpujarras uprising. It raises the question of the roles played by local priests and religious authorities in their parishes, and how indigenous peoples interpreted the act of concealing and protecting these images in the mountains or other secluded areas. In this way, images were sometimes miraculously found anew and unharmed, and incorporated into local devotions. One event stood out while the French were in the Yucatan, as one of the hidden artifacts did not escape harm. According to Maçuca, the French set fire to a box containing the books of the local church in Ycab, which was being kept in the home of the indigenous cantor.[62] Carrying the smoldering chest to the French captain, the cantor allegedly complained he "suspected that a Morisco who came with the said French had done it."[63] Maçuca lamented that these actions went unpunished by the captain and added that he heard that the Morisco was circumcised.

When Francisco Pat, one of the indigenous witnesses to the destruction of the church, appeared to testify, he described the actions in more detail, although he referred to the man as a *gitano*, or gypsy, not a Morisco. According to Pat, "One of the French, who was called the gitano, burned the books of the church, and that afterwards the boys of the church and a son of Pablo Pat, mayordomo of the church . . . whose name was Pedro Pat arrived to throw water on the box where the said books burned, and they put out the fire. To this witness it seemed that the French were Lutherans because they were people of evil lifestyles (mal vivir) and he did not see them pray except at night when they sang some songs that this witness did not understand."[64] Maçuca also described how the Morisco ate meat and eggs with the French on Friday and tried to force the indigenous men to do the same. According to Maçuca, "The Captain told the Indians to eat meat, that he would absolve them and give them [papal] bulls for a coin because he had the power of the pope to do so, and one of them, who he thinks was the Morisco, rubbed an Indian's chin with meat because neither the said Indian nor the others wanted to eat it on Friday."[65] Pedro Suchil, an indigenous man from Guatemala who also testified in the case, described what befell Pablo Pat, one of the *principales* of Ycab, when he refused to eat meat on Friday: "They rubbed his lips with the meat and his face too," in front of the gathered indigenous witnesses.[66] Suchil also described the destruction wrought at the church as he saw how "one of the French, who was called the gitano, with a harquebus lighter . . . burnt part of a book of the church. To this witness, the actions of the French did not seem right, because they slept in the church and urinated in it, and dirtied it."[67]

While the Morisco in question was not alive to stand trial with the French and testify, and the only description of him comes from witnesses, it is not inconceivable that a Morisco accompanied the French on their raids in Yucatan. Moriscos moved easily between France and Spain during this period, and years later, at the time of the expulsion, some Moriscos settled in France or passed through on their way to other parts of Europe and the Middle East.[68] A few even became Protestants.[69]

In their rejection of the Trinity and use of material objects such as statues to represent Christ, the Virgin Mary, and saints, Moriscos and Protestants were perceived as having something in common. Iconoclasm played a role in both religious conflicts in sixteenth-century France and during the Alpujarras uprising. The minority status of both Moriscos and Protestants in predominantly Catholic societies may have also led to similar patterns of persecution.[70] Their responses were reflected in the doctrinal similarities concerning images. Both Moriscos and Protestants privileged the word of God over graven images and condemned their worship in Catholic churches. Louis Cardaillac provides evidence that Morisco authors of polemical texts in Spain were aware of the writings of contemporary Spanish reformers. The links are clear in two manuscripts by Morisco authors who copy passages from Cipriano Valera's treatises on the pope and his authority, and on the Mass, listed on the Inquisition's index of prohibited works.[71] María Ruiz's depiction of her brothers' actions in the Alpujarras was more than just part of the polemic from an inquisitor's perspective of the uprising, portraying violence out of fear. It was grounded in actions in response to increased persecution, that had a logic of its own. Nevertheless, among many Spaniards, iconoclasm came to be associated with Moriscos and Protestants, as one of the threatening markers of their separation from Catholic community and disloyalty to the nation. Maçuca's assertion that a Morisco, rather than a gypsy, burned church papers and tried to force Pablo Pat to eat meat is revealing in this respect. Regardless of who he actually was, the image of the perpetrators was pervasive.

Knowledge of iconoclasm and religious outbursts among Moriscos in Spain also crept into everyday interactions in Spanish America, lending perilous meaning to potentially innocent gestures. In 1560 Hernando Beltrán, a resident of the mining district of San Martín in

New Spain who was reputed publicly to be a Morisco, was accused before the ecclesiastical court of the cathedral chapter of Guadalajara, for "a few words that he uttered against our holy Catholic faith."[72] Miguel Galindo, another resident of San Martín, testified that he and Anton Catalan overheard Beltrán muttering words during Mass that "scandalized him and left him in shock."[73] According to Galindo, when the priest was reciting the Pater Noster during Mass, "at the point when they say 'on earth as it is in heaven' . . . [Beltrán] said 'it is not yet that time.'"[74] Because Catalan was new to the area, he searched for someone who could identify the speaker and learned that the man was the Morisco, Hernando Beltrán. Alonso Verdugo, also present, testified that during the prayer Beltrán had said, "It is getting late. . . . [He then] turned to the left to look at [Beltrán], to know who had said these words, and he was shocked to hear them."[75] Verdugo claimed that Beltrán then left, and remained "outside the church . . . where the cross is and he strolled around there until they finished consuming [the Eucharist] and the said Mass had ended."[76]

Several days later, Beltrán was summoned before the ecclesiastical court to respond to these accusations. Beltrán testified that he was born in a small Spanish town five leagues from Baeza, in Andalusia, and that he was indeed the son of a Morisca. He had left Spain twenty years previously and had resided in Florida for four or five years before moving between various pueblos in New Spain.[77] Beltrán argued that he had been diligent about going to confession and taking communion "like a Christian, and he had earned the jubilees that had occurred during this time like a Christian."[78] He insisted that the reason he stood at the doors of the church hearing Mass outside "was because his house was open and he did not have anyone to guard it, and he did not want anyone to enter it to rob him or steal what he had in it."[79] Beltrán added that while the priest was reciting the Pater Noster, he "was standing, hearing the said prayer and commending himself to God, and that . . . when he was about to stand up, as he had not stood from the beginning, he had said 'it is late,' and this confessant said it for this reason, because he had not risen in time, and not to offend God."[80]

Beltrán's judges remained unconvinced by his argument, perhaps in part because he was a Morisco. Nonetheless, he received a minor sentence, which stated that he had acted "more out of ignorance than malice."[81] The judges ordered Beltrán to pay ten pesos toward repairs of the church and to appear at Mass carrying a candle as penance.

They also ordered him to leave his indigenous mistress and bring his wife, who was in Mexico City, to live with him in San Martín. Beltrán's alleged behavior was less dramatic than that of Catalina de Ibiza and her family, but the reaction to what he said was representative of contemporary suspicions surrounding Moriscos.

Because María Ruiz's appearance before the Inquisition was voluntary, and because she insisted that during the past three years, her belief in Catholicism was genuine, inquisitors gave her a minor sentence. They ordered that her reconciliation into the church be done in secret, inside the tribunal and that she renounce her errors before God, while carrying a candle and wearing yellow penitential garb.[82] Inquisitors told Ruiz not to speak of her trial to anyone and gave her the spiritual penance of fasting on Fridays, praying the rosary on Sundays and feast days, and visiting Friar Diego de Orozco at the church of Santiago Tlatelolco, who would "instruct her in the things of our Holy Catholic Faith until she might be and is completely instructed in them."[83] The correspondence between Mexican inquisitors and the Supreme Council of the Inquisition in Spain stressed the importance that Ruiz's penance take place in secret. In their report to the Suprema, inquisitors noted that it was "with the understanding that if her punishment were public, it would allow these hidden heretics, or others, to not want to denounce themselves."[84]

The atmosphere of suspicion engendered by the polemics in Spain seeped into speculations about peoples' backgrounds, in a land where many were immigrants but tried to maintain close ties with others from their birthplaces.[85] Accusations that an individual was a Morisco were often leveled by those claiming to have shared a common hometown in Spain. In 1617 Friar Alonso Díaz, the commissioner of the Mexican Inquisition in Huamantla, wrote to inquisitors about accusations against the landowner (*estanciero* and *labrador*) Pedro Hernández, mentioning a potential conflict as Hernández reputedly refused someone who asked to borrow money.[86] In 1616 Hernández was denounced before Mexican inquisitors because "he is considered to be a Morisco among his neighbors, and he goes to Mass on very few feast days, spending them doing household things and scolding those who go to hear it."[87] One of the witnesses, Pedro López, a small farmer on the estancia, claimed that Hernández was considered to be a Morisco "because everyone from his homeland says he is a Muslim of the ones from Granada."[88] López noted that Hernández did not attend Mass and made the people on his estancia work on feast days, "and [he] has ordered them to not observe any more Sundays."[89] López also testified that the man who was renting the estancia to Hernández, Alonso Moreno, had called him a "Muslim dog (*perro moro*) and that he would prove it."[90] Finally, López testified how one evening while Hernández was having dinner he was visited by a Spaniard (*gachupín*) from Old Castile, Diego Martín de Castro, who upon entering said "Praise Jesus." Hernández replied furiously, "Here there will be no 'Praise Jesus,' but rather good night, from God to your graces."[91] A year later, Martín de Castro was finally located in Tlaxcala and forced to testify. Martín de Castro described how one evening, while working for Hernández, watching the Indians harvesting crops, as the sun was setting, he had said, "Praise Jesus, which is a sign that they [the Indians on the estancia] cease work, to which the said Pedro Hernández said, 'these dogs do not know Jesus Christ,' referring to the Indians, and he has heard that they called him a Morisco but he does not remember who [said it]."[92]

Ideas beyond religiosity also circulated about Moriscos, extending to occupation and occasionally even skin color. In 1611 in Santiago de Guatemala, Nicolás de Oliva faced accusations that he was a Morisco. Accusations leveled against Oliva addressed a range of attributes that included lineage, purity of blood, religiosity, reputation, customary practices, dress, occupation, and physical appearance. During the trial, witnesses debated whether Oliva was a Muslim or a Christian, in language inflected with assumptions about his religious identity. The range of factors that played into his trial suggests the complicated nature of social standing and legal status in the early modern Iberian world. Oliva's case was unfolding at the time of the expulsion of the Moriscos from Spain, when Moriscos were increasingly being racialized in the writings of advocates of expulsion. Through debates over the position of Moriscos at the imperial level, and individual negotiations of status in the courtroom, it becomes possible to identify competing conceptions of identity: some commentators advocated the immutability of characteristics like blood, while others promoted more fluid conceptions of status shaped by reputation.

The reasons Oliva's accusers gave are revealing. Gaspar Bernal de Reyna testified how he was talking to a man from Gracias a Dios (in the Honduras province) named Pedro de la Portilla who worked in the province of San Salvador. In Suchitoto, one of the pueblos he passed through, Portilla had encountered Oliva, whom he called a "bad Christian and they understood he was a Morisco because he shows it in his color, and in his trade, because he was a *buñolero* [maker of buñuelos, or buns], an occupation used ordinarily by Moriscos in Spain."[93] What did Portilla mean by referring to both Oliva's color and trade? His statement highlights two elements present in discourses about suspected Moriscos: public reputation, actions, and behavior, as opposed to genealogy and attributes transmitted by blood. Words like "complexion" and "color" had a range of meanings that included both physical appearance and moral qualities that could indicate trustworthiness.[94] Oliva's occupation was, in the minds of his contemporaries, a clear indication that he must be a Morisco. The association between Moriscos and being a buñolero may have been reinforced by a popular *romance* by Lope de Vega that had wide circulation and may have contributed to its dissemination in Spanish America.[95] Portilla declared that it was common knowledge that Oliva was a buñolero, and he had been seen "making *buñuelos*, and as a result he is understood to be a Morisco."[96]

Portilla testified that Oliva owned an estancia with livestock and a dye works (*obraje de tinta*) near Suchitoto, and whenever trouble occurred, "they heard him call upon Muhammad, saying these words, 'Ah Muhammad.'"[97] Portilla reprimanded Oliva, exhorting him to invoke instead, "Our Lady or her blessed son, that they would favor him, and not to call Muhammad." Portilla continued, "In this province they said he was a Morisco, and what aid could he receive from Muhammad? Therefore everything turned out badly for him."[98] To Portilla's chagrin, Oliva ignored his advice. Differing opinions over which sacred figures to invoke played a role in relations between Christians and Moriscos. Receiving aid, whether through the cult of the saints, the Virgin Mary or Christ, was considered ineffective if not sacrilegious by some Moriscos who practiced Islam, although it was employed by others. Likewise many old Christians believed only bad things could result from invoking Muhammad.

Bernal de Reyna, the other accuser, noted that Portilla and Oliva were involved in a dispute over Oliva's estancia and over a debt. By September 1613 an inquisitorial investigation had been opened against Oliva in San Salvador, Guatemala. Dominican prior Friar Miguel Garzon summoned Portilla to testify. A merchant, Portilla had stopped in Oliva's house for fifteen days to collect from him a debt of 1,500 *tostones*. During this time, Portilla claimed to have heard Oliva "many times during the fifteen days, say on any occasion which offered itself, 'ah Muhammad.'"[99] Portilla repeatedly admonished Oliva to stop, telling him, "'Look, they say you are a Muslim,' and the said Nicolás de Oliva replied to this witness, 'I cannot.'"[100] Portilla added that he had heard Oliva was a man "who had little fear of God or of his conscience. . . . [He was also] a man of bad conduct who with great ease denies debts that he owes, both with his signatures and without them, under oath . . . He did not see in the house of the said Oliva either cross or image or . . . rosary, nor is the Christian doctrine taught in his house to the people in his service."[101] Religious identity was an important point of contention in many of the cases because *encomenderos* and other Spaniards in charge of indigenous laborers were responsible for their catechization and attendance at Mass on Sundays and Catholic feast days. Portilla's testimony also illustrates the implications of linking religious identity with qualities such as trustworthiness in business relationships.[102]

Portilla then raised questions concerning Oliva's birthplace. While he had heard that Oliva was from Valencia del Çid, on one occasion two years previously he was talking with a group of Spaniards about Oliva, and one of the men, Pedro Hidalgo, had called Oliva "a circumcised Muslim dog from Greece."[103] On other occasions, Portilla had heard Oliva claim he was from Mallorca, "so that sometimes he says that he is from Valencia del Çid and at others from Mallorca."[104] Portilla also testified that another resident from Gracias a Dios had confided that Oliva had told him he was circumcised. Portilla ended his denunciation with a vehement proclamation: "As long as he has known him, he has not seen him cross himself or pray or do anything that resembles anything Christian. In his house he walks around in short open breeches made of a coverlet (*calzon de manta corto abierto*) and a shirt of the same and a dirty rag wrapped around his head in the usage and dress of a Morisco."[105]

Generally associated with indigenous dress in Mexico and Central America, the *calzon de manta* here operates alongside the "toca," or head covering, as a marker of "Moorish" difference. Recent studies have noted the persistence in sixteenth-century Spain and Spanish America of styles of dress borrowed from Muslims and Moriscos, incorporated into regional identities or used by the elites and not primarily associated with Islam. Dressing as Moors, sitting on the floor, and performing *juegos de cañas* was unremarked upon by the Spanish nobility, until exhibited on public occasions in front of other European nobles and ambassadors, allowing them to project in their public discourses an increasingly racialized image onto Spain as a "Moorish nation."[106] Pedro de Valencia's frustration with limpieza de sangre as applied to Moriscos indefinitely can be read in this light, as Spaniards became conscious of their image in other parts of Europe. Yet Oliva's accusers did not view his clothing as something positive, associated with nobility, but rather a marker of difference that added weight to an inquisitorial denunciation. Clothing was increasingly noted in colonial Spanish America as being connected to an individual's perceived public status and reputation. Dressing as an Indian, mestizo, Spaniard, or Muslim carried connotations about ethnic or religious identity, performing it before the community in a way that was "public and notorious." This had legal implications.

Circumcision also factored into denunciations. When a carpenter named Pedro Hidalgo Tinoco testified against Oliva, he recounted a conversation they had had while he was making him an obraje on his estancia. Oliva told Hidalgo Tinoco that he was Greek and that he had been a captive. Upon hearing this Hidalgo Tinoco declared, "The Greeks give tribute to the Grand Turk and they give him their first son, and according to this, that is what you must have been. You must be circumcised."[107] Oliva replied quickly, "I am joking, as I am only from the Kingdom of Catalonia."[108] When asked if he called Oliva a "circumcised dog from Greece," Hidalgo Tinoco admitted that he had, because Oliva would not pay him for the work he had done on the obraje, but that he only said this because of what Oliva had told him, not because he heard him invoke Muhammad.[109]

The next witness was Pedro de Cuéllar in San Salvador. He described how he had met Oliva in Seville in 1579 and had seen him there "in the house of a Morisco buñolero engaging in the same occupation of buñolero."[110] Cuéllar testified that Oliva had lived in the province of San Salvador for fourteen years. He had been married to an indigenous woman before his current wife, a mulata described by other witnesses as the daughter of a mulata and a Spaniard.[111] Cuéllar also stated that he did not know where Oliva had been born, although he had heard others say in Mallorca, and that he had been a renegade.[112] Cuéllar said that Diego Sánchez, who had spent a lot of time on the estancia, had seen Oliva "one day, naked, passing by in a canoe on the Lempa River that passes near the estancia . . . and he saw that he did not have a foreskin on his member."[113] Sánchez had asked Oliva what had happened, and Oliva replied that it had been removed due to an illness. After relating Sánchez's account, Cuéllar added that he had heard Oliva had been a captive in North Africa, and he had heard him speaking in Arabic although he did not understand what he was saying.[114] Ideas about what made someone a Morisco circulated in Spanish America and infused the denunciations that surfaced during local conflicts. Insults such as those leveled against Oliva threatened public reputations and resulted in ecclesiastical court cases.

* * *

In colonial Spanish America, ecclesiastical authorities were concerned with spreading Catholicism and regulating indigenous religiosity, with the aim of creating a model Catholic republic. Not only secular priests and members of religious orders, but also encomenderos were responsible for ensuring the catechization and religious participation of indigenous peoples laboring on their *encomiendas*. Attending Mass, going to confession, and taking communion regularly were important markers of devotion. Public displays of heterodoxy in communal devotional spaces undermined Spanish imperial projects, and authorities attempted unsuccessfully to restrict emigration to the Americas to individuals who could prove that they were old Christians. The complaints voiced by Sotomayor and others about the "scandalous," "public," and "notorious" nature of a Morisco's conduct during Mass can be contrasted with individuals who acquired a public reputation for piety, even if they did not possess the requisite "purity of blood." The lawyer (*solicitador de causas*) Gaspar de Cabrera, a "descendant of the Muslims of Tunis," was tried by the Inquisition of Seville in 1583 for invoking Muhammad.[115] However, he was absolved because "it was found that he was held to be a good Christian, and as such, was a member of the brotherhood of Nuestra Señora del Rosario, and of other brotherhoods."[116]

When focusing on public interactions and ideas about Moriscos, one cannot ignore the importance that personal piety and internal belief held for the individuals involved, specifically the importance of ideas about salvation that informed public perceptions of religiosity. Inquisitors asked accusers to scour their memories and consciences in order to denounce anyone acting against Catholic doctrine. Likewise, those appearing before inquisitorial tribunals repeatedly voiced concerns over their salvation and doubts about their faith, even at moments that would not have been in their best interest.

Through the confessional--and by extension, the Inquisition--the interior spaces of private religiosity fell under the scrutiny of ecclesiastical authorities. By undergoing public penance such as appearing in penitential garb in an auto–da–fé, an individual's private beliefs became public, thereby transforming their legal status permanently. In this context, Spanish authorities solicited and invoked customary practices in order to categorize and regulate behavior in ways that had legal implications.

Individuals in Spanish America who were accused of being descendants of Muslims and Moriscos, or who were called "dogs" and insulted publicly, used the courts to create and maintain status in a society in which purity of blood became increasingly important. Furthermore, some Spaniards writing at the time of the expulsion became concerned that the slur "perro moro," applied frequently to Moriscos, prevented them from fully assimilating, in response to a political struggle that was increasingly casting religious identity as an innate characteristic, transmitted by blood.[117] Pedro Aznar Cardona referred frequently to Moriscos as dogs throughout his work justifying the expulsion, while Pedro de Valencia decried this insult, because its emphasis on lineage rendered the idea of Morisco assimilation impossible.

Perceived by many authorities as being unassimilated, Moriscos were cast as disloyal subjects in official discourses about the emerging Spanish nation. This also resonated in everyday interactions "on the ground," as knowledge about Moriscos and Muslims and conversations about religiosity crossed the boundaries between religious communities. Images of Moriscos, as constructed in the court records, influenced an individual's status in his or her community. What made someone a Morisco could vary depending on the denunciation. Accusers cited a range of attributes, some of which went beyond prayer and religious practice to language, dress, and occupation.

CHAPTER 5

Healers and Diviners

Morisco Practitioners in the New World

Healing illnesses could become a particularly fraught matter for ecclesiastical authorities, practitioners, and clients because in the Americas there were few trained physicians and pharmacists. Even in Spanish cities, their services were too costly for the majority of the population. University-trained doctors and pharmacists, licensed by the Tribunal de Protomedicato, at best had mixed outcomes in curing disease.[1] As a result, many relied on the services of folk practitioners who had a reputation for the success of their cures.

Medical practice sometimes overlapped with so-called magical practice (*hechicería*), as the provenance of a particular remedy gained significance during the course of ecclesiastical and secular authorities' attempts to define what constituted an appropriate means of curing. Accusations involving healing were more ambiguous than those concerning hechicería pertaining to love magic and divination, as in the latter the source of supernatural power, in the minds of religious authorities, was always the Devil. Instead, when trying curanderos or *saludadores*, inquisitors and bishops had to carefully determine the provenance of the remedy. Was its purported effectiveness due to the natural properties of plants and medicines, to sanctioned figures such as Christian saints or the Virgin Mary, or to the tricks performed by the Devil to subvert God's power? Ecclesiastical authorities diligently attempted to regulate the uses of images of saints, Christ and the Virgin, and Christian prayers in cures because they were concerned about their misuse or misinterpretation. They endeavored to allow only well-trained priests to administer these. However, the religious faced the problem that clients in search of a cure placed great value on the curative properties of Catholic holy figures and relics, and sought healers who would incorporate these into their cures. At the same time, they were worried about the potential for the Devil to invade or inhibit proper cures. Similarly, North African Muslims and some Moriscos attributed the "virtue" of remedies to come from the Qur'an, Muhammad, holy people who crossed religious boundaries (Mary, Christ), and to spirits (djinns) that could be either good or evil.

This chapter explores the tension between everyday negotiations among local peoples, and Spanish authorities' attempts to condemn practices they associated with Muslims. Spaniards, North Africans, and indigenous peoples entered into conversations and exchanged remedies in the towns where they resided. Yet fears concerning the presence of Muslims in Spanish America spurred some old Christians to denounce individuals for practices that ranged from learning healing rituals in North Africa to praying in Arabic and invoking Muhammad. These inquisitorial testimonies against Moriscos and North Africans often invoked the presence of indigenous peoples in strategic ways. Accounts of daily exchanges were reshaped into narratives that undermined Spanish imperial authority in the Americas.

Sixteenth-century Spanish treatises concerning hechicería provide descriptions of the various types of ritual specialists who performed cures, from the point of view of ecclesiastical authorities. In the *Reprouacion de las supersticiones y hechizerias* (1538), Pedro Ciruelo forwarded the argument that hiring healers or performing cures that were not sanctioned on theological and medical grounds constituted a sin.[2] Curing by *ensalmos*, by uttering words and drawing sacred characters, does not possess "natural virtue" because "the will of men cannot bestow natural virtue upon the works they do."[3] Rather, only God can infuse objects with virtue: "Herbs, stones and other natural things were created at the beginning of the world by only the will of God and not by the will of any man."[4] To Ciruelo, because language was the product of centuries of interactions among people, and not divinely granted, it could not provide a source of licit healing power. As a result, the ensalmos recited by the *ensalmadores* and the *nóminas* they carried were blasphemous because the resulting cures constituted "false miracles" brought about by the "secret operations of the Devil."[5] Those who healed using their breath, the saludadores, were similarly suspect.

FRANCISCO LÓPEZ DE APONTE: A CASE STUDY

A 1659 *Relación* printed and disseminated by order of the Holy Office
of the Inquisition in Mexico City related the exemplary punishment
meted out to individuals who appeared in the auto–da–fé of that
year.[6] These sensationalized accounts highlighted the charges against
those sentenced and described their demeanor as they faced death
at the stake. They circulated to remote regions in Spanish America
long after the auto–da–fé had ended, making public the sentences
and stigmatizing the families of the condemned. Intended to induce
fear of heresy and a sense of communal rejection, the authors of the
Relación emphasized the dire consequences of impenitence and exag-
gerated the points leveled against those who were sentenced. One
of those executed in the 1659 auto–da–fé was Francisco López de
Aponte, accused of making heretical claims and of being a *saludador*,
or healer. More than his actions as a healer, the *Relación* stressed
López de Aponte's assertion that Muslims were faithful precisely
because they did not acknowledge the virginity of Mary following
the birth of Jesus. At a time when Marian devotion became symbolically associated with the Spanish naval victory at Lepanto and the
expansion of Catholicism, denial of the virginity of Mary was seen as
a particularly grave transgression. Shocked friars who visited López
de Aponte in the inquisitorial prison witnessed "the fierceness of this
Demon. He was the most rash heretic, and the greatest, who has ever
been seen in the Inquisitions to date, and the most ignorant, obstinate
and unashamed to be found among men. . . . [He was] the declared
enemy of the Holiest Virgin Mary . . . denying in a foul-mouthed way
her wholeness and purity."[7] The apocalyptic tone of this particular
Relación, which included explicit references to Saint John and the
Apocalypse, stressed how the cities of antiquity, as well as Africa and
the "three Arabias" were all being "profaned by the same Sect, and
with another thousand deceits."[8] The *Relación* emphasized conve-
niently that the presence of the Inquisition in Spain, Italy, and the
Americas prevented the spread of heresy to these regions that were a
beacon of Catholicism.

The trial transcript of Francisco López de Aponte's case, however,
presents a very different version from the one proclaimed publicly
on the scaffold. López de Aponte was denounced primarily for his
actions as a healer. His statements concerning the virginity of Mary
and questions regarding his adherence to Catholicism only surfaced

later, as his trial gained momentum. On 7 November 1656, María Buitrón appeared before Mexican inquisitors to denounce events that had taken place two months previously. In her deposition, Buitrón described how López de Aponte had been summoned to the house of her aunt Margarita Pulido to heal her ailing eyes. According to Buitrón, López de Aponte had claimed to be a "white Moor, of the ones who had been favored" by King Alfonso.[9] She described how, as a saludador, he carried a bag full of pieces of wax "like agnus," papers, and relics to cure illnesses.[10] López de Aponte had been visiting Pulido in her home, at her request, in order to perform cures on her eyes, but had in the process scandalized several of the people present.

Buitrón described how, "when he cures the eyes of the said woman with a mouth swab [hisopillo], he applies it first to his mouth, saying, 'in the name of the Holiest Trinity,' and he also applies to his mouth the cloth or rag with which he cleans her eyes, before cleaning them."[11] Several witnesses commented on his method of curing with his breath. Buitrón's daughter, Augustina de Buitrón Muxica, described how she overheard López de Aponte say on several occasions "that he has virtue in the breath of his mouth, and in his hands, because he removes slow fevers, and that wherever he places his hand, there cannot be any illness, nor can he have it [illness], and that this was by the grace that God gave him, and it was bestowed upon him by his mother."[12] To the inquisitors this was suspect as a practice used by some Morisco and North African healers, which had nothing to do with "natural" remedies but rather with diabolic intervention. Religious authorities in Spain, as elsewhere in Europe, considered cures in which no obvious natural remedy was used to be the result of a pact with the Devil.[13] Although the practice of using breath to cure dates to Late Antiquity, marabouts, or Muslim religious leaders in North Africa during the early modern period, transmitted their healing power, or baraka, through saliva and touch.[14] An aljamiado manuscript detailing the miracles carried out by Muhammad also highlighted the importance of breath. The manuscript further described Muhammad as "he who with only touching his hand to an injured leg, healed it, and he who with only the saliva in his mouth spit in the eyes of a blind man, [and] returned to him his sight."[15]

Not only Morisco religious leaders but also doctors and healers used aljamiado manuscripts that circulated clandestinely. By the early sixteenth century, as a younger generation of Morisco doctors was increasingly denied a university education, more authority was given to the medical knowledge transmitted orally within their families and in these texts.[16] Although Moriscos were barred by the 1560s from being licensed as physicians at most Castilian universities, the sick often turned to Morisco healers and even the Spanish royal family sought the expertise of Morisco doctors.[17] The reputation of Arab medical knowledge in medieval Europe lingered in the popular imagination into the sixteenth century. The University of Valencia allowed some Moriscos to be licensed as physicians into the early seventeenth century, and there were also informal ways they could become doctors and obtain approval by the Protomedicato even if they did not hold an official degree.[18] After the University of Granada was founded in 1531, a few prominent Moriscos such as Alonso del Castillo and Miguel de Luna obtained degrees in medicine there.[19] Nonetheless, the more conservative and exclusionary position assumed by the University of Alcalá de Henares was more commonplace. The position of Morisco medical practitioners was precarious due to the climate of suspicion: those who were not successful in their cures could be accused of poisoning. The 13 September 1607 Actas de las Cortes de Castilla reveal some of the anxieties old Christians had about Morisco doctors. The Cortes de Castilla banned Morisco doctors from practicing their craft, citing the prohibition against Moriscos bearing arms: if they could kill old Christians with arms, and medicine was just as dangerous, why should they be permitted to practice it?[20] Furthermore, they argued, the Moriscos' propensity for rebellion made them more likely to hate old Christians. Moriscos should not hold the occupation of doctor because of "some deceit that they may engage in, because the more honorable the profession of doctor is, the more serious is the deceit that can be committed within it."[21] Again, trustworthiness was linked to religious and ethnic identity, and it was invoked to justify measures to exclude Moriscos. Such suspicions could also shape local perceptions of remedies undertaken by Muslim or Morisco healers.

Outside learned circles, knowledge about healing was transmitted orally, within families and through daily exchanges.[22] In Spain, inquisitors and ecclesiastical authorities scrutinized the activities of Morisco doctors and healers for elements they associated with Islam, highlighting these for prosecution. They banned circumcision and punished *retajadores* (circumcisers) for continuing to visit the homes of newborns.[23] Relations between Morisco healers and the sick became strained. While some Moriscos were sought out as healers, others faced suspicions that they would circumcise Christian babies or deliberately fail in their cures and kill their clients out of hatred of Christians.[24] The Synod of Guadix in 1554 prohibited Morisca midwives from practicing in Granada and Morisco doctors from treating Morisco patients, given the worry that they would continue to incorporate perceived Islamic elements into their medical cures.[25] Another synod in Granada in 1572, under Archbishop Pedro Guerrero, explicitly condemned the practices ecclesiastical authorities associated with Moriscos. The synod prohibited "superstitions with papers, divination, saludadores, *ensalmadores*, *santigüeras*, and prayers of the blind."[26] It also warned Morisco doctors "under pain of excommunication not to cure with things that did not possess a natural virtue for the illness they intended to cure."[27] Religious and ethnic tensions in Spain swept across the Atlantic and inflected relationships between practitioners and their clients in Spanish America.

The degree to which any of these practices was characteristic of, or can be attributed to Muslims and Moriscos, is subject to debate. While scholars who have worked specifically on Morisco magic argue for the applicability of some of the remedies found in aljamiado texts to Moriscos, practices across medieval and early modern Catholic Europe also resemble those attributed to Moriscos.[28] While ecclesiastical authorities were less concerned with the actual medicines used for healing illnesses, they stepped in when the interpretation of the curative materials invoked prayers or religious figures and could result in their misinterpretation, or heresy. When trying Morisco practitioners, inquisitors further noted their use of talismans bearing short Qur'anic texts, and invocations of God and Muhammad in Arabic. Inquisitors were especially concerned with keeping such knowledge from new converts, whether Moriscos or Amerindians. They labeled healing, in addition to practices of divination and love magic, with the stigma of hechicería, or "magic," an illicit remedy associated with the Devil.

There was thus in the early modern Iberian world a thin line between what clergy considered acceptable practices and the dreaded use of hechicería. Recent works on Morisco "magic" have based much of their analysis on the earlier works of Edmond Doutté, Idries Shah, and Toufic Fahd, concerning North Africa and the Middle East. Many of these earlier works argue for the universality of "magic" and fail to situate practices within their social and political contexts.[29] Yvette Cardaillac-Hermosilla, who composed the only systematic study of healing, divination, and love magic among Moriscos, argues that what ultimately distinguished Moriscos from old Christian practitioners was their faith in Islam.[30] As a result, Moriscos considered God to be the source of the power of the remedies. Yet what do we make of the variations in individual Moriscos' religiosity, or how many of the elements labeled Morisco also appear in Jewish and Christian remedies in medieval and early modern Europe?

Dror Ze'evi has noted a similar tendency to universalize among historians who have analyzed dream interpretation in Muslim societies, echoing research conducted in the 1960s. The emphasis of these older works on the prophetic nature of dreams across time periods and cultures overshadows inquiry into the meaning that dream images might have held for contemporaries.[31] Composers of treatises and manuals for dream interpretation engaged with one another, and their texts also changed depending on the priorities of the societies using them. Insights can be gained here for approaching the practices of Moriscos and North African Muslims in the Iberian world. Ze'evi notes how Muslim scholars drew from Greek and Roman thought in their treatises. Later Arabic translations of such texts allowed Middle Eastern Islamic ideas about dream interpretation to reach Christian Europe through Spain, Sicily, and Byzantium.[32] Translators of dream manuals might alter passages to make them suitable for monotheist Christian, Muslim, and Jewish readers. Richard Kieckhefer likewise traces how knowledge about magical practice circulated from the classical world across the Mediterranean, into both Africa and Europe. From this perspective, magic can be considered a crossroads where different cultures came into contact. During the medieval period, Christians in Europe borrowed practices from Jews and Muslims, as texts and people traveled.[33]

While it is difficult to reconstruct the social world surrounding magical practices, when filtered through testimonies in the inquisitorial trial records, it is necessary to explore the meaning that they held for practitioners and clients alike. While some practices might appear to be universal when examined from a distance, they were always embedded in social and political contexts that would have changed spatially and temporally. This political context would have had very specific implications for practitioners, clients, and the ecclesiastical authorities who sought to control their activities in the context of the Counter-Reformation. The fluid population of the early modern Iberian world, where Europeans, Africans, and indigenous peoples interacted with each other, and Catholics, Jews, and Muslims came into contact in the Mediterranean, provided ample opportunities for individuals to exchange remedies.

On 17 December 1657 the inquisitors summoned Margarita Pulido to testify against López de Aponte. They asked her if she knew why she had been called to appear before them, and she answered that she assumed it was because she had called in a *curandero* who claimed to be a "moro blanco" a year ago, to cure her eyes in the house of her niece, María Buitrón. Pulido described how López de Aponte would "put on her forehead a bag that he said contained relics, and he blew the breath from his mouth into her eyes, placing his tongue on her eyes, telling her that it was by the grace that God had given him."[34] It was perhaps López de Aponte's unorthodox claims surrounding the use of relics in his cures that began to preoccupy his clients. As María Buitrón and Augustina Buitrón Muxica gathered around Pulido during her cure, they saw López de Aponte remove "a white piece of paper from a bag of relics that he carries and he showed it to [the women who] . . . saw drawings of four Christs on the said paper. . . . [He then] folded the said paper and he put it in his mouth . . . placing it on his palate, and having taken them out he said the said Christs were just drawings, and he put the paper back in his bag."[35] The barber Gerónimo de Ortega, who lived in the same house as Pulido, was also treated by López de Aponte. He testified that on the first day that López de Aponte came to cure him of his syphilis (*enfermedad Galica*), he "did not speak a word; he just put a patch on the sole of his foot covered in granules which he thought was of *tecomaca* and dragon's blood (because this witness knew something about pharmacy), and before making the said patch he put in his mouth the things from which he made it, saying that he had virtue in his mouth because he had a Holy Christ on his palate and it gave virtue to those things so that they could cure the illness and that his mother had given him this grace."[36]

Ortega also described how López de Aponte referred in an indecent way to the small silver image of the Virgin of Guadalupe that he carried for his cures. Buitron's other daughter, Antonia Rangel, offered to make López de Aponte another bag in which he could carry the image. When handing it to Rangel, López de Aponte told her, "Here, you take that woman," and on other occasions he would ask for someone to bring him the image of the Virgin by saying, "Bring me that woman."[37] Such a disrespectful way of referring to the Virgin shocked Ortega and made him doubt López de Aponte's piety.

He also used other images in his cures. Interestingly, when López de Aponte's goods were confiscated by inquisitors, they discovered the papal bulls he had been claiming to heal with were actually "printed conclusions dedicated to Saint Ignatius whose image was engraved over the lettering as is customary."[38]

López de Aponte reputedly made several other disconcerting claims. Antonia Rangel testified that one day when she had expressed a wish to go to heaven, López de Aponte told her to "wait until he had died and then hold on to him and she would go to heaven."[39] To this, a shocked Rangel replied that he should "watch out that they both did not end up in hell."[40] López de Aponte later told her that he was a saint "because he was told this by a woman whom he had consoled for an affliction that she had . . . [and the woman told him that] this saint has consoled me."[41] He also claimed on several occasions to be a theologian (*tehologo*), who could confess sins and provide spiritual guidance to Rangel and the others.[42]

Itinerant healers who aspired to be holy persons had a long history in the Mediterranean world. Had he learned his practices in North Africa, as one of his accusers claimed, López de Aponte would have encountered numerous cults surrounding holy people. Sossie Andezian has described these cults using the concept *zyâra*, meaning visit, rather than the Christian notion of a cult of saints.[43] Zyâra expressed the "relationships that men and women entertained with human beings, dead or alive, who were invested with supernatural powers [baraka]."[44] Their sanctity was linked to a "state of grace," which followed a vision or a dream. Possessors of baraka were able to foretell the future, read minds, and heal by prayer and touch.[45] During the fifteenth and sixteenth centuries, maraboutism experienced a shift as lettered Andalusian emigrants spread Islam to rural areas in the Maghreb. During this period, sainthood became hereditary. By the seventeenth century a variety of actors who ranged from marginal wanderers to fully integrated members of society, and who were considered to be born with baraka, provided moral guidance as well as healing.[46] Sufis also acted as popular healers. By 1500 Sufism had grown to become a popular movement with Sufi tarīqas springing up across Ottoman lands.[47] López de Aponte may have been familiar with some of these movements had he traveled to Algiers, as one of the accusations claimed, or even encountered them in Spain.

Another source for López de Aponte's concepts and practices for curing may lie in and around the city of Granada. A. Katie Harris has examined the sacred meaning of the Sacromonte caves for Granadan Moriscos. These caves gained a reputation as a Muslim pilgrimage site during the fifteenth century. During the sixteenth century, Granadan Moriscos did not graze livestock near the caves due to rumors that it had *"zulaha*, which in our language means saints."[48] They claimed the Sacromonte emitted "supernatural lights" associated with baraka from the tombs of saints.[49] Moriscos attributed healing powers to the caves. They picked herbs on the mountainside that they thought had absorbed healing properties, and they brought the clothing of the sick into the caves to absorb the curative forces.[50] Could López de Aponte have incorporated some of this local knowledge, either from North Africa or from Spain, into his own practices? He certainly incorporated Nahua plants such as tecomaca into his cures.

Healing by the grace of God also held meaning for Catholics. In early modern Italy, living saints came to embody sacred power that could be used to cure illnesses.[51] All sectors of society participated in these devotions to individuals with charismatic power who performed miraculous cures. Living saints and their cults at times faced repression from the church, although some of them were eventually canonized.[52] A number of objects facilitated the healing of Catholic believers, and some aspirants to holiness included sacramentalia such as the Agnus Dei in their repertoire of remedies.[53] Contemporaries found their visions and miracles to be credible, even if inquisitors were skeptical of them, projecting their own idea of what constituted a "genuine" holy person.[54] López de Aponte seemed aware of the use of the Agnus Dei and images of saints in cures, although it becomes clear that he blundered in using them. To what extent was he performing for a Catholic audience, attempting to gain their confidence in his power as a healer, but still using other methods he may have believed to be effective, such as breath, saliva, and plants?

It was in the midst of these statements and actions that López de Aponte uttered his opinion on Muslim attitudes toward the Virgin, further scandalizing those present. The ailing barber, Ortega, related how, while Pulido was being cured, López de Aponte told another man that "Muslim women, when they wanted to give birth, would invoke the Holy Virgin to help them."[55] Because he was in pain, Ortega did not follow the conversation closely, but related how soon after, Antonia Rangel had suggested, "Muslims said that because they lacked faith and the said Francisco López responded that it was rather the excess of faith that the Muslims had in not believing it."[56]

Upon hearing this exchange, Ortega exclaimed for them to "throw out that man from there, since he did not want to be cured by him because the inquisitors should take him out in an *auto* for the nonsense that he was saying."[57] According to Rangel, the man with whom López de Aponte was speaking had said, "Muslims believe in God and they only denied the virginity of the Holy Virgin Our Lady after she gave birth."[58]

While this exchange echoes the polemics between Muslims and Christians in Spain concerning the virginity of Mary, López de Aponte's claim that the Virgin also had significance for Moriscas is accurate. Mary's representation in the Qur'an parallels that of Jesus, as a pious human being whose life and miracles attest to the power of God. In the Qur'an, Mary is presented as a holy woman, who was neither divine nor the mother of God. She is associated with miracles, for which she is venerated, although their power originates in God.[59] Because the Qur'an does not specify whether Mary remained a virgin following the birth of Jesus, who is recognized as a prophet in Islam, Iberian Muslims and Moriscos held varying opinions on the matter.[60] Yet many considered Mary, along with Muhammad's daughter Fatima, and his youngest wife, Aisha, to be a model of feminine virtues and piety whose virginity before marriage, religious devotion, and motherhood were exemplary.[61] Popular devotions to Mary were present among Muslims and Moriscos in Spain and North Africa. Because the Qur'an represents Mary as having given birth to Jesus beneath a date palm, dates were thought to possess a protective quality that Muslim women could invoke during their own pregnancies.[62] In 1494 the German doctor Hieronymus Münzer was shown a rosary by an elderly Granadan Muslim made from dates of the kind that were carried by pregnant Muslim women. Münzer wrote, "An old man showed me a rosary made from date pits, saying that they were from the palm tree from which Mary ate, during her flight from Egypt. He kissed it saying they were very useful for pregnant women, as he had experienced."[63] In his account, Münzer also mentioned the Granadan Moriscos' veneration of the Virgin, Saint Catherine, and Saint John, noting that some would even name their children after them.[64] The *Libro de dichos maravillosos* provides a recipe for a talisman to be given to a woman about to give birth. The instructions state that she should tie it to her left leg and remove it once the baby emerges: "In the name of God, the Merciful, the Compassionate. God bless our lord, the noble Muhammad. Fetus! Come out of the narrowness and the hardness of the womb and the anguish of the belly to the house of the world. Come out, by the power of The One who created the world and modeled it in the most perfect form. My God, help, just like you helped Mary, daughter of Joachim, when she gave birth to Your holy servant. Facilitate it in the same way to the owner of this note."[65]

López de Aponte's case suggests how perceptions of Muslims influenced everyday interactions in colonial Spanish America. Gaining insight into his past is difficult given the conflicting testimonies at his trial. To his clients, he may have intended to pass himself off as a Muslim. This could prove an advantage under certain circumstances, due to the growing reputation in Europe of Arab and Muslim expertise in medicine and magic. In early modern Italy, for example, notions of the exotic and foreign held a strong attraction for itinerant peddlers of remedies and their clients.[66] Some Italian-born charlatans adopted names that suggested exotic locations such as "Il Barbaresco," "Il Turchetto," and "Il Persiano."[67] Others may have been renegades in Ottoman lands who returned to Italy as reconciled Catholics and peddled the medical knowledge they could have acquired there. It was not uncommon for individuals residing in the lands bordering the Mediterranean to have had contact with the Ottomans; some were even taken captive and converted to Islam.[68] David Gentilcore has studied cases of charlatans in early modern Italy that resemble that of López de Aponte. For example, in 1735 Domenico Antonio Franchi styled himself as the creator of the Balsamo della Porta Ottomana and as a Turkish convert to Catholicism. Franchi claimed to be the son of the physician of sultan Mehmed III, who had learned the recipe for his balm at the Ottoman court.[69] A number of charlatans were thus able to "profit from Europe's fascination—a mixture of fear and admiration—with the Ottoman Empire, the prestige of Arabic medicine (and the marketability of their spices)."[70] But this strategy could be turned on its head. While individuals could dress "alla Turchesca" in front of their audiences or during Carnival, in more quotidian settings such attire could inspire unease and prosecution.[71] This distinction was even more pronounced in Spanish America, and it was possibly what made López de Aponte's clients suspicious. These images had a basis in lived realities across the Mediterranean as various peoples interacted with one another in changing political settings.

López de Aponte's origins were obscure. He might even have been from North Africa as the *alcalde mayor* of Motines, Captain

Cristóbal Flores de Medrano was tracked down to testify. In the town of Colima, Flores de Medrano told the local commissioner that he had met López de Aponte while he was living in Mexico City. Flores de Medrano claimed he had called López de Aponte a hypocrite and told Pulido and everyone who would listen that López de Aponte was "the greatest liar" and warned them against using his services because he would end up before the Inquisition.[72] He also stated that he heard López de Aponte was "by nation a Muslim or a Turk because he spoke with a strong accent."[73] Inquisitors supported Flores de Medrano's assertion, noting that López de Aponte was unfamiliar with the basic tenets of Catholicism, and uttered the Pater Noster, Ave Maria, Credo, and Salve Regina "in poor Romance."[74] They complained, "He knows neither the Christian doctrine nor the commandments, and, when he was examined, the little that he said of the four prayers was poorly grasped for a man of such age. If he were a Catholic, it is impossible that he would not know them."[75]

When confronted by inquisitors, López de Aponte presented a very different account of his life. He stated that he was born in Faro, Portugal, as were his parents and grandparents on both sides.[76] He maintained vehemently that he was a "refined Spaniard and neither a foreigner nor a white Moor."[77] By calling himself a Spaniard he may have been claiming belonging in the Republic of Spaniards, as a white European. Throughout his trial he denied constantly the charges against him. López de Aponte stated that as a boy he had run away, first to Ayamonte and then to Seville, having learned the trade of a cooper along the way. As a young man in Cádiz he enlisted as a soldier on one of the galleons, on which he sailed to Havana where he married. Following several more transatlantic voyages and a suit for divorce filed by his estranged wife in Havana, López de Aponte settled in Mexico City to work as a cooper. He claimed that he was sought after as a healer in Mexico City, and he stressed that he used only natural remedies for his cures. Nevertheless, individuals began to insist he was a *zahorí* and requested his services as a treasure hunter and diviner, skills he denied ever possessing.[78] According to López de Aponte, a man whom he had been curing once approached him, saying, "They had told him he was a zahorí and that he cured with the virtue he possessed." To this, López de Aponte replied "that he was not a zahorí. He had treated the eyes of many people with honey (*miel virgen*) and crystallized sugar (*azucar candi*), and they had been cured. Perhaps this was a virtue that God had given him, and he placed on their eyes a print of the Santo Cristo del Buen Viaje (Holy Christ of the Good Voyage) of Havana, who was a very miraculous saint."[79] López de Aponte then described how rumor spread that he was a zahorí, following a conversation he had had with Antonia Rangel about a tailor with whom she was having a relationship. When López de Aponte related the details of her story to the tailor, he was asked how he knew these things. López de Aponte replied, jokingly, "because he was a zahorí and he knew it."[80] However, the tailor and others took his statement seriously and began asking him to foretell future events.

Rather than attempting to ascertain López de Aponte's actual status, whether as a Muslim, or someone who claimed to be one to lend legitimacy to his cures, or even someone accused falsely of being a zahorí and a moro blanco, what becomes interesting are the assumptions underlying his trial. The polemics surrounding peninsular Muslim-Christian relationships spilled into ideas about who possessed the power to heal and how effective cures could be performed. A healer, especially one who claimed to be a saint whose power was bestowed by the grace of God, needed to demonstrate exemplary piety when conducting healing rituals. López de Aponte's references to Muslim beliefs concerning the Virgin Mary worried his clients, causing them to question the provenance and efficacy of his cures. In producing the *Relación* of the auto–da–fé, inquisitors emphasized López de Aponte's statements about the Virgin, casting him as an impenitent Muslim and heretic. This propagandistic move further linked associations between religiosity and actions, as news of his trial and his execution was disseminated throughout Mexico and to other parts of the Spanish world.

***

López de Aponte's case and others raise a number of questions about the appearance of practices attributed to Muslims and Moriscos in Spanish America. How did knowledge of these practices cross the Atlantic, and what was considered by contemporaries to comprise Morisco magical practice? How did Morisco practitioners and clients conceive of their actions? While they shared knowledge about the Virgin Mary or Christ, Christian and Muslim attitudes differed toward these religious figures, producing points of friction in doctrine that could lead to denunciations. In the early modern Spanish world the confessional played a central role in directing some practices and stigmatizing others. In this multiethnic, multiconfessional society exchanges were occurring that authorities tried unsuccessfully to control. However, such actions could become grounds for prosecution. On the Peninsula, religious conflict between Christians and Muslims set the tone for Spanish authorities' priorities when it came to regulating customary practices involving healing. Both Morisco and old Christian practitioners incorporated religious elements into their remedies, and it was on these practices that inquisitors focused most of their attention.

Despite official concerns, emerging networks of practitioners and clients allowed individuals on both sides of the Atlantic to tap into forbidden knowledge as they exchanged remedies. It is important to examine both contemporary conceptions of what constituted Morisco practices and how these ideas and stereotypes crossed the Atlantic to gain a new life in the Americas. As Francisco López de Aponte's case shows, these had profound implications for relationships between ritual specialists and the people who sought their expertise.

CHAPTER 6

"Polvos del Gran Turco"

Moriscos and Magical Practice
in Spanish America

At the end of his *Relación*, Álvar Núñez Cabeza de Vaca recounts a compelling anecdote about a Morisca in Castile who foretold the outcome of the Pánfilo de Narváez expedition, before the ships departed for the Americas. This Morisca from Hornachos warned one of the ten women about to accompany Narváez that if any of the men were to venture inland, they would perish. However, if anyone survived, "God would perform great miracles through him."[1] Cabeza de Vaca then noted that "the entire voyage had occurred to us in the same manner that she had told us."[2] Seemingly disconnected from the main narrative, but nonetheless related in the final lines of the *Relación*, this story reveals the importance that Morisco men and women held, as diviners, in the imagination of individuals about to depart for distant and dangerous lands. Perceptions of Moriscos as capacious practitioners of love magic and divination, as seekers of buried treasure, or as healers, appeared not only in Spanish Golden Age literature but also in daily encounters in Spain and Spanish America.

Spanish and Portuguese emigrants to the viceroyalties of New Spain and Peru brought with them both knowledge of and a market for rituals they associated with Muslims and Moriscos. In Spanish America they also intermingled with sub-Saharan African and indigenous ritual specialists whose repertoire included rich medicinal traditions.[3] The performance of these practices, and the questions asked of the ritual specialists, would have held degrees of resonance or familiarity across various social groups in colonial society. At the same time, individuals might seek recourse to other practitioners, even as the material objects used in the rituals and the extent of social acceptance or stigmatization varied as bishops and inquisitors became involved in defining and regulating them. Reputed Morisco and North African remedies for healing, love magic, and divination crossed the Atlantic and were transformed during the course of daily exchanges in the New World.

Moriscos and Muslims who carried their knowledge with them overseas continued to face inquisitorial scrutiny and suspicion in Spanish America. Old Christian, converso, and Morisco emigrants from Europe brought their own remedies with them, and these combined "on the ground" during the course of informal interactions. The prevalence of love magic cases in southern Spain certainly influenced patterns of magical practice that individuals carried with them to the Americas.[4] As was the case with Muslim healers, Morisco women were viewed as especially skilled in love magic and divination, but also as potentially dangerous. On both sides of the Atlantic, women established relationships in which they shared remedies that might aid them in the face of abusive or indifferent sexual partners.[5] Ecclesiastical officials stigmatized these networks among women, and at times they were prosecuted by the Inquisition, to the degree that their prevalence threatened more orthodox forms of Catholicism. The political context involved in creating this new informal religious culture, as specific remedies were exchanged, merits close examination in order to gauge the meaning of magical practice in Spanish America. Many questions surface: What significance did the actual practices hold in a constantly changing, religiously and politically charged setting? To what extent did it matter that Muslims and Moriscos were invoked and approached when individuals chose a remedy or a practitioner? In what ways, if any, did the power dynamics between members of different religious communities influence not only the selection of a particular practitioner, but also the reception of their performance, in ways that reflected the instability of social relationships?

MEANINGS OF "MAGIC" AND "HECHICERÍA"

Analyzing magic as a category is controversial. There are problems in defining what precisely is meant by "magical practice," and in the ways that scholars have related it to the concepts of "religion" and "science."[6] Practices attributed to Muslims and Moriscos must be examined according to the categories that contemporaries would have found familiar. More precise language to describe these practices, such as "love magic," healing, and divination can be more useful than the vague term "magic." In other instances, broader terminology such as "unofficial ritual" may be more appropriate.[7] Nonetheless, it is difficult to avoid using the term magic. Jonathan Z. Smith points to the difficulty: magic is "not only a second-order term, located in academic discourse. It is as well, cross-culturally, a native, first-order category, occurring in ordinary usage which has deeply influenced the evaluative language of the scholar."[8] The historiography on peninsular Morisco magic, as well as on witchcraft in colonial Spanish America, wrestles with these issues. Indeed the translation into English of the Spanish term hechicería, used in much of the inquisitorial documentation concerning the practices under study, as witchcraft or sorcery, can lead to problematic assumptions about the actual practices taking place.[9]

What terms were used by contemporaries to refer to magical practice and ritual specialists? In the *Tesoro de la Lengua Castellana o Española* (1611), Sebastián de Covarrubias Orozco defines *hechizar* (to ensorcell) as "a certain type of incantation with which they bind the person who is *hechizada* (ensorcelled) in a manner that perverts their judgment and makes them love that which, being free, they would abhor (this is done with explicit or tacit pact with the devil)."[10] Covarrubias notes a linguistic connection between *hechizar* and *fachizar*, derived from *fascinum*, and suggests that women are more likely to make use of hechicería "because the devil finds them [women] to be easier, or because they by nature are insidiously vindictive and also envious of one another."[11] Covarrubias also distinguishes between *magos* as "wise philosophers" (magi) and individuals whose powers, aided by the Devil, attempted to supersede nature, using "the magical arts, condemned and prohibited."[12]

Pedro Ciruelo and Martín del Río, from whose work Covarrubias draws, believed similarly. In the *Reprouacion de las supersticiones y hechizerias* (1538), Ciruelo defined hechicería and superstition before breaking them down into their various parts or practices. His stated motive in writing was to prove that these violated the first commandment, constituting idolatry in their implicit recognition that the Devil had greater authority over nature, creation and free will than God. Hechicería arose after Christ's redemption of mankind as a "hidden and dissimulated idolatry" that the Devil introduced into the world to tempt people to return to serving him.[13] By definition, "any work that a man does to obtain some benefit, or to excuse something evil: if the things he places on it, and the words he says there possess neither natural nor supernatural virtue to have that effect, then that operation is vain, superstitious and diabolical: and if it reaches fruition it is by secret operation of the devil."[14] As a result, "hechicerías and superstitions should be greatly punished by prelates and judges and be cast out of the land of the Christians: as very evil and poisonous: and very harmful to the honor of God."[15]

The Jesuit Martín del Río, who drew from the extensive reports of the Society of Jesus' missions in India and elsewhere to write the *Disquisitiones Magicae* (1608), noted that "idolatry and witchcraft go together."[16] To Del Río, magic was "the handmaid of moral turpitude," and "immensely strong" among heretics: "Witness the Muslims in Africa and Asia, the heretics of Germany, France, and Britain, and the apathetic Catholics called *politici* in Italy and other places."[17] He then claimed that "as a result of the Moorish occupation of Spain, the magical arts were virtually the only subjects being taught in Toledo, Seville and Salamanca."[18] Drawing from the works of Jesuit theologian Juan de Maldonado, Del Río argued that the cause of magic was when "evil spirits take up residence in heretics" whom they use "to deceive humanity."[19] Again, belief in and practice of the magical arts was the work of the Devil, which could only be counteracted by the preaching of the Gospel in the Jesuit missions around the globe. Later in his work, Del Río addressed the power that evil spirits have over the soul, translating from Spanish to Latin a Toledo Inquisition case from 1600 of Roman Ramírez, a Morisco accused of "having received knowledge of medicine from an evil spirit."[20] Del Río details the practices Ramírez allegedly kept, including observing the feasts of Ramadan and Zahor, praying the zala, and performing ritual ablutions. According to Del Río and by extension the inquisitors in the case he was citing, Ramírez "dedicated his soul" to an evil spirit in exchange for "expertise in the cure of many secret, hidden (occultae) illnesses by means of herbs, fumigations, and superstitious incantations."[21] Del Río recalled the portion of the trial when Ramírez is summoned to expel 101 spirits who possessed a woman on her wedding day, a story incorporated by Mexican playwright Juan Ruiz de Alarcón in his *Quien Mal Anda En Mal Acaba*.[22] Elite representations of magical practice in works by Del Río and Ciruelo must be compared to the everyday descriptions of remedies, which appear in inquisitorial testimonies.

MORISCOS AS SORCERERS: PERCEPTIONS IN IBERIAN
POPULAR CULTURE

Spaniards in the fifteenth and sixteenth centuries were familiar with
"Moorish" culture and members of the nobility actively participated in and adopted some of its elements.[23] These included wearing
the toca, playing juegos de cañas, and writing romances that portrayed Muslim-Christian interactions in a favorable light. Barbara
Fuchs argues that this differs from later expressions of Orientalism
in France and Britain because Iberian Christians, having coexisted
with Muslims for generations, did not consider them to be alien or
an exotic "other." Rather, travelers from northern Europe portrayed
Spain as a "Moorish nation" following their observations of Spaniards. In some ways, this consideration also holds true for practitioners of magic and their clients, who would have sought remedies
without necessarily considering them scandalous or illicit, before
ecclesiastical authorities stepped in to define them. Nonetheless the
goals of inquisitors and bishops to define, delimit, control, and eradicate "magic," labeling some practices licit and others demonic, were
informed by political imperatives that complicated prior regimes of
coexistence. Stereotypes of Moriscos as possessing knowledge of hidden treasure, or being adept at magical practice, pervaded popular
culture as is reflected in Spanish Golden Age literature. Miguel de
Cervantes, Lope de Vega, and others represented Moriscos in a variety of these roles.

A case from 1606 is suggestive of how descriptions of magical practice made their way from the Mediterranean to Spanish America, in
the stories told by individuals who had traveled in North Africa. Juan
Alonso, a Genoese man living in Mexico City, denounced himself to
inquisitors at the insistence of his confessor, for attempting to practice divination. Alonso claimed that he had shared knowledge about
his experiences with magic while living in Algiers with his friend,
the weaver Francisco Español, who had left the viceroyalty of New
Spain in a recent fleet and returned to Spain. Alonso told inquisitors
that he had been selling clothes in Algiers nine years earlier, when
news arrived that Murat Reis "the Elder," admiral of the Ottoman
navy and Algerian privateer, had been captured by the galley fleet of
Malta.[24] Wondering whether this was true, Alonso approached "an
old Muslim woman who was in a room in the house of the janissaries.
Speaking with him and two Mercedarians who were there to ransom

captives, she told them that she knew how to find out. She then called to a boy and wrote in the palm of his hand some letters inside some lines that said the following: Asasaro, Asason, Asis, Tasisen, Galisen, Enchip, Enchip, Yselgan, Elende, Aulu, Massa. And over these letters she spilled ink so that it appeared to be as if in a mirror, and she cast a bit of resin in some lit coals and told the boy to ask the image that was inside the ink if Murat Reis was imprisoned or injured, and the Muslim woman said the image had cloth on its head which was a sign that he was injured."[25] Alonso, "out of curiosity," then asked the woman to teach him how to make the lines and letters that she had made, which she did.[26] Alonso also told inquisitors how on another day, he, along with "companions of his from Marseilles who were [in Algiers], called a Muslim boy and made, in the palm of his hand, the said lines and letters, to know whether it was true what the Muslim woman had said."[27] Alonso said he did not repeat this act until his exchange with Francisco Español in Mexico City. Francisco had asked him to "put on a piece of paper the said lines and letters, which he did, but does not know if he used them."[28] Inquisitors were especially concerned that knowledge of these practices would spread. At this point Alonso, realizing that he was on dangerous ground if he were actually teaching others, stressed his ignorance of what Francisco had done.

SACRED WRITING AND THE TRANSATLANTIC TRANSMISSION OF PRACTICE

Alonso's case and others raise a number of questions about the appearance of practices attributed to Muslims and Moriscos in Spanish America. How did such knowledge cross the Atlantic, and what was considered by contemporaries to comprise Morisco magical practice? How did Morisco practitioners and clients conceive of their actions? While they shared knowledge about the Virgin Mary or Christ, Christian and Muslim attitudes differed toward these religious figures, producing points of friction in doctrine that could lead to denunciations. In addition to religious figures common to Islam and Christianity, Moriscos and North African Muslims invoked Muhammad and incorporated inscriptions from the Qur'an into their amulets and curative powders.[29] However, in conducting rituals for Catholic clients, Morisco practitioners tended to use elements drawn from Christianity that their clients would have considered powerful. In the early modern Spanish world the confessional played a central role in

directing some practices and stigmatizing others. For example, confessors encouraged individuals to denounce themselves to the Inquisition if they had used a healer who employed religious elements in their
cures, not approved of by the Catholic Church. These tended to be
routine self-denunciations in which the recipient of the cure claimed
ignorance and was reincorporated into the church, while leaving the
ritual specialist she or he consulted vulnerable to inquisitorial charges
of hechicería. Authorities tried diligently yet unsuccessfully to control
these types of exchanges.

Many North African and peninsular Morisco remedies used written Arabic that was thought to possess healing qualities and usefulness in love magic, which crossed the boundaries of religious
communities. In sixteenth-century Spain, a clandestine network
of religious leaders (alfaquíes) who were literate in Arabic enabled
aljamiado texts to circulate within small circles of specialists.[30] The
alfaquíes appear as the manufacturers of talismans in the inquisitorial
records from Valencia.[31] Aljamiado miscellanies such as the *Libro de
dichos maravillosos* contained instructions for making the talismans.
These works detailed the materials to be used in their manufacture
and the astrological considerations indicating the most auspicious
moment to produce them.[32] Nonetheless, the talismans' power was
derived primarily from the written word, rather than from astrological associations. In Spain, Muslim and Morisco practitioners copied
Qur'anic verses and religious invocations in Arabic from similar texts
onto pieces of paper, or onto the body, to use for healing.[33] For example, aljamiado manuscripts instructed Morisca midwives how to give
women who were late in giving birth "magical words" to drink, or
a talisman to wear between their legs, that bore crosses and "magical characters."[34] Women who experienced problems with lactation
were instructed to draw "letters possessing a magical character" and
tie them onto their left leg.[35] Qur'anic verses, sacred letters (*fawatih*)
found at the beginning of some *suras*, and religious invocations such
as "basmala," "Allah akbar," and "ya Allah," were all inscribed onto
pieces of paper, objects, or the body, to be used in magical practices.[36]
The suras chosen for this purpose bore frequently some relation to the
actions they were used for. The power within the sacred writings was
transferred from the texts to a person's body by dissolving the paper
in water, or washing the writing in saffron or rose water, and admin-
istering it as a drink, burning the paper and inhaling it (*sahumerio*),
or writing it directly onto a piece of bread or on almonds.[37]

The case in 1591 against María Peraça, a Morisca born in North Africa and taken to the islands of Lanzarote and Canaria as a slave, provides valuable physical descriptions of the pieces of paper (nóminas) used for love magic. Cases from the Inquisitions of Seville and the Canary Islands illuminate those depicted in the records from New Spain, describing the actions of practitioners in the port cities that were centers for colonial trade and emigration. Peraça was tried for attempting to return to North Africa, along with a group of other North African slaves. Many of them had arrived on the island as Muslims. After having been baptized forcibly they attempted to return to North Africa despite having to face charges of apostasy before the Inquisition if they were caught. One of the women captured with Peraça testified that she visited a local Muslim man who gave her a "quartilla written in saffron with letters that look like beetles, and he told her to carry it on her right breast, and the knots that he had given her previously, on the left, and with this, the man whom she wished to marry would not be able to marry anyone else, even if he wanted to."[38] The evening she had attempted to flee to North Africa, Peraça had also placed "two small bundles [enboltorillos] of red taffeta, like nóminas," underneath the mattress of her mother's bed.[39] The notary who confiscated her possessions when she was arrested testified that "inside her small coffer, they found something like a nómina of red cloth, and another nómina of very old yellow taffeta."[40] When the inquisitors opened the wrapped objects, they found inside one of them "a quartilla of paper written on one side with characters and letters that appear to be Arabic, and on the other [side] they found a bit of white wax, and inside it a piece of paper that was smaller than a quartilla, with the same characters and letters as the other one, and all the said letters had such little color that they were difficult to see."[41] The other nómina of yellow taffeta contained "many round papers, and in the middle of them, a piece of wax that appeared to be white, and it was very dark."[42] Peraça later said that the Muslim gave her these pieces of paper "so that she carry them, the one on her right side and the other on her left, and with this she would have peace with her husband, and that the wax that was on one of them was from Our Lady of the Candelaria."[43] The reference to the Virgin of Candelaria, patroness of the Canary Islands, as bestowing power over these remedies, as practices crossed the boundaries between religious communities, suggests how Christian images also played a role in the sacred system that was emerging from the exchanges between old Christians and Moriscos.

These practices held different meanings for Moriscos and old Christians, both of whom sought practitioners who could carry them out. In the auto–da–fé in Seville in 1583, two Moriscos were sentenced to the galleys for using pieces of paper to cure illnesses. Antonio Luys, a North African who had been baptized in Tangier and resided in Seville, was tried for giving the sick nóminas with Arabic texts for them to carry that "called on Muhammad to protect them."[44] According to Antonio Luys, by using those papers, "they would be freed from much evil, and many good things would happen to them."[45] Hernando Muñoz, another North African who worked as a porter in Seville, was arrested for planning a rebellion with other Moriscos. Royal authorities found "papers written in Arabic with invocations of Muhammad" on his person and remitted him to the Inquisition.[46] Muñoz finally confessed that he "carried the said papers so that Muhammad would help him with his freedom and free him from the courts."[47]

The use of talismans bearing Qur'anic verses held special significance for some Moriscos, and they appear regularly in the inquisitorial record. According to a marginal note from an aljamiado manuscript from the Morisco community in Aragon: "A good Muslim should never be without amulets, because the person who goes without them is like a house which cannot be closed because it does not have a door. In a house without a door, all who wish to can enter. In a person who goes about without amulets, the devils enter from all sides."[48] Amulets and talismans such as the hand of Fatima proscribed by the Synod of Guadix were favored by many Moriscos and North African Muslims, and they were manufactured by local alfaquíes. Belief in djinns, or spirits who ordered worldly matters and could be either beneficial or harmful, was widespread among Moriscos.[49] Because djinns could cause illness or misfortune, possession of the appropriate talisman was necessary to protect the user from harm. Inquisitors labeled djinns as devils, interpreting them within a Catholic framework that likened the actions of Muslim and Morisco healers to demonic pacts. Further cases from Seville attest to the importance of carrying talismans. In 1592, a Morisco living in Seville named Juan Martín was accused by five witnesses of possessing pieces of paper with Qur'anic verses, which he carried "hidden on his person, like nóminas."[50] Martín confessed that a Muslim had given them to him, telling him that "they were from Muslims and the Qur'an of Muhammad and that he received them knowing this, and they were written in Arabic, and he believed that because they were from the Qur'an . . . they could help him heal from his illnesses. . . . He also believed that carrying other papers of the same sort, that the said Muslim gave him for a friend, a Morisco who was in jail, that he would be freed from prison, and thus he took them and believed that because the said papers were from Muslims, they would aid both of them."[51] Supernatural and spiritual remedies for securing freedom from slavery circulated among Muslim and Christian captives in the Mediterranean world. These remedies, and others, made their way to Spanish America, transmitted by practitioners who claimed to have acquired this sought-after knowledge from Muslims or Moriscos.

Examples from the Mexican Inquisition indicate how individuals had encountered practices in Spain and North Africa that they attributed to Muslims, and they suggest possible pathways along which ideas about magical practice moved. Ecclesiastical authorities stigmatized even the most seemingly innocent of these actions and, upon their confession, urged individuals to denounce themselves before the Inquisition. In 1606 Juan de Monteagudo presented himself before the commissioner of the Inquisition in Veracruz. Monteagudo confessed that the previous year, before sailing to the Mexican port of San Juan de Ulúa, he was in Puerto de Santa María, near the port city of Cádiz, where he lay, "sick and *ligado* by some women who disliked him."[52]

While looking for someone to cure him, Monteagudo was told that "in a galley there was a Muslim who cured all illnesses, and he could heal him."[53] Monteagudo soon met with the Muslim healer, who "took an iron grate and a plate, and wrote on them in his Arabic language, and he does not know what [the words] meant."[54] The healer instructed Monteagudo to mix water that had been poured into one of his shoes with rose water and use it to "wash the letters that the said Muslim had written on the said grate and plate, and with the same water, to wash all of his body. With this he would become well."[55] Monteagudo said he did not think more about having sought the aid of a Muslim healer, until, "by order of his confessor, [he] was enlightened of his grave fault," and denounced himself to the Inquisition.[56] Structures of authority such as the confessional shaped perceptions of illness and what constituted a licit cure, by creating a sense of wrongs done if these were ineffective. Monteagudo maintained that before speaking with his confessor, he had not realized he had done anything wrong.

In Puebla de los Ángeles, during the 1620s, several cases were brought against people using rituals associated with Muslims and Moriscos. In 1621 Andrés, an indigenous slave from the Philippines, was accused by the comisario of the Mexican Inquisition in Puebla, Doctor Pedro García de Herencia, of "selling powders to attract women, which were sent to him by the Grand Turk."[57] García de Herencia complained that Andrés "goes about selling powders to many people, [powders] which he says have the virtue that [when] women carry them on their person, and perfume themselves with their incense . . . men will die for them. [He says] . . . that the Grand Turk sent them to him with some papers that he carries, that are full of characters."[58] Andrés's references to the Ottoman sultan, and his use of papers that were presumably written in Arabic in carrying out love magic, are reminiscent of the actions of Morisco practitioners in Spain. By referring to the "Grand Turk," Andrés was perhaps invoking the legitimacy and attraction that this image would have had for those seeking his aid, an image that is echoed in the trial of Francisco López de Aponte, who reputedly cast himself as a moro blanco to perform cures using saliva and his breath.[59] The possibility that an indigenous man, even from the Philippines, could invoke the Grand Turk heightened authorities' concerns, and it also raises the question of what effect his practices might have had on local networks.

How did remedies for love magic attributed to Muslims and Moriscos reach Spanish America, despite restrictions on the dissemination of beliefs and practices associated with Islam? What impact might they have had on Spanish authorities' anxieties about the infiltration of this knowledge into indigenous communities whose faith was already considered tenuous? The papers that Andrés carried, bearing "characters" that he attributed to the Ottomans, are reminiscent of those circulating among Spanish Moriscos and North African Muslims.[60] Furthermore, they were used in the Philippines, which was under the jurisdiction of the viceroyalty of New Spain, as the documents sent from the commissioner of Manila to Mexican inquisitors demonstrate. These documents from the 1620s record that Juan, an indigenous man from the island of Terrenate used "certain burnt papers on which there were certain words, all written in Moorish," for seducing women.[61] Another case mentions an indigenous woman who tied leaves together, on which were "written certain words in the Moorish language."[62] Antonio de Morga, who had been a Spanish official in the Philippines, as well as alcalde de crimen of the

Audiencia of Mexico and a *consultor* for the Mexican Inquisition, described the majority of the population, both male and female, as literate, using characters that "resembled Arabic," written from right to left on "the leaves of trees and on canes, on the bark of which on this island there are many."[63]

Andrés's claims that he received his papers directly from the "Grand Turk," reflect practices that he carried with him from the Philippines, where there was a growing Muslim presence by the seventeenth century. In his *Sucesos de las Islas Filipinas* (1609), Antonio de Morga presented a history of the Spanish conquest of the Philippines that included descriptions of the peoples inhabiting them. Morga described the conflicts between Spaniards and the Muslims inhabiting the islands of Jolo, Mindanao, and Terrenate, and the "moros Malayos" in Cambodia who actively resisted Spanish colonization. Furthermore, Morga noted networks of merchants moving from Borneo into Luzon Island and Manila, intermarrying with and teaching the local population about Islam. According to Morga, these marabouts (*morabitos*) gave the native peoples "pamphlets [*cartillas*], ceremonies and the means of observing them, using some *ghazis* they brought with them, and now many, and the most principales, began . . . to be Muslims, circumcising themselves and adopting Muslim names, so that if the expedition of the Spaniards had been delayed any longer, this sect would have spread throughout the whole island, and also across the others, and it would be difficult to uproot."[64] Alongside the Dutch, the "moros" remained a source of anxiety for colonial authorities, as expressed in the language of the official documents and in Morga's account: In Mindanao and Jolo, "the Muslims rebelled against the Spaniards."[65] Echoing Spanish commentators' descriptions of Muslims in other parts of the world, they characterized the peoples of these islands, "as Muslims, and as such, facile and of little steadfastness, restless and given to disquiet and wars; every hour and in diverse parts, they acted and rose up."[66] Juan de Esquivel, the field marshal in charge of suppressing one of the uprisings, regretted that although he and the other captains labored for "the punishment and pacification . . . they could not achieve this."[67]

Following Spanish military incursions into the Philippines, a number of the Muslims living there were enslaved and brought to New Spain. In a letter composed in 1614, Diego de Nobela, the *beneficiado* of the Motines region on the Pacific coast of Michoacán, lamented to inquisitors the prevalence of Philippine Muslims in the ecclesiastical provinces of Motines and Zacatula. He complained that many, "when they were conquered, they were adults, and because in their land they had followed the sect of Muhammad, they are circumcised, and some are still [being circumcised], even after they have been baptized."[68] Nobela worried that they would set a bad example, "because they are among the *naturales*, [who are] simple people, who, with little effort will fall into novelty."[69]

More information about Andrés arises in the accusations against María Delgado for practices she claimed to have learned from Moriscas in Spain. One of the witnesses, Luisa de Cuéllar, whose lover had left her for another woman, had heard about Andrés's powders and went to consult him. Andrés visited Cuéllar in her home, where she asked him to "give her some powders to bring back the said man who was hers, and reduce him again to her friendship, and . . . [he] gave her three types of powders."[70] Andrés instructed Cuéllar that "some were for her to put in the water the said man was to drink, others for her to sprinkle on her head, [and] others for her to carry on her body."[71] Cuéllar said she gave the powders to the man twice, in his water, and "after three months he left the other woman and returned to her."[72] Cuéllar also testified that she had sought the aid of María Delgado, who possessed similar knowledge of love magic. Delgado told Cuéllar to send her a string from the man's undergarments ("una sinta de los calsones"), in order "to tie" (*ligar*) him.[73] While the *ligadura*, or *aiguillette*, was a standard form of love magic that appears in denunciations across the Mediterranean, the Spanish and Spanish American cases emphasize the salience of Morisca practitioners who could teach their craft to old Christians.[74] Cuéllar said she would give Delgado the string, because "in Spain, a Morisca had showed her this . . . in order to discern where her suitor was."[75] Another witness against Delgado, Juana de Reinoso, claimed that she had given her a "root . . . that a Morisca gave her in Castile and the said root had the virtue that, if women carried it with them, men would die for them, and give them anything they requested."[76]

Other cases from Puebla concern divination and suggest how knowledge associated with Morisco practices could have reached New Spain. They also shed light on the remunerative aspects of magical practice. In 1619 Francisca Maldonado appeared, "without being summoned," before Doctor Pedro García de Herencia, the comisario of the Inquisition in Puebla de los Ángeles.[77] About twenty days previously, Maldonado had been sitting at home in her drawing room, "sad and melancholy because of the many debts that she had, and no way of paying them," when her slave Catalina arrived with a proposition.[78] Catalina told Maldonado "not to be upset because God would remedy [her problem]" and to "look for someone who would practice divination, to know if that man would feel compassion for her, and to know his heart, and . . . [Maldonado] replied that only God could know the heart of that man."[79] Catalina then revealed that "when she was a prisoner in the jail of Seville, she saw a Morisca who practiced divination with beans, a piece of charcoal, and a paper, while saying 'in the name of the Father and of the Son, and of the Holy Spirit and of Saint John.'"[80] Catalina also noted that the Morisca's performance proved to be ineffective, and that she "assumed the Morisca did it to take her money" since she was paid by others to practice divination.[81] Maldonado told inquisitors that after Catalina left, she took a "fistful of beans, a piece of paper, and charcoal and . . . threw it all into a room" but did not pay attention to see "what attached to the bean or the charcoal to the paper."[82] A few weeks later, Catalina was summoned before inquisitors to testify. She said that "when she was imprisoned in the jail of Seville for a debt of her masters, a Morisca was imprisoned, one of the ones they expelled from Spain."[83] On her first night in jail, the Morisca approached Catalina, asking "what would she give her in return for divination to determine whether she would be imprisoned for a long time."[84] Catalina gave the Morisca some money, at which point she proceeded to tell the future with beans, charcoal, and papers, "but all of it was a sham and a lie."[85]

The Morisca in the Seville jail was not unique in requesting payment for her services. Some Spanish Moriscas indeed charged for providing remedies and supplemented their low incomes by practicing love magic and divination for others. Others acted as midwives or healers. Many of these women were poor or had been enslaved or exiled from Granada following the Alpujarras rebellion. Payment ranged from food and clothing to jewelry to a few coins and would not be returned if the remedies or cures failed to work. These Moriscas were integrated into local social networks through their activities and expertise, even though at the margins of the law because of ecclesiastical condemnation.[86] New Spain also had a thriving community of curanderos, diviners, and practitioners of love magic who charged for their services. Many of these individuals were indigenous or Afro-Mexican, and some were slaves, who sought to bolster their status by performing these rituals. Acting as a healer or ritual specialist had the potential to bestow *honra* upon an individual, a form of honor and authority that was gained through activities and positive attributes publicly recognized within one's community.[87]

In 1537 a group of women was denounced before the ecclesiastical tribunal in Mexico City, under Bishop Friar Juan de Zumárraga, for practicing hechicería. The group included two Morisca slaves who allegedly sought to obtain their freedom. The testimonies of three of the women stand out. They described the entangled network of prac-titioners in their community in Mexico City. In exchange for items of clothing, blankets, or wine, they performed remedies that ranged from healing, to love magic, to incantations that would free a person from captivity. Marta, a black slave accused of hechicería, described how another slave, María Despinosa, came to her for help in obtain-ing her freedom papers (carta de libertad). According to Marta, Des-pinosa chastised her for taking a long time in performing the hechizos and told her she would find another woman who had helped to free a Morisca named Luisa. Marta described how Despinosa then began to cry, saying, "All I do is give what I have to Moriscas to do hechizos for me."[88] Inquisitors targeted Despinosa's piety and attitude toward Catholicism. She was also the only woman in the group sentenced to perpetual exile from the Indies.[89] One of the witnesses, Alonso de Palençuela, stated that when Despinosa was at his house, they began conversing about two Moriscas in the silver mining town of Taxco. Despinosa told him that "those Moriscas go about in a troubled man-ner, entering and leaving the house of their masters . . . with this devil of confession."[90] He stated that Despinosa said this out of ignorance (*sympleza*), a statement that was later confirmed by Despinosa who added that she did not hate the confessional.[91] The prosecutor for the Holy Office pointed out that Despinosa had been sentenced previously for renouncing her baptism (*renegado de la crisma*), and demanded successfully that she be exiled to Spain.

SUPERNATURAL REMEDIES FOR ILLNESS: MORISCO HEALERS

While official channels such as the Protomedicato were increasingly trying to regulate who could become a licensed physician in both Spain and Spanish America, residents of the viceroyalties of New Spain and Peru complained of the scarcity of doctors and the high cost of summoning them to their sickbed. Unregulated healers were much more attractive, being less expensive and more amenable to including in their cures religious elements that were also thought to influence individual bodies and health. Each community had slightly different prayers and figures to whom they appealed to cure illnesses, but over time they borrowed from each other.[92]

While old Christians may have doubted curanderos who failed to incorporate a proper dose of Catholic piety in their remedies, Moriscos in Spanish America may have sought the aid of healers whose cures they found familiar. For some, this created the opportunity to avoid the spiritual remedies forwarded by Catholic priests, surrounding sacraments such as the Eucharist.[93] For others, the Christian-Muslim polemics, present in local knowledge, spurred denunciations even concerning a patient's behavior on the sickbed. In this context, the sickbed came to be a place in which old Christians and Moriscos associated, at times sharing their expertise in medicine and at others encountering conflict.[94] In 1624, when Gregorio Faxardo was ill in his hacienda of Santa Catalina near Sombrerete, in New Spain, he was asked to confess, take last rites, and pray for God's mercy for his sins. According to scandalized witnesses, "In no way did he appear . . . to do such a thing, or incline himself toward such acknowledgment that he should have as a Christian."[95] Finally, Faxardo's doctor, Captain Diego de Bañuelos, summoned Friar Andrés de León to administer the sacraments to Faxardo, but that "before doing so, he [Faxardo] released a thousand oaths."[96] One of the witnesses, Miguel Sánchez Montión, took Faxardo to be a "bad Christian" because of his blasphemies, and because he never saw him "pray outside the church, and [when he was] in it [it was] with poor example and little veneration."[97] Sánchez Montión also noted that once when Bañuelos was bleeding him, Faxardo exclaimed, "this blood is Muslim, and on another occasion, many days later, he declared . . . that his lineage and relatives . . . descended from the Muslim kings of Granada."[98] If true, Faxardo's claim to noble status and descent from prominent Granadan Muslim families is worth considering. It is interesting that Sánchez Montión chose to repeat this to inquisitors, as in Spain the claim to descent from the Granadan and Moroccan nobility brought with it a series of economic privileges and exemptions from the restrictions placed on the majority of the Morisco population.[99] The claim would have its echoes in those of the indigenous nobility in New Spain and Peru, who assumed privileges under Spanish rule by highlighting their noble lineage predating Spanish arrival, and participation in the early conquests. Could this have been Faxardo's attempt to defend himself against allegations of blasphemy?

Frustrated by the doctor who insisted on bleeding him and calling in a priest to administer the Eucharist, Faxardo summoned an indigenous healer named María to determine what had been ailing him because he believed his illness was caused by hechicería.[100] According to Bañuelos' testimony, María confirmed Faxardo's fear that he was suffering from a "*bocado.*" She then proceeded to draw crosses on Faxardo's stomach and to burn things she found on him associated with his illness, including three worms and a bat, using incense that she had removed from "a piece of holy *copal* that was in the box with the Eucharist."[101] After she had performed these cures, Faxardo claimed he saw a figure pass by his bed and felt terrified. María told him, "do not be afraid. Take courage, as this is the devil that was inside the bocado they gave you . . . not only to take your life, but also to take away your soul."[102]

The bocado that appears in Faxardo's trial, while rare in Spanish and Latin American witchcraft cases, bears striking resemblance to the concept of *Tukal* as a cause of illness among healers in North Africa. According to anthropologist Renée Claisse-Dauchy, who conducted extensive interviews with healers in Morocco, Tukal is translated as "something that is given to be eaten."[103] This corresponds to the literal translation of the Spanish word "bocado." Tukal is referred to as an entity that personifies the illness, that can't be cured by other means and persists in the way that Faxardo's did. Its symptoms similarly include fatigue and intense stomach aches. While it is problematic to draw too many correspondences between the actions of twentieth-century healers and those operating in the sixteenth century, some insights can be gained. The interviews conducted by Claisse-Dauchy describe not only the practices conducted by Moroccan healers, midwives, pharmacists, and fqihs, but also their social context, history, and texts.[104] While the social context changes over time, the texts being used were consistent, with some fqihs consulting medical treatises written by Arabs in the twelfth century.[105] In this way, a basic knowledge of illness and cures could have remained consistent, even if the structures of transmission and client-practitioner relationships were very different in Morocco, in a society that did not condemn its healers and force their practices underground.

In the early modern Spanish world, however, such actions became grounds for prosecution. On the Peninsula, growing religious tensions set the tone for Spanish authorities' priorities when it came to regulating customary practices involving healing.[106] Both Morisco and old Christian practitioners incorporated religious elements into their remedies, and it was on these practices that inquisitors focused most of their attention.[107] The following day, Faxardo told Bañuelos, the doctor, about his experience with the indigenous healer. Bañuelos proceeded to reprimand him, saying that these were "illusions of the devil and evil things."[108] Faxardo then became angry with Bañuelos and asked him why he said what he did, "as these were things that involved crosses and things of Christian appearance."[109] References to use of "things of Christian appearance" seem to take on new meaning and resemble Francisco López de Aponte's incorporation of Catholic images into his cures. Some practitioners may have reasoned that ecclesiastical authorities would leave them alone if they incorporated Christian images into their remedies. Ysabel de Morales, the *"morilla partera"* tried in 1537 in Mexico City for curing the evil eye with rosemary incense while muttering sacred words, provided witnesses to come in her defense. Through her lawyer, Morales claimed the words she uttered were "of devotion" (*de devoción*) and she made the sign of the cross over those she attempted to cure.[110] One of her clients who testified on her behalf claimed she used words that were "good and healthy . . . words of Our Lord and Our Lady."[111] Morales was eventually sentenced to seclusion in a monastery to receive religious instruction. The prosecutor stated she cured with her breath and without using medicine and noted that she harvested the herbs she collected for her cures, including nine coriander seeds and rosemary, at certain times of the day. Interestingly, instructions for collecting these herbs and using them in cures appear in the aljamiado texts, but there is no direct evidence in the trial that Morales was a Morisca.[112]

Faxardo's recourse to an indigenous healer makes sense in the context of Iberian and Morisco healing practices. Local knowledge of remedies that were infused with Catholic or Islamic significance was shared by both old Christians and Moriscos in Spain. The *Misceláneo de Salomón*, an aljamiado text that circulated among the Moriscos, shows Solomon prescribing cures for various illnesses that combined pharmacopeias with the appropriate talisman or amulet for each ailment. These talismans or amulets could be inscribed with the names of God, Muhammad, the angels, or short Qur'anic texts.[113] Catholic prayers and saints also made their way into the practices of Morisco ritual specialists. Morisco healers used incense and sacred words to expel devils and demons from patients' bodies.[114] By using an indigenous healer, Faxardo was also attempting to distance himself from the tense atmosphere of the sickbed and the pressure to die publicly as a Catholic. María Ruiz's experience being forced to take communion in Mexico City when she was ill suggests that a failure to take the sacraments would have brought down condemnation from those who had gathered around her sickbed: physicians, neighbors, and the local priest. Even the spaces surrounding birth and death became politicized during the course of encounters between Moriscos and old Christians on both sides of the Atlantic.

※ ※ ※

In both Spain and Spanish America, conflicts over religious matters could surface during everyday interactions between old Christians and Moriscos. This was especially manifest in the exchanges of remedies for binding a loved one, freeing oneself from a perilous situation, or performing a cure. Some religious symbols were shared, but they could be interpreted differently in the context of the Christian-Muslim polemics. Many old Christians perceived Morisco doctors, healers, and medical specialists to have special expertise in curing illnesses. As the cases from New Spain show, Moriscas were also sought out for remedies that ranged from obtaining love and ensuring the fidelity of a spouse or lover, to obtaining freedom from enslavement, to finding lost objects and possessions.

Beyond Christian symbols, the pieces of paper used for healing and love magic, thought to bear Qur'anic verses, may have been perceived as especially threatening. Spanish ecclesiastical authorities' failure to control the manufacture of these papers, the knowledge of their content, and their transoceanic dissemination increased anxieties about the presence of Morisco practices in the New World. Both Muslims and Christians invoked sacred texts in cures, and their use represented another arena that Counter-Reformation authorities were trying to restrict. The confessional presented one tool for authorities to label certain remedies as heterodox, at once collecting new information about their practice and referring practitioners and clients to the Inquisition for penance. It taught individuals to scrutinize their own actions and, by extension, those of their neighbors, for illicit activities.

In everyday interactions "on the ground" in Spanish America, exchanges of remedies crossed the boundaries between religious communities. In spite of numerous restrictions, not only Moriscos and North Africans themselves but also practices attributed to them crossed the Atlantic. Knowledge of cures for illnesses traveled from North Africa and Spain, via ports in Seville or the Canary Islands, to Spanish America. This fluidity of exchanges preoccupied Spanish authorities. While the royal decrees prohibiting Muslim and Morisco emigration, and the inquisitorial correspondence emphasized the concern that Moriscos could pose a religious threat to indigenous souls by encouraging them to convert to Islam, these fears were unfounded. But in the realm of daily exchanges, remedies and cures did indeed cross the boundaries of class and caste, and of the vast ocean.

CHAPTER 7

Honor, Lineage, *Ovandina*

The Dynamics of Accusations
and Religious Intolerance

In 1621, a scandal erupted in Lima following the publication of Pedro Mexía de Ovando's *La Ovandina*. In his text, which was only the first part of a work that promised to be four volumes long, Mexía de Ovando extolled the noble origins of a number of Lima's families. Shortly after its publication, the enemies of these families brought the *Ovandina* to the attention of inquisitors, claiming that many of those listed were descendants of Moriscos and conversos, who paid Mexía de Ovando fifty ducats to be included in his book.[1] They produced and circulated an anonymous satirical poem challenging the *Ovandina*. Within a year, Lima inquisitors assembled and burned the existing copies, declaring the work damaging to the Republic.[2] However, when inquisitors at the Suprema in Madrid examined the text, they concluded that the Limeños had overreacted. They declared that the *Ovandina* should not be censured because it promoted the crusading spirit of Reconquest by encouraging young men to take up arms and conquer non-Christian peoples. Their decision in this case invoked Spain's history of Reconquest, the memory of which was closely associated with arguments in favor of colonizing the Americas. Yet to the people of Lima, genealogical distinctions drawn along religious lines acquired urgent importance for defining status. How could a book detailing the lineages of local families cause such an uproar?

Authorities feared works such as the *Ovandina* could be used in court cases to support claims to noble status or offices. Libelous pamphlets also circulated during this period, that attempted to cast individuals as new Christians and to bar them from certain privileges.

Even verbally calling someone a Muslim or a Jew in a public setting often carried legal consequences. Being publicly considered a Morisco could mean the loss of status, offices, or encomiendas, and it called into question one's right to remain in the New World. Individuals in the Spanish Americas who were accused of being descendants of Muslims and Moriscos, or married to Moriscas, used the courts to create and maintain status in a society in which purity of blood played an important role. Public reputations were shaped by litigation, as well as by the publication and circulation of manuscripts and printed works that cast families as old Christians. These works could be, and were, carried into the courtroom as tangible evidence of nobility and by extension purity of blood.

Memory and local interpretations of the Reconquista, which continued to gain importance in Spain during this period, also transformed relationships in Spanish America. Local competitions over status placed increasing importance on lineages, despite the challenges of tracing these in a transatlantic setting. A family's participation in either peninsular or American conquests was recorded in histories and legal documents, often with detailed descriptions of specific battles and the heroic deeds their ancestors performed.

INSULTS AND THE COURTS

In 1636 in the Peruvian coastal town of Huaura, Nicolás de Zamudio Oviedo accused a local priest Licentiate Juan de Angulo of using injurious language against him. Zamudio Oviedo complained to the ecclesiastical court in Lima that the priest had called him a Morisco and insulted him before several people. One witness summoned by Zamudio Oviedo testified that Angulo, "at the entrance to the inn of the said town, said loudly . . . to the said Nicolás de Zamudio, 'Morisco, drunken dog,' repeating these things two or three times." The witness also recalled that "there were many people on the street."[3] In his deposition, Zamudio Oviedo claimed that Angulo had "the custom of slandering and mistreating the residents [of Huaura] . . . because he is a priest he does and says anything he wants to." He insisted that this "grave crime is worthy of exemplary punishment."[4] The gravity of the priest's transgression lay in challenging someone who claimed to possess papers documenting noble lineage, because Zamudio Oviedo had emphasized his status as an "hijodalgo notorio de executoria," or a notable hidalgo who possessed a *carta executoria* attesting to his high status.[5] Zamudio Oviedo's complaint, and similar suits in the Peruvian viceroyalty, show how accusations concerning religious identity were made public, disputed, and altered in the early modern Spanish world.

Two of the witnesses described the events leading up to this exchange. Zamudio Oviedo had advised the merchant Juan Gómez Castellanos to leave his position as mayordomo in the confraternity of the Santísimo Sacramento in Huaura.[6] Overhearing their conversation, Angulo chastised Zamudio Oviedo for suggesting that Gómez Castellanos leave. The priest's authority within his community in Huaura undermined Zamudio Oviedo's suit. The witnesses that Zamudio Oviedo summoned on his behalf were ambivalent. One of them, Diego Guerra, stated that although he had heard Angulo call Zamudio Oviedo a Morisco, he considered the priest to be an honorable man. Guerra testified that after the exchange, Angulo had said that he only called Zamudio Oviedo a Morisco because he himself had told him "that he was the son of a Morisca who sold cooked beans, and of a gentleman."[7] Zamudio Oviedo eventually could not proceed in the case because of the lack of willing witnesses to testify against a priest.[8]

Concerns over lineage and religious identity had become deeply ingrained in early modern Spanish society.[9] Through successful litigation resulting in a ruling that they possessed limpieza de sangre, by providing witnesses to declare that they were considered publicly to be old Christians, individuals could gain social standing despite their actual background.[10] Conversely, public statements such as Angulo's that an individual descended from Muslims or Moriscos, if proven in court, could result in the forfeiture of lands, offices, and prestige. The consequences could affect a family for generations. Insults that implied Muslim or Jewish ancestry, such as calling an individual Mustafá or Don Moisén in front of witnesses, led to a proliferation of lawsuits across Spain because the burden to restore personal reputations fell on the offended parties.[11]

Some benefited financially from conflicts over status. Sevillian genealogists, or *linajudos*, scoured parish archives in search of damning evidence that an aspirant to the city council had a Muslim or Jewish grandparent. Linajudos used these documents to extort payment from those applying for public office or membership in a military order.[12] The practice became so pervasive that by the 1620s Philip IV attempted to limit the number of times someone could be brought to court for lack of limpieza. He established the rule of "three positive acts," after which a candidate was officially "limpio" and could not be charged again. These reforms were directed more toward protecting old Christians from slander than incorporating new Christians into Spanish society.[13] Contemporaries also disagreed over whether public reputation or documentary evidence was more reliable for proving old Christian status.

Families in Spain who wished to gain offices or enter the nobility faced a dilemma. Because conversos were widely believed to have married into old Christian families during the fifteenth century, to gain status and wealth, many noble families fell under suspicion by the sixteenth century, to the extent that Spanish theologians worried that Spain was labeled internationally a nation of "*marranos.*"[14] Imperial competition that cast Spaniards as Muslims and Jews also played a role in hardening Spanish rhetoric and policies toward new Christians. Propaganda spreading this perception undermined Spain's title to the Americas, granted by the bull *Inter Caetera*, and increased anxieties about new Christian presence both on the Peninsula and in the Americas. By the late sixteenth century, a number of treatises began to address the issue of national honor, and this concept also played a role in everyday interactions in colonial society. Moriscos entered into concerns over limpieza to a lesser extent than the conversos, as their detractors viewed them as having remained Muslims and rejected intermarriage with Christians.[15] According to Friar Agustín Salucio, who proposed a reform of the purity of blood statutes in his *Discurso acerca de la justicia y buen Gobierno de España en los estatutos de limpieza de sangre*, stigmatizing the lineages of Moriscos and conversos would encourage them to leave Spain for North Africa as opposed to becoming integrated as good Catholics.[16] Salucio was making a legal point in his characterization of conversos and Moriscos. He argued that under the old Concilios, converted Jews were excluded from office because "they suspected justly that they were not truly Christian, but rather enemies of the name of Christ, in the way that today we suspect the Moriscos."[17] In this way, Salucio distinguished the recently and forcibly converted Portuguese Jews, and Granadan and Aragonese Moriscos, from the "new Christians" who had been considered good Catholics for several generations.[18] Using language grounded in legal terms, Salucio argued that it was the *justo recelo* (justified suspicion) of their disloyalty, rather than their position as *gente infame* (infamous people) that warranted their exclusion from status and honor.[19] While conversos appear more frequently in denunciations involving social standing in both Spain and Spanish America, the legal position of Moriscos and considerations of their difference also came into play. The concern of Salucio and others over *justo recelo* extended fears of disloyalty to both Portuguese Jews and Moriscos.

An examination of the precise status of the Morisco population on the Peninsula, and how their cases differed from those of the conversos, is necessary to discern the social and legal position of Moriscos in Spanish America. By the end of the sixteenth century, many Castilian Moriscos had become integrated into old Christian society. When faced with expulsion and royal prerogatives that placed them in the same category as the Valencian and Granadan Moriscos, the Castilian Moriscos argued that they were old Christians. Definitions of what constituted a good Christian varied, and they were influenced by both the historical memory of a family's conversion to Catholicism or role in the Reconquest, and whether their religious behavior and piety were "notorious."[20] For example, in order to prove exemption from the expulsion decrees, some Moriscos presented certificates of nobility.[21] Others, such as the Moriscos in Talavera de la Reina, claimed that their ancestors had accepted baptism voluntarily in the thirteenth century.[22] The Granadan Juan de Xaení stated in court that he was an old Christian because his family had converted from Islam before the fall of Granada in 1492. He proffered papers that exempted his family from the prohibition that Moriscos travel and bear arms.[23]

Due to the difficulty in defining Morisco and old Christian status, and the diversity of the population that could be labeled Morisco, both authorities and Moriscos attempted to argue a variety of positions both for and against the expulsion. By taking their cases to court, many individuals labeled Moriscos in Castile were able to claim old Christian status. Few Valencian Moriscos took advantage of this legal recourse.[24] In 1609 a group of Granadan Moriscos wrote to Philip III that because they were "good and faithful vassals" their community should not be expelled; only individuals should receive just punishment for their impious deeds.[25] Officials were especially fearful that the so-called *mudéjares antiguos* blended in with the old Christians so much that they would escape expulsion.[26] Local priests and bishops in Castile also advocated for the Morisco population in their dioceses. In order to determine who was "notoriously" Christian, Philip

III had asked the Castilian bishops to examine Morisco "language, dress, traditions, confession, attendance at mass, religious foundations, interactions with old Christians and vows of chastity as *beatos*."[27] Through the physical act of carrying out these interrogations, local authorities fermented a conceptual link between customary practice and religiosity. Contemporaries debated what it meant to be a Christian, and whether Christian status was the result of "ancestral origins" or "good works."[28] This debate was also important in Spanish America. It arose in the definitions of virtue and nobility that began to appear in printed histories and genealogies, definitions that found their way onto both the pages of the *Ovandina* and the written opinions of the inquisitors who reviewed the work.

Moriscos in Spain used a number of labels and legal claims to argue for their position in society. As a category, Morisco also held contrasting meanings for many Spanish authorities. In face of mounting persecution of Moriscos in Spain, becoming a "good and faithful Christian," gained currency on both sides of the Atlantic as individuals negotiated their status in the courts. In Spanish America, the presence of new Christians in the Republic of Spaniards raised a new set of concerns. Royal decrees prohibited Moriscos from settling in the Americas because authorities feared they would have a corrupting influence on local religiosity. These fears spilled into accusations that individuals descended from Muslims or Moriscos and into local power struggles. Cases of insults linked to Morisco status, such as Zamudio Oviedo's suit, became one way of countering defamation in the public realm of the courtroom. Through successful litigation that resulted in a legal decision, individuals could restore their honor and produce a record of their lineage. They could then refer to these documents as proof of their status if they were taken to court again.

Insults concerning Morisco status were even directed against inquisitorial officials. On 22 August 1629 in the town of Celaya in the diocese of Michoacán, in New Spain, Friar Juan de Yrayzoz wrote indignantly to the inquisitorial tribunal in Mexico City that Friar Cristóbal Martínez had called him a *moro calabrés*, or Calabrian Moor. In his letter, Yrayzoz stated that because his status as commissioner for the Inquisition in Celaya was his "greatest honor . . . and the greatest emblem of his limpieza," Martínez's remark was particularly damaging.[29] According to Yrayzoz, being called a moro calabrés was a "statement so harmful to the limpieza that is required of those who serve this holy tribunal," and therefore "by having the proper decorum and obedience," he was obligated to bring this to the inquisitors' attention.[30]

The charges were so injurious and compelling that on that same day, a case was opened against Martínez at the ecclesiastical court in Celaya. It was presided over by Bachiller Jacinto López de Mesa, whose testimonies and account the local commissioner for the Inquisition, Franciscan Friar Tomás de Zavala, later included in the report he forwarded to Mexico City.[31] López de Mesa stressed that disciplinary action was needed against Martínez for causing public scandal and that his punishment "serve as an example and correction to the other priests."[32]

On 18 September, Zavala opened his local investigation of the events in Celaya. Representing the inquisitorial tribunal in Mexico City, Zavala collected testimonies from two of the witnesses examined by López de Mesa, as well as statements from Yrayzoz and Franciscan Friar Diego de San Joseph, which he forwarded to inquisitors in Mexico City. San Joseph supported Yrayzoz, recounting how they had been standing outside their monastery of San Francisco, where Yrayzoz was the guardian, when Martínez passed by. Yrayzoz asked Martínez if he could have a word with him, and Martínez, "without taking off his hat, or stopping, said that he did not speak to his enemies."[33] When Yrayzoz exclaimed that Martínez must have few friends if he considered him to be his enemy, Martínez replied that he had only "very honorable friends."[34] Yrayzoz told Martínez that he could consider him his friend, and Martínez called him a moro calabrés.

Luis Enríquez and Joan de Quintanilla, although they had been summoned originally by Yrayzoz because they had been present during the exchange, provided a different version of the event. Enríquez, testified that, as Martínez was passing, Yrayzoz turned to San Joseph and said loudly, "Padre, be my witness . . . Martínez is a mestizo."[35] Enríquez claimed not to have heard Martínez's reply because he spoke softly, only that he told Yrayzoz to "be quiet because you are a friar."[36] On 7 October, Joan de Quintanilla, who had attempted to avoid testifying and was not located until this later date, told Zavala that while he was sitting in his house, facing the church of San Francisco, he heard Yrayzoz yelling at Martínez that, "because he was a *pícaro mestizo*, he only associated with pícaros."[37] In his letter to the inquisitors on 9 October, Zavala concluded that because both Enríquez and Quintanilla were Martínez's friends and dependents (*criados*), their testimonies were unreliable. He also suggested that the judge was biased because he was "a very good friend" of Martínez.[38] San Joseph, in contrast, was "a religious who in this province receives esteem and trust" and who held "honorable offices."[39] Zavala, responding to the need to describe Martínez's status (calidad), wrote that Martínez supported himself from his *chaplaincy* and was "the son of humble parents, and by nature is arrogant and foulmouthed [*mal hablado*]," and as a result the townspeople disliked him.[40]

In a letter to inquisitors on 22 October, Martínez described the events that took place and requested that if Yrayzoz and San Joseph had to bring a case against him, "that it be with the secrecy to which this holy tribunal is accustomed, without scandal or note of my person and honor" as he was well known in Celaya.[41] Martínez made certain to refer to the written *opiniones* and *pareceres* supporting his status, held in Celaya. It is interesting that he appealed to the secrecy of the Inquisition to guard his honor and not make the scandal public unless he was proven guilty, as opposed to the public shaming that rumor and a more visible court case could incur. Martínez wrote that Yrayzoz had approached him with such anger, he thought he bore him ill intentions and he tried to avoid him. According to Martínez, Yrayzoz then proceeded to "insult me, calling me publicly pícaro, mestizo, and shameless, which offended me greatly, having as I have in that town a good and honorable reputation, and being as I am clean of [tainted] race, and a Spaniard on all four sides [*abolengos*]."[42] Several days after this exchange, Yrayzoz "put in the baptistery of the church of the said convent, in an obvious place, and visible to all who enter, a table and on top of it a silver cross covered in a black veil." Yrayzoz then ordered his conventual, Friar Diego de San Joseph, to act as notary while he presided at the table as judge. Martínez complained that "with great note of the place, [he] began to fulminate against me, calling witnesses."[43] Yrayzoz had proceeded to tell those present that Martínez had "committed a grave crime against the holy Catholic faith, making a case for the Inquisition, out of the very particular grievances that he has with me."[44] Martínez was thus speaking out against the publication of a private dispute that called into question his honor and his authority in the community as priest. When Zavala arrived in Celaya, he summoned "with notable publicity" those who had witnessed the dispute.[45] According to Martínez, Zavala appeared before a "great crowd of people, since it was a holiday, with the insignia of the holy office on his chest, conveying that he had to investigate an inquisitorial case. Because the dispute occurred just before this, all the residents of the said town knew that it was against me, causing . . . notable scandal and dishonor to my person, being as I am a priest . . . and the son of good parents, in good opinion and reputation in the said town."[46]

In the insult cases prosecuted by Zamudio Oviedo and Yrayzoz, a priest's authority within the community influenced the willingness of witnesses to testify on their behalf. Witnesses expressed anxiety about testifying against either priest. It is unclear how either case was resolved. Martínez's trial ended with his letter appealing to inquisitors to proceed in secret, so as not to damage his honor further. Zamudio Oviedo's trails off, and it is unclear whether it was resolved, or moved like Martínez's to the inquisitorial level for further scrutiny. What is salient in both cases is the language used to delineate preoccupations over status. How the memory of lineages was manipulated and recast within local communities in Spanish America continued to be a concern into the seventeenth century.

ENCOMIENDA DISPUTES: A CASE STUDY

By the mid-sixteenth century, encomiendas, or grants of indigenous tributaries, produced increasing friction in colonial society. Originally granted by the Crown to the first conquerors of a region, with the passage of the New Laws in 1542, they were no longer hereditary, but remained in the possession of those who had won them for only two generations.[47] This led to a growing number of denunciations, as others sought to secure the encomiendas for themselves. In 1554, Cristóbal de Monroy summoned witnesses in the Spanish city of Alcalá de Henares to testify against Diego Romero, an encomendero residing approximately five thousand miles across the Atlantic, in Santa Fe, New Granada.[48] Monroy had traveled to Spain to prove that Romero was the son of a Muslim slave woman, hoping to dispossess him of his encomienda. Monroy's efforts to trace Romero's lineage were not unique and resembled other inquiries conducted by the linajudos in Spain.[49] Genealogical searches assumed a dynamic of their own in Spanish America, as new generations of Spaniards disputed claims to offices and encomiendas. Transatlantic trials invoking purity of blood, such as Romero's, reveal much about the nature of the debate concerning status in the early modern Spanish world. They also illuminate how individuals could carve small spaces for themselves by manipulating their status through litigation.

Diego Romero formed part of the initial 1537 Gonzalo Jiménez de Quesada expedition to conquer and settle the region that is today Colombia and Venezuela.[50] Romero and most of the survivors settled permanently in the New Kingdom of Granada.[51] Many acquired encomiendas, claimed noble status, and formed part of the colonial elite.[52] By the mid-sixteenth century, following the passage of the New Laws in 1542, the right to hold encomiendas produced increasing friction in colonial Spanish American society.[53] In contrast to the viceroyalty of Peru where the application of the New Laws was met with violence, encomenderos in New Granada turned to litigation to attempt to secure their encomiendas in perpetuity. The legal circumstances surrounding the initial distribution of encomiendas in New Granada are murky. While Jiménez de Quesada granted them to the men participating in the first expedition, he lacked full royal authority to do so.[54] His brother and successor Hernán Pérez de Quesada, lacked similar authority and assigned encomiendas carelessly to three or four individuals at a time.[55] When Alonso Luis de Lugo became governor of New Granada in 1543, he initiated legal action against wealthy encomenderos and convinced them to surrender their titles so that he could redistribute them in a more legitimate way.[56] However, he granted the encomiendas to his allies, rather than returning them to their previous holders, sparking lawsuits over their possession, including denunciations that Romero was a Morisco.[57]

In 1558, Diego Romero was charged formally with being a Morisco, who, because of his Muslim lineage, had no right to his encomienda. In a statement against Romero, the prosecutor in this case emphasized the consequences of possessing a Morisco lineage: "Because the said [Romero] is the son and the descendant of Muslims, and in accordance with your laws and ordinances of the Indies, he should be cast out and exiled from them, and his Indians should be [removed]."[58]

For his part, Romero claimed he was one of the first conquerors of New Granada, and he compiled a document detailing his services to the Crown.[59] Romero argued that regardless of whether he was an old Christian, he had emigrated before the prohibitions were issued and therefore should remain. Romero's lawyer stated that the council should exonerate Romero because the charges were leveled by his enemies, especially Monroy, who had no encomienda. Furthermore, Romero was an "Old Christian of pure lineage, born and raised in . . . [Spain]. He passed more than thirty five years ago to the said New Kingdom of Granada, and he was among the first conquerors of it, and he served your highness so that he should be . . . sustained by the land and not cast out and exiled."[60] By invoking his status as one of the first conquerors and producing a service report, Romero emphasized his legitimate claim to his encomienda.[61]

Distinctions formed quickly between the men accompanying Jiménez de Quesada, who styled themselves first conquerors, and subsequent arrivals.[62] Tensions grew between the first conquerors, who attempted to establish their seniority, and the university-educated bureaucrats sent from Spain to assume posts of governance. Contemporary chroniclers noted that some of the insults leveled by these men at the conquistador group targeted their claims to noble status (*hidalguía*) in an attempt to reduce their collective power.[63] How people conceived of status and honor in sixteenth-century New Granada is important to consider, especially as the number of hidalgos in the Jiménez de Quesada expedition exploded, from four to twenty-seven.[64] Except for the original four who possessed official titles of nobility, the rest of the men, including Romero, claimed in their service reports to be recognized hidalgos whose nobility was common knowledge and legally proven by court testimony.[65] They had to cultivate and maintain their honor publicly, through actions and possessions, because what was "public and notorious" became an index of their social standing.[66] Although conquerors aspired to titles of nobility, coats of arms, lands, and public offices, the king was not forthcoming in granting the first two. Consequently, encomenderos based their hidalgo status on their activities as local officeholders, their control over land, and indigenous tribute.[67] They also emphasized exemplary behavior and religiosity because encomenderos were responsible legally for supervising the religious indoctrination of indigenous peoples under their jurisdiction.[68] This made religious identity a point of friction.

In 1561 Romero produced his service report in which he described his deeds during the conquest.[69] His account, and those of witnesses during his trial, presented contrasting views about achieving social advancement and honor through actions rather than descent. The telling of personal histories in official documents and in the courtroom made knowledge public, authenticating it for the community, albeit temporarily if new suits were filed. The concept of conquest, whether in a medieval Iberian, North African, or New World setting, imbued these histories in ways that bestowed honor and status to the participants. Romero stressed the qualities that made him a recognized

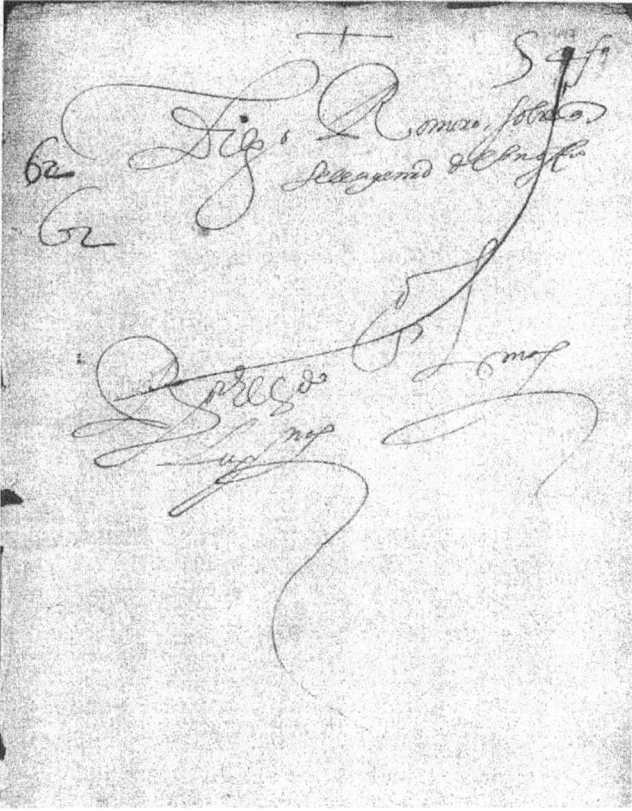

Figure 2. Diego Romero's service report. Spain. Ministerio de Educación, Cultura y Deporte. Archivo General de Indias. Patronato 154, N. 3, R.1, imagen 9.

hidalgo, which included holding the office of chief constable in Santa Fe, fighting indigenous groups on horseback, and professing loyalty to the Crown. Romero insisted that his household was "very sumptuous and well-maintained like any good hidalgo."[70]

The testimonies against Romero targeted specifically his claims to be an old Christian and a hidalgo. Prosecutor Licentiate García de Valverde presented an account of Romero's life in Spain, based on information collected in Alcalá by Monroy. According to García de Valverde, Romero was born the son of North African Muslims in Oran. His family had been enslaved by Cardinal Francisco Jiménez de Cisneros during Oran's conquest in 1509. Romero was taken to Alcalá de Henares, baptized, and given the name Diego Hurtado.[71] Romero

had been the slave of the royal accountant Bañares in Alcalá, until he
murdered a woman and fled to Spanish America with a false license.[72]
It was in the Americas that he changed his name to Diego Romero.
These events had occurred seventeen years prior to Monroy's investi-
gation, approximately in 1537. The prosecutor pronounced Romero a
Muslim "of lineage and of nation."[73]

Romero's accusers painted differing portraits of Romero that
invoked contemporary assumptions about status. Witness Francisco de Salas claimed that he had known Romero's mother María,
a slave in Bañares's household who was eventually freed. Salas had
also seen Romero in Bañares's house, "going about in the clothes of
a well-off man."[74] He encountered Romero again in Seville, where
they "embarked together . . . to conquer Santa Marta and from
there . . . they went to win the New Kingdom and this witness
returned to Spain."[75] Salas learned that Romero had remained in
Santa Fe as "one of the ones who won the said Kingdom and was
given an encomienda as a conqueror. He is presently in the said city of
Santa Fe a very rich man."[76]

For three years, Romero languished in jail, waiting for his transatlantic trial to be resolved. In 1558 the prosecutor requested that a
second investigation take place in Alcalá de Henares and that Romero
be taken there to face witnesses. He also ordered that doctors inspect
Romero for evidence of circumcision, a sign that he had been a Muslim.[77] Romero's lawyer protested that this treatment was irregular:
Romero should not be examined by the doctors because this would
shame him as a hidalgo; and whatever they found would be incon-
clusive, as it could be the result of illness rather than circumcision.
Romero argued that the physical descriptions of him by witnesses
did not match his person. He insisted he was a hidalgo from Toledo,
rather than the slave with dark skin (*moreno*) and curly hair (*crespo*)
from Alcalá they claimed to remember.[78]

Monroy meanwhile marshaled witnesses against Romero in Santa
Fe. New Granada's governor, Miguel Díez de Armendáriz, provided
damaging testimony: "In Oran, [Bañares] used the mother of the
said Diego Romero, a Morisca and a Muslim woman at the time. He
wanted to bring her to Spain but because it was forbidden to remove
in the ships any infant, Romero's mother was leaving unwillingly with
the said royal accountant Bañares her master, who, to please her and
not lose her, wrapped Romero, who was of tender age, in some clothes
and a sack from the ship, and in this way [Bañares] took him covertly

out of Oran and brought him to Spain with his mother who had borne Romero not by the royal accountant but by a Muslim man."[79] Next, Alonso Téllez, secretary of the Audiencia of Santa Fe, testified how he had tried to buy a man in Alcalá from the heirs of Bañares who was said to be the son of a slave from Oran. Téllez was told that Diego had been freed by Bañares and was shown his freedom papers.[80] Another witness testified that he had heard that Romero had carried his freedom papers before losing them during the conquest of Santa Marta.[81]

Other witnesses provided variant accounts of Romero. Captain Gonzalo Suárez said that in both Seville and Santa Fe, "he heard it said publicly [by men who had participated in the conquest] that the said Diego Romero was the son of the royal accountant Bañares whom he liked greatly, and that always in the said expedition, and for a long time after, the captains who were stationed under this witness had treated [Romero] like an honorable soldier and a free person and they honored him."[82] Another witness recalled how, when Téllez arrived from Spain, he had appealed to Téllez on Romero's behalf, saying that although "some people . . . tried to say that he had been bought," Romero was in fact "honorable and held as such."[83] By participating in the conquest and styling oneself a hidalgo, some individuals were able to contest accusations that they were not old Christians. Regardless of Romero's actual birth, testimonies from his trial reveal the arguments considered plausible by contemporaries about how a North African slave could have risen to the status of encomendero. Romero's lawyer also argued successfully that he should not be sent to Spain to face trial but rather wait for the witnesses' declarations to reach the court in Santa Fe. This created complications for both Romero and his accusers, as the testimonies in Alcalá de Henares took almost three years to assemble. During this time, Romero petitioned successfully that his case be closed because the two-year period granted to the prosecution to collect evidence had expired.

In examining the conquest and settlement of Spanish America, and the ensuing conflicts over encomiendas, it is important to consider the role that the historical memory of the Reconquista played, as well as early modern Iberian images of Muslims and Moriscos. Attitudes in Spain toward the Moriscos were directly influenced by contemporary conflicts between Spain and the Ottoman Empire. The simultaneously unfolding histories of the conquests of Oran and New Granada, tied together in the mental worlds of those involved in Romero's case deserve further exploration. Members of early expeditions were not all old Christians because restrictions on emigration were still lax and often circumvented. Moriscos emigrated to the Americas and some acquired encomiendas. When they did, less fortunate old Christians could profit if they could prove that an individual descended from Muslims. Repercussions were severe: the accused were subject to losing their status and possessions, as well as exile from the Americas. Yet distances across the Spanish world hindered the full enforcement of the laws. Diego Romero ultimately won his case and kept his encomienda, regardless of whether or not he was a Morisco.

MORISCOS, INQUISITORS, AND THE DYNAMICS
OF RELIGIOUS INTOLERANCE

Ever since the establishment of an inquisitorial tribunal in Lima in 1569–70 to regulate orthodoxy in the Peruvian viceroyalty, officials' backgrounds fell under local scrutiny as they became caught up in the virulent disputes following the civil wars. Viceroy Francisco de Toledo oversaw the establishment of the Lima tribunal, noting already the potential for conflicts over jurisdiction as inquisitors asserted their claims to power in a politically turbulent viceroyalty.[84] Toledo's initial concerns, expressed to the Council of the Indies, foreshadowed subsequent conflicts between viceroys and inquisitors. During the visita of the Inquisition of Lima conducted by Doctor Juan Ruiz de Prado between 1583 and 1594, Inquisitor Antonio Gutiérrez de Ulloa was accused of "favoring and honoring in excess some people who are in the opinion of being conversos and Moriscos . . . who have used the Inquisition and treated it as if they were very old Christians and ministers of the Holy Office, of which there has been much notice and scandal."[85] The visita sparked numerous denunciations that inquisitorial officials descended from Moriscos or conversos. Many of those who brought complaints against Gutiérrez de Ulloa were themselves inquisitorial officials who were aware of the controversy surrounding the appointment of officials that occurred periodically since the inquisitorial tribunal in Lima was established.

Concerns that new Christians had gained access to offices of Lima's inquisitorial tribunal had already been raised several years earlier in letters that inquisitors sent to the Suprema in Madrid. In 1590 Licentiate Antonio de Arpide y Ulloa referred to these letters, stating that when the tribunal was first established, "no persons could be found who could prove their limpieza, as is done in Spain, and because of this there was a lack of officials."[86] In order to address the scarcity of officials to police the faith in the frontier regions as the empire expanded, the Suprema permitted the appointment of officials without the exhaustive investigations required in Spain.

By the last decade of the sixteenth century, Lima inquisitors continued to wrestle with the problem, as further correspondence with the Suprema suggests. On 30 April 1590 Gutiérrez de Ulloa and Ruiz de Prado reported that the Lima tribunal lacked sufficient number of officials to oversee the ratification of witnesses during trials. They also pointed out that checking whether every candidate to be a familiar was an old Christian was overly time consuming as investigations into limpieza had to be remitted to Spain before any decisions could be made.[87]

On 20 December 1590, Arpide y Ulloa reported to the Suprema that the testimonies taken for familiars and commissioners two decades earlier as the tribunal was being established in Lima were questionable. These posts had been filled hastily to meet demands to send inquisitorial officials to the viceroyalty of Peru, with little attention paid to confirming whether they were old Christians. Arpide y Ulloa wrote that "during the first years that this Inquisition was established, having informed your grace that there were no people whose limpieza could be examined in the way it is done in Spain and that because of this there was a lack of ministers, your grace . . . gave us license to name familiars and commissioners, taking down whatever information possible. Because of this, the information from those times is all of little value, and those who provided information only gave the side of either their father or mother and were not asked for more."[88] Arpide y Ulloa noted that while the Lima inquisitors were conscious of the deficiencies of these early *informaciones*, little was being done by 1590 to reevaluate the officials and replace them if necessary, in spite of being able to send for more detailed reports of their limpieza.

These concerns were credible to contemporaries, as correspondence surrounding the establishment of the inquisitorial tribunals in the Americas attests. On 12 February 1569, Pedro Alcedo wrote a letter to the Suprema while he was in Seville, awaiting his departure for Lima. Alcedo complained that he had yet to receive the royal orders (*despachos*) organizing the establishment of the tribunal in the Peruvian viceroyalty. He expressed concern that the armada threatened to leave without him and his dependents, and they were confused and needed the necessary papers to present at the Casa de Contratación in order to be able to travel to the Indies. Alcedo stated, "They will oppose us if your grace does not remedy it because they say that if all the people or dependents who in our company need to go with your grace's licenses, and they do not have reports of their limpieza, they will not let us pass."[89] According to Alcedo, they had not had time for "each dependent to go to his homeland and prepare an *información* because they are all from different and very distant parts."[90] Alcedo requested that the Casa de Contratación "give us free authorization [*recaudo*] for all the licenses, assuming that each one is assured of the people who are in his company and house, that they are old Christians."[91]

By the end of the sixteenth century, accusations began to surface concerning the purity of blood of some officials. For example, in 1590 Luis Remón, the notary and familiar of the Inquisition in Quito, wrote to the inquisitors in Lima that another familiar, Antonio Freile de Zamora, was married to a Morisca. Remón told inquisitors that Freile de Zamora's wife was "the daughter of Francisco Moreno from Guadalajara, and they say he is a Morisco [*de nación morisco*], as Francisco de Albadan, silversmith, will testify. He is from that city and was sent into exile to serve in the galleys."[92] According to Remón, Freile de Zamora had asked to be appointed a familiar in order to receive the protection granted to inquisitorial officials. Freile de Zamora had just finished his duties as notary of the visita of the Royal Audiencia of Quito. Remón claimed that the reason Freile de Zamora had applied to the post of familiar "was to use the Holy Office, as a familiar, against so many principal people whom he dealt with in the inspection. . . . And fearing that he had mistreated those whom he had inspected, and that they would complain, and follow him to Castile, he attempted this in his defense."[93] Similar accusations involving the abuse of inquisitorial power by conversos and Moriscos surface in Ruiz de Prado's visita.

Witnesses summoned by Ruiz de Prado to testify about Gutiérrez de Ulloa's competence as an inquisitor provided vivid accounts of his association with new Christians. In 1586, royal accountant Juan de Cadahalso Salazar described how Inquisitor Gutiérrez de Ulloa "has had in his house as his dependents (criados) and friends (allegados), and he sat them at his table, the said Rodrigo Arias and Luis García and Pedro Enríquez and a Juan de Llerena . . . all of them are in the opinion of being conversos and Moriscos and all of them have used the Inquisition and done its business as if they were very Christian and its ministers, going with the high staff of the Inquisition to Callao to inspect the ships that arrive in that port."[94] In 1588 Cristóbal Ruiz Tostada, the notary of confiscations of the Inquisition, provided more details about one of the men at the table, Luis García. He noted that García, who was a familiar and "very close to" Gutiérrez de Ulloa, was a converso and was married to a Morisca.[95]

In response to these charges, Inquisitor Gutiérrez de Ulloa replied that "if in this land familiars had to provide such detailed reports [of limpieza] as are required, this inquisition would be without [familiars] until [the reports] arrived from Spain."[96] He dismissed charges that he had knowingly appointed familiars who were married to Moriscas. He argued that in the case of the familiar Alonso de Valera Morales, only one witness had claimed his wife was a Morisca, and he pointed out that "it would be unjust if because one witness, who perhaps is motivated by hidden animosity, says that someone lacks limpieza, without providing any proof of this, that a man should be excluded who, in everything else is very competent."[97] Gutiérrez de Ulloa's frustration became evident as he wrote, "To say that Rodrigo Arias and Pedro Enríquez are conversos or Moriscos or are held in that opinion, I could not say (with clear conscience) because I do not know. Their having remained in my household was because they are from (*naturales de*) eight leagues of my homeland, and the parents of Rodrigo Arias were dependents of my parents, and of other relatives."[98] Ties to home communities remained strong, and networks of patronage through family, household, and place of origin also played a role in who emigrated to the Americas and what opportunities were available to them once they arrived.[99] Ruiz de Prado's response at the end of the visita acknowledged the difficulties in screening potential officials. He charged the tribunal, under Gutiérrez de Ulloa, with having failed to carry out the required investigation of familiars and of having admitted "persons who are notoriously lacking the necessary qualities."[100] However, Ruiz de Prado allowed that it was better to have qualified familiars who were married to Moriscas than officials who themselves descended from Moriscos or conversos: "Although it is true that here there are few or no persons who can be trusted regarding these things with the necessary qualities, but in this there is more or less, because there are some who in themselves have them [the qualities] and in their wives they do not, and it seems there would be less harm done to use these instead of someone who has so many defects in everything."[101] As Ruiz de Prado's assessment shows, anxieties that Moriscos not only emigrated to Spanish America but also incorporated themselves into the elite, through service during the conquest, appointment to offices, or marriage, arose from a number of contradictions in the enforcement of colonial legislation.[102] In light of these anxieties, individuals who were suspected of possessing new Christian ancestry also turned to printed works to protect their status.

THE *OVANDINA*, HISTORIES, AND GENEALOGIES OF NOBILITY

The importance of lineages appearing and circulating in published histories, thereby becoming "public and notorious," drove individuals to seek out chroniclers or genealogists to compose accounts of their families. In 1636, the bishop of Cuzco, Fray Fernando de Vera, wrote a letter to his nephew in Spain, Jacinto de la Vera, who wanted to join the Order of Saint John. The bishop advised his nephew to, "strive to become a friend of historians, and of those who write lineages; of historians so that in what they write they produce a *memoria* of you . . . and of the genealogists so that they produce a memoria of your lineage, and the house of your forebears."[103] Members of the elite, or those who aspired to elite status, became increasingly invested in creating public accounts of their lineage. Possession of a carta executoria or a record of méritos y servicios provided a degree of protection. Yet these documents could be challenged, and individuals became involved in lengthy disputes.

The publication of the *Ovandina* spurred not only inquisitorial denunciations but also satirical poems that circulated, making public an alternate version of Lima's family histories. Inquisitors included one such poem in the file they sent to the Suprema. The poem demanded Ovando to explain why anyone should believe him, "if it is all invention/ taken from your archive/ mixing hidalgos from clay/ covering them with sheepskin/ and making them of the golden fleece."[104] It continued with a reference to Mateo Rosas de Oquendo's 1598 satire of Lima: "You do not know that Oquendo told/ of this Peru the truth/ and to remedy this you/ commit those excesses/ nobles for fifty pesos/ we can easily call them."[105] In Lima, tensions grew between the first generation of conquerors and those they perceived as newcomers, who did not participate in the conquest and should not take away their land and labor grants. These generations of Spaniards debated what constituted true nobility, although it was likely part of a larger transatlantic debate about the relationship between status, lineage, and good works that also found its expression in the inquisitorial inquiry into the *Ovandina*.[106] Contemporaries commented on the ease with which lineages were altered and a number of them composed satirical works. For example, Friar Buenaventura de Salinas y Córdoba extolled the transformative powers of the viceroyalty of Peru (1630): "Upon reaching Panama, the river Chagre and the South Sea baptizes them, and puts a Don on each one: and reaching this City of Kings [Lima], all dress in silk, descend from Don Pelayo and the *godos* and *archgodos*, go to the Palace, claim rents and offices, and in the churches they affirm themselves between two columns, open like the Colossus of Rhodes, and order Masses for the soul of the good Cid."[107]

In 1622, once the *Ovandina* was in their hands, inquisitors in Lima scoured the text alongside the reports of Spanish inquisitorial tribunals, connecting the names of families in Lima with those who had been tried in Spain. Licentiate Gaspar de Valdespina, the prosecutor in the case, composed an account of these names, which was sent to the Suprema in Madrid along with a copy of the *Ovandina*. Valdespina accused Mexía de Ovando of having created a scandal by including persons held to be new Christians in the *Ovandina* and of having "stolen many pesos . . . from the said persons, and if they had not paid him, he did not include in the said book many qualified persons."[108]

A copy was also sent to Friar Antonio de Peñaranda in the Convento del Rosario in Lima who condemned the *Ovandina*. Peñaranda highlighted its potential to be used in individual constructions of nobility. He judged the books of the *Ovandina* to be "harmful to the King and the Kingdom because they try to bestow nobility on many people who are notoriously lacking it. . . . If he continues to write, as he promises, they could ennoble all the vassals of His Majesty in all his kingdoms by which neither the king will have subjects nor the Republic personal services. Notwithstanding that this book is not an executoria litigated in court . . . it is a public instrument, printed with royal authority and the approval of learned men whose qualities in any time carry no small weight."[109] Peñaranda then expressed concern that the circulation of the *Ovandina* would unleash a barrage of court cases in which the families would try to formalize their status by using the book as proof of their nobility. Peñaranda accused Mexía de Ovando of altering the surnames of families in order to link individuals to noble families in Spain. For example, "In this way he says that Maldonado and Baldonado are the same name, and Gorgia and Borgia also, and on this he bases . . . the antiquity of a household, founded on so little that is solid, as can be seen in many names in which, when the first letter is changed, the meaning is changed also."[110] Peñaranda's concern over altered spelling is also echoed in trials of Moriscos who obtained false licenses to pass to the Americas. Some individuals were able to take advantage of the inconsistencies in spelling names in order to associate themselves with families with similar last names who were known publicly to be old Christians.

The opinion of the friars in Madrid who reviewed the case in 1623 can be contrasted with the uproar in Lima. Friars Diego de Barrasa and Francisco Berdugo concluded that Peñaranda's censure of the *Ovandina* was excessive. They disagreed with his concern that the *Ovandina* could bestow nobility upon Lima's families because "those who are not 'limpio' now, nor ever possessed limpieza, will be the same in one hundred years, because the memory of deficiencies in lineages is preserved from parents to children as an entailed estate [*mayorazgo*], as the experience of many rich and principal houses in Spain shows, that the lack of lineage that they had is as present now as it was when it happened, whether it was two hundred or four hundred or six hundred years ago."[111] They argued that Mexía de Ovando was not at fault for desiring what so many conquerors did—"And assuming that the New World has commenced during our own times, there is no inconvenience . . . that all who have conquered it and have gone to live in it, should presume to be noble and virtuous, which is what the author intends, for the extension of the faith and conquest of the rebels."[112] Barrasa and Berdugo concluded that the *Ovandina* promoted good customs (*buenas costunbres*), "indeed, young men of our time could learn from the ancient Spaniards who fought against the Muslims to dedicate themselves to the drill of arms and the militia in order to defend our holy Catholic faith."[113]

During the sixteenth century, Spanish writers forged histories of their cities that examined their ancient origins. Their depictions of the founders of these cities and the customs of their citizens, whether they were Goths, Visigoths, Romans, Jews, or Arabs, were used to make strategic arguments that had legal implications. In early modern Spain, genealogists developed an obsession with tracing family lineages back to the *reyes godos*, or the Gothic kings, who fought against Muslims during the eighth century. Memories of participation in the wars of Reconquista were also maintained and made their way into official documents. Witnesses in both Spain and Spanish America were summoned to attest to an ancestor's heroic deeds in medieval battles, and these were recorded and copied carefully in investigations of limpieza de sangre. Histories, including the *Ovandina*, also described actions during the Reconquista, perpetuating its memory in ways that had consequences for daily interactions in Spanish America. Even indigenous peoples became aware of the importance of these genealogies for Spaniards and in their own histories compared the *godos* with their own ancestors to claim certain privileges.

For example, the Jesuit Jerónimo Román de la Higuera wrote a history of Toledo that argued in favor of its converso population.[114] He forged documents proving that there was a Jewish population in Iberia that predated Christ, so that the conversos could not be considered accountable for charges of "deicide" that justified to some their status as "rebels" and continued exclusion from public offices and other privileges. Román de la Higuera stressed the Iberian Jews' appeal to the apostles to indoctrinate them, placing them among the first converts to Christianity. He argued in favor of ennobling converso families in Toledo and allowing them to gain benefices in the church.[115]

The controversy over the Plomos del Sacromonte was driven by a similar impulse to protect elite Granadan Morisco families. To sixteenth- and early seventeenth-century Granadan historians, the relics and lead books provided physical evidence for their reinterpretation of Granada's history that emphasized deep continuities in the Christian devotion of the city's inhabitants.[116] With the threat of expulsion looming, these elite families continued to petition the Crown for privileges to be considered old Christians and not subject to expulsion. They composed histories that cast their lineages within a peninsular context, before the Muslim conquests during the medieval period. Like many Spaniards at the time, they claimed descent from the godos. Many were members of families who collaborated with the Christian armies during the conquest. Others claimed to descend from the Nasrid nobility, which had petitioned successfully to be exempt from taxation, like the Spanish hidalgos, under Christian rule. In order to prove hidalguía, they would have to demonstrate they were either baptized prior to the forced conversions and should thus be considered old Christians, or that they descended from noble Muslim families who had served the Crown.[117] These petitions increased after the Alpujarras rebellion, as Morisco merchant families also joined the elites and petitioned to avoid expulsion.[118] They intermarried with old Christian families, joined confraternities, and military orders, actions also taken by the conversos during the late fifteenth and early sixteenth centuries.

As members of the Granadan Morisco nobility, the Granada Venegas family was exempt from a number of restrictions imposed on Moriscos, such as bearing arms, joining military orders, and traveling to the Americas. Following their actions in suppressing the first Alpujarras rebellion in 1499, the Granada Venegas family petitioned the Crown successfully to join the military order of Santiago.[119] How they achieved noble status, and the arguments they used in court to maintain their claim, sheds light on the strategies used in the Spanish American cases.

Some of the elite Morisco families composed histories of their lineages in order to claim old Christian status. For example, the Granada Venegas family commissioned publication of the *Origen de la Casa de Granada, señores de Campotéjar*, which attempted to link their family to the royal lines of the godos.[120] Using both genuine and falsified documents, the Granada Venegas family cast their ancestors as hidden Christians living under Muslim rule who aided the Christian kings during the Reconquista. They also attempted to affiliate themselves with the royal house in Zaragoza.[121] They argued that although they had not been technically Christians while living under Muslim rule, they had upheld a "moral attitude similar to that required by the Church and political actions that approximated those of the Christian princes."[122] To this end, the Granada Venegas family sponsored literary gatherings for historians and chroniclers composing similar works, such as Ginés Pérez de Hita and Miguel de Luna.[123] In his *Guerras civiles de Granada*, Pérez de Hita presented a genealogy of various Granadan noble families, linking them to the Nasrid nobility and describing their services to the Christian kings, in a way that echoed the genre of méritos y servicios.[124]

A preoccupation with participation in conquest also entered into the incorporation of leading indigenous families into the local colonial elite. In Peru, the *kurakakuna* had held the prestigious position of intermediaries under the Incas, and they learned Inca legal and religious practices in Cuzco before bringing them back to their communities across the empire. Under Spanish rule, the kurakakuna converted to Catholicism and adopted the Castilian language and legal practices. In exchange for organizing their communities for the Spanish tax and tribute systems, they were granted privileges akin to those of the hidalgos.[125] A number of portraits of Andean elites were painted, in the style of Spanish portraits of the nobility, as well as genealogical paintings featuring the dynastic Inca rulers. These paintings were also presented as legal documents and carried into the courtroom. One example is that of Leonor de Soto who, in 1586, tried to claim a land grant, presenting a painting of herself from Cuzco in 1571. Its iconography implied she was the daughter of an Inca princess and her father, Hernando de Soto, dressed as a member of the military order of Santiago, had arrested Atahuallpa during the conquest of Peru. In 1603 a group claiming descent from the Incas sent a painting of the genealogical tree to Garcilaso de la Vega el Inca, in Madrid, to request exemption from tribute at the Spanish court.[126] These tropes and uses of the past persisted into the seventeenth century and were still being used to advocate for privileges in colonial society.

***

Whether in the form of insults issued publicly in front of the entire town, or through the circulation of libelous pamphlets, accusations that an individual descended from Muslims or Moriscos carried dire consequences. The accused could lose not only their property and social standing but also face deportation from the Americas. Like Zamudio Oviedo, anyone denounced for being among the "prohibited" or behaving in a suspicious way carried the burden of bringing the case to court to defend their public reputation. Accusers were cognizant of the circumstances that lent credibility to their claims— Moriscos did emigrate to the Americas and some acquired encomiendas, and some Moriscas did marry into elite families. As the cases against the inquisitorial officials in Lima show, distances across the Spanish world hindered the full enforcement of the laws restricting access to secular and ecclesiastical offices. Opinions on how to implement the legislation differed as well. In Madrid, inquisitors considered that the work of Mexía de Ovando promoted the crusading spirit of the Reconquest, whereas in Peru, families excluded from the *Ovandina* regarded their omission as a threat to their honor and social standing.

Due to contradictions between the legislation and experience, both accusers and the accused could bend the rules to their own purposes. Legal decisions obtained in court were used to contest new allegations.

Documents detailing noble status such as the cartas executorias or relaciones de méritos y servicios were brought into the courtroom to support claims to old Christian status. Even printed works such as the *Ovandina* were invoked to render the genealogy of a particular family "public and notorious." These attempts to define public status, in language that was steeped in religious terms, were being redefined on both sides of the Atlantic, as individuals, both in the courtroom and on the streets, grappled with their position in colonial society.

In addition to negotiations of status in the courtroom, images of Muslims and Moriscos circulated in Spanish America and had an impact on colonial society. Arguments about waging war "by fire and by blood" against indigenous groups, arising during the Mixton War and other conflicts on the edges of the Spanish Empire, echoed debates over Morisco "rebels" in Spain, albeit with very different results.

CHAPTER 8

Images of Muslims and Moriscos in Spanish America

While most of this book has focused on the experiences of individuals accused of descending from Muslims and labeled Moriscos, this chapter analyzes the implications of this dynamic, specifically the role that visual and verbal images of Muslims and Moriscos played in a colonial Spanish American context. Representations of Muslims and Moriscos circulated in Spanish America in a variety of forms, further displaying peninsular anxieties in a transatlantic context. As Spanish officials were defining their empire as Catholic and their global role as champions of Catholicism, their language concerning belonging and exclusion in the emerging Spanish nation was changing. Their ideas about civic status, about freedom and enslavement, were also wrapped up in ideas about religious loyalty and descent. For some early modern Spaniards, Moriscos embodied potentially disloyal and rebellious subjects liable to enslavement and exclusion from the body politic. Through a variety of public discourses, localized events assumed symbolic global status, as accounts of their occurrence were disseminated to distant parts of the empire. For example, reports of the Alpujarras uprising or battles against Ottoman forces reached the viceroyalties and were met with celebratory sermons and public festivity. Circulation of these tidings produced a growing sense of belonging to a Spanish Catholic community and a global empire. Images of Muslims and Moriscos played a role in discourses about membership in the Spanish nation, empire, citizenship, civic status, and community.

On 26 April 1572, Mexican Viceroy Martín Enríquez wrote to Philip II expressing his delight at the Spanish victory over the Ottoman fleet at the Battle of Lepanto. Triumphal accounts circulated throughout the empire for months after the battle on 7 October 1571. The viceroy told the king that once the dispatches reached New Spain, "these servants and vassals of Your Majesty have demonstrated the contentment and joy that is required. And after giving many thanks to Our Lord through general and particular processions, they have begun to perform displays of joy which they continue, being such loyal servants and vassals."[1] While the battle of Lepanto was never as decisive as the contemporary reports made it seem, the victory bolstered Spanish commentators' praise of Philip II and their evocation of him as a messianic monarch. Occurring almost jointly with the royal forces' suppression of the second Alpujarras uprising by 1571, news of both these Spanish military victories provided grist for claims that Spain's global empire was divinely favored. The messages embedded in sermons and other celebratory accounts created a sense of imperial belonging for all Spanish vassals, who were symbolically set against the Ottomans and the rebellious Moriscos. Public performances and recitations of the Spanish victory transmitted this ethos to indigenous peoples, incorporating them into the empire, in contrast to Muslims who were emphatically excluded. This empire-wide sense of connectedness among Catholic Christians may have resonated in the aftermath of native uprisings such as the Tupac Amaru I rebellion in the Andes in 1570 and missionary complaints of incomplete evangelization of indigenous peoples. By the early seventeenth century, extirpation campaigns in the Americas followed the contours of inquisitorial cases against conversos and Moriscos, connected to growing anxieties on the part of imperial officials about the faithfulness of their native vassals.[2]

In carrying out their projects overseas, Spanish authorities became preoccupied with defining customs and describing peoples who made up the empire as it was expanding and incorporating new types of people. This process was highly debated and negotiated, and the ways individuals and communities were characterized publicly had an impact on their legal status and social standing. In this context, arguments to categorize Moriscos as rebels and apostates were projected onto seminomadic indigenous groups whom Spanish soldiers wanted to enslave, despite the New Laws prohibiting Amerindian enslavement. Reiterated images of disloyalty and rebelliousness, as applied to Moriscos and some native communities in the Americas, could be used to define their status as subjugated bodies—and forward claims that they were less civilized and lesser citizens.

SHIPS OF TURKS AND MOORS: REPRESENTATIONS OF MUSLIMS IN SPANISH AMERICA

Shortly after news of Lepanto arrived in Mexico, a curious case was brought before the Audiencia of Nueva Galicia, in northern New Spain. This case raises the question of the extent to which indigenous peoples removed from the viceregal centers heard about Turks, Muslims, or Moriscos, and how they interpreted these figures. On 21 July 1573 Pero Ximénez, an indigenous merchant who traveled the Pacific coast of New Spain, appeared before the Audiencia and Royal Chancery of Nueva Galicia to present a letter written by the corregidor of Centiquipaque, Alonso Álvarez de Espinosa. With the help of translators, Ximénez testified before the president and judges of the Audiencia that Álvarez de Espinosa had given him the letter in Compostela and told him to make his way to the Audiencia "very quickly because they had seen along the coast many ships that were said to be of Turks or Moors."[3] Ximénez reported that while he was on the peanut farm of Manuel Fernández, "which is close to the sea," the majordomo of the farm named Madriaga called out to Ximénez "in the Mexican language." Madriaga told him, "Look at the sea—ships were sailing there. Only God knows if they are Moors or Turks!" Ximénez turned to look at the sea where he "saw many large ships sailing that morning. They said there were ten ships that the said Madriaga claimed were heading in the direction of Purificación. This witness does not know what type of people were on the ships, nor who they were, only that they said there that if they were Christians and friends they would stop to disembark and come to land to eat and drink."[4] Ximénez then testified that when he arrived in Compostela to sell fish and cotton he "heard it said publicly by all Spaniards that the said ships were sailing along the coast and that this was public and notorious."[5]

In August, the judges of the Audiencia and Royal Chancery continued to receive missives concerning the strange ships. One of the more telling letters was written by Juan Fernández de Ijar, who urged the Audiencia to pay great attention to the events unfolding along the southern coastline of Nueva Galicia, "because it is something that matters greatly to the royal Crown that your grace first order an inquiry because they say that a Morisco who is on a cacao plantation of Gerónimo Pérez sounded this alarm, and then order that they see whether he is circumcised and send him to be punished. As for him and others of his quality, neither Greeks nor Slavs nor any other types who appear to be strange and vassals of the Great Turk, do not permit them to land within fifty leagues of the southern coast."[6] Fernández de Ijar added that in the plaza of Purificación he had encountered "seven vassals of the Great Turk, all men of the sea, the spies of the princes, all are in diverse clothing as they see is required for what they are doing."[7] After receiving this news, the president and judges of the Audiencia ordered Diego de Bolaños y Paniagua, the alcalde mayor of Compostela, to go in person to the area where the ships had been sighted to investigate the matter. This was perhaps in response to a letter written by Alonso García who expressed concern that no Spaniards had sighted the ships. García noted that the ships had been reported only by indigenous peoples living in the coastal towns whom Spanish authorities considered to be less reliable witnesses than Spaniards.[8]

Reports of ships full of Turks and Moors sailing the coast of Nueva Galicia and sighted by indigenous witnesses raise a number of questions about how these images that are traditionally associated with the Mediterranean crossed the Atlantic, to reach the Pacific coast of Mexico. They suggest that not only Spaniards but also Amerindians were aware of contemporary peninsular images of Muslims and Moriscos, images that included fears that the Ottomans would invade Spain with the help of Moriscos.[9] Such images are present in an array of sources. Parish priests preached sermons celebrating the battle of Lepanto and announcing the Bull of the Santa Cruzada. Inquisitors read edicts of faith that included references to practicing Islam. Inquisitorial and ecclesiastical court cases of Moriscos in the Americas also conveyed peninsular attitudes toward Islam and colonial anxieties over religious identity and allegiance. Many of these instances reflect the unease with which Spanish authorities approached the intermingling of Muslims or Moriscos with indigenous peoples. Representations of Santiago decorated local churches, and the dances of *moros y cristianos* were enacted as early as Fray Toribio de Benavente Motolinía's description of the conquest of Jerusalem staged in Tlaxcala in 1539.[10] Ongoing debates concerning the practice of "just war" and the enslavement of seminomadic indigenous groups inhabiting the northern frontier of New Spain, or the South American borderlands, provided another source of transmission for these anxieties.

Participants in the early campaigns of conquest would have had close associations with contemporary battles in North Africa and even the final sieges on Granada. Their conduct in the Americas and early military engagements against indigenous groups followed patterns with which they were familiar. Initial descriptions of the Aztec capital of Tenochtitlán by Hernán Cortés, Bernal Díaz del Castillo, and others referred to the sacred structures as mosques and drew parallels with the North African towns many of them had encountered on previous military campaigns.[11] In his *Historia verdadera de la conquista de la Nueva España*, Bernal Díaz del Castillo refers at several points to Spanish soldiers' treatment of the Amerindians: in the province of Pánuco, they "robbed the pueblos, and took the women by force, along with blankets and chickens, as if they were in the land of Muslims, stealing whatever they found."[12] Spatial understandings, as well as the underlying descriptions of the peoples who inhabited these newly encountered areas, affected both Morisco emigrants and indigenous peoples.

One arena for the representation and transformation of peninsular relationships involved the dances of conquest, some of which were introduced by the friars into colonial Mexico and enacted battles between Muslims and Christians. Spaniards invoked Santiago for protection during the conquest of Mexico, Peru, and other regions, echoing Iberian Christian armies' calls on this saint during the battles of Reconquista. Indigenous peoples also appropriated the symbolic battles staged between Muslims and Christians and applied them to campaigns carried out by settled native communities like the Nahuas against the seminomadic "Chichimeca." By the end of the sixteenth century, for example, the Chichimeca were cast in the role of the "moros," conquered by settled and "civilized" Nahuas. In northern New Spain, indigenous peoples had acted alongside Spaniards in the attempts to suppress the Chichimeca.[13] In their histories and legal documents, the Nahuas of central Mexico contrasted themselves with the seminomadic groups, emphasizing their own position as Christian converts who had been congregated or settled in towns.[14] Spanish missionaries promoted these idealized models of Christian society and Hispanized colonial relationships, which they transmitted to indigenous audiences in the sermons they preached, in colonial art forms decorating the walls and façades of churches, and in performances staged in the outdoor chapels on the doctrinas. Colonial images in Mexico and elsewhere in the Americas experienced a similar shift, depicting Santiago not only as *matamoros*, or Moor-slayer, but also as *mata-indios*, or Indian-slayer.[15]

Some moros y cristianos dances were held to commemorate important events across the Spanish empire such as the Spanish victory over

the Ottoman navy at Lepanto. A suggestive description of the festivities to commemorate the battle of Lepanto survives for the Peruvian
highland city of Cuzco: "The evening that the joyous and prodigious
news of the victory of . . . Don Juan of Austria against the power of
the Turk by sea was heard here . . . His excellency immediately that
night ordered the corregidor . . . of this city to illuminate it every-
where. In this way the corregidor and all the cavalry of the city came
out on horseback with many fires and lights made by the Indians."[16]
The residents of Cuzco then gathered the following Sunday for a
"very solemn" procession as the religious orders and clergy filed out
of the cathedral to the Indian Hospital where the priest preached the
sermon. The sermon "proclaimed the victories that God had granted
His Majesty and the thanks that should be given to Him, so that
the *naturales* understood the favors that God was bestowing on the
Catholic King for being Christian, and that there was no power that
prevailed over his neither by sea nor by land."[17] Andeans were not
only made aware of the Spanish victory, in terms that exalted imperial rights to its possessions, they participated actively in the celebrations. The festivities continued on the night before the next feast day,
when a festival of lights (*fiesta de lumbres*) was declared throughout
the city, the neighboring Indian towns (*poblaciones de indios*), and
on the fortified mountaintop of Sacsayhuaman, overlooking the city.
On the mountainside that had remained a sacred space for the Andeans, the people of Cuzco witnessed the "fireworks of *ichu* grass carried on lances, and the houses of his excellency . . . with five towers
of so many and such bright lights, that they seemed to be embracing.
In this way, the night passed with much music of minstrels and songs
and festivities of the Indians."[18] The following evening, celebrations
continued "in the plaza of the cathedral with a battle of fiery galleys
which the said church had and many firecrackers and fireworks. The
lights and fires, the music and songs and battles of the Indians lasted
almost the whole night."[19] On the following days there were bullfights
and a castle was assembled in the plaza for games, followed several
days later by a performance "about some Muslim women who were
taking water from the spring when the Christians arrived to besiege
the castle, and the Muslims defended themselves, and there were
many firecrackers and fireworks."[20] These vivid celebrations in which
both Spaniards and Andeans performed the power of the monarchy
and triumph of Catholicism would create a lasting impression. Spanish authorities certainly recognized the impact of such ceremonies on

community cohesion. By royal decree, Spain's victory at Lepanto continued to be celebrated across the empire and commemorated in sermons years after the event took place.

Spanish priests and missionaries were also ordered to preach the Bull of the Santa Cruzada not only in Spanish towns but also in Indian parishes. This papal bull granted indulgences in wars against so-called infidels either to those who fought or who contributed alms that would fund the military campaigns. Originally granted to participants in battles of Reconquista, the bull was extended to the Americas by Pope Gregory XIII in 1573.[21] Detailed instructions were given to missionaries before they set out to collect funds and inform people across the empire about the ongoing wars against the Ottoman Empire. Through these sermons, indigenous peoples came to know a particular image of Islam and Muslims in the Mediterranean, driven by propaganda of the Roman Catholic Church and the Spanish Crown. Thomas B. F. Cummins has shown that Bulls of the Holy Crusade constituted meaningful physical objects, as some Andeans were buried with their copies of this document, which they would have purchased to contribute to the church's campaigns against Muslims, with the ultimate goal of attaining personal salvation.[22] Sermons preached in Quechua after the bull was issued in 1600 emphasized the benefits bestowed upon the bearer that would reduce their stay in purgatory, although the bulls themselves were only valid for a limited period of two years' time, after which they had to be renewed with another donation.[23]

NEW LAWS, OLD PRACTICES: MUSLIMS AND THE DEBATES OVER AMERINDIAN ENSLAVEMENT

During the mid-sixteenth century a series of heated debates took place across the Iberian world concerning the status of the seminomadic peoples inhabiting the regions north of Mexico City, who were known collectively as the Chichimeca. Increasing conflict between Spaniards and indigenous groups on the northern frontier of New Spain, occurring approximately between 1531 and 1585 and referred to by the Spanish as the Guerra Chichimeca, raised a number of ethical concerns in both Mexico City and Spain. Ongoing debate concerning the legitimacy of Spanish conquest of the Americas called into question the justifiability of conducting warfare against and enslaving the "barbarous" Chichimeca.[24] In contrast with the academic debates of theologians in Spanish universities, the specific and often conflicting interests of miners, estancieros, colonial officials, soldiers, and missionaries in settling the northern frontier in spite of indigenous resistance shaped these debates in Mexico.[25] The juridical position of non-Christians and "new Christians" in Spain was echoed in the ways that colonial authorities attempted to make sense of and justify their policies toward Amerindians.

During the sixteenth century European writers became increasingly interested in producing genealogical accounts of peoples in the far reaches of the globe. This interest was accompanied by a greater attention to ethnological detail as Spanish travelers and thinkers attempted to gather information about those whom they were attempting to conquer and convert. New categories of classifying peoples emerged from their writings, which in turn had an impact on issues that ranged from the juridical questions of who possessed dominion or sovereignty over land to who could be enslaved. Muslims and Moriscos presented familiar reference points for Spanish writers who incorporated them into descriptions of indigenous peoples, presenting parallels between Ottomans and Aztecs, or Arabs and the Chichimeca, as they began to organize non-Christian peoples into hierarchies of civility and barbarism.[26] These categories emerged both implicitly and explicitly in northern New Spain in the debates over whether to enslave the Chichimeca.

Between 1569 and 1574 Viceroy Martín Enríquez convened a series of theological juntas in Mexico City. During the course of these meetings the principal debates concerned the ethics of waging war against the Chichimeca who were implicated in the escalating robberies and murders of Spaniards along the routes to the silver mines in Zacatecas.[27] While Amerindians were theoretically protected by the Crown from enslavement as vassals of the king, and by the papal decree in 1537 with the Bulla Veritas Ipsa (Sublimis Deus) that affirmed their humanity, local interests far removed from institutions of central authority often reinterpreted "just war" arguments to fit their demands.[28] These debates over the status of the Chichimeca occurred in the midst of growing indigenous resistance to Spanish presence in their lands that began during the 1550s and became especially tense after the "great rebellion" of 1561.[29] The social context in northern New Spain changed rapidly after the establishment of silver mines in Zacatecas after 1546, as the seminomadic peoples who lived along the newly constructed Spanish roads were being persecuted increasingly by Spanish settlers. Spanish reports from this period onward portrayed these peoples, labeled collectively as "Chichimecas," in a negative light.[30] Some reports further compared them to Moriscos and Muslims in crafting arguments to legitimize their enslavement.

The position of the missionaries attempting to evangelize the Chichimeca differed significantly from that of the soldiers and miners whom they accused of enslaving Amerindians under the pretext of a "just war" (*buena guerra*) without distinguishing between those who were peaceful and those who were aggressive, whose subjugation would for some justify a defensive war.[31] Some missionaries, such as Guillermo de Santa María, an Augustinian who had more than twenty years of experience living among the Guamares and Guachichiles, advocated pacifying the Chichimeca by reducing them to small settlements. He hoped that a sedentary lifestyle would promote religious instruction and conversion to Catholicism. Santa María considered that this objective could only be made possible through the cessation of the campaigns "by fire and sword" against the Chichimeca that he and others condemned as opportunistic attempts to enslave them.[32] Soldiers and other individuals with interests in expanding and protecting the mining enterprise at Zacatecas such as Pedro de Ahumada Sámano often advocated the enslavement of the Chichimeca and used arguments drawn from the experience of Reconquista in Spain to justify their position.

Both the accounts by Guillermo de Santa María and Pedro de Ahumada Sámano compare the Chichimeca to North Africans, albeit to very different ends. The *Tratado de los chichimecas de nueva España*, a manuscript attributed to Santa María who likely composed it in 1575, provides a window into these colonial debates concerning "just war" and the enslavement of the Chichimeca.[33] Santa María may have accompanied Gonzalo de las Casas, a Spanish soldier involved in the venture to transport the silk industry to Mexico, on a campaign to subdue the Chichimeca. At this point, he may have given him a copy of the treatise.[34] Santa María's *Tratado* consists of both an ethnological description of the various groups comprising the Chichimeca and a discussion of the cases in which war and enslavement could and could not be inflicted justifiably upon the Chichimeca. At the beginning of the ethnological portion of his work, Santa María states that "this name of Chichimeca is generic, applied by the Mexicans (ignominiously) to all the Indians who roam freely as vagabonds, without having a house or cultivated lands, and who could well be compared with the alárabes."[35] This is the only time in which he makes specific mention of alárabes, a term that sixteenth-century authors applied to Arabs and North African Muslims. In his early seventeenth-century dictionary, Sebastián de Covarrubias Orozco defines alárabe as a resident of the Arabian peninsula.[36] Another contemporary source, Luis del Mármol Carvajal's *Descripción general de África*, uses the term more broadly to refer to the Arab conquerors of North Africa and their immediate descendants.[37] Neither reference taken on its own is helpful for understanding the possible implications of the comparison between Chichimecas and Muslims. Santa María's reference to alárabes at the beginning of his work raises the question of what this comparison might have meant to sixteenth-century Spaniards who were evaluating their right to occupy the lands north of Mexico City and enslave indigenous groups who displayed resistance.

In his treatise Santa María proposed a civilizing program for the Chichimeca that affords insights into the political and strategic uses of ethnological writings. He also provided a critical response to Spanish officials who argued that the conflict with the Chichimeca comprised a generalized rebellion, thus justifying defensive war and their enslavement. Santa María uses the term alárabes to refer to a semi-nomadic people whose description in contemporary accounts paralleled that of the Chichimeca. References to Turks, Arabs, Muslims, and Moriscos in documents on the conquest and enslavement of Amerindians tend to appear as discrete instances that the authors do not elaborate upon. However, to contemporaries they would have evoked familiar images and would have carried cultural and legal implications.

José de Acosta's references to Muslims in the *Historia natural y moral de las Indias* (1590) shed greater light on the ways that Europeans conceptualized "other" peoples according to familiar categories.[38] In a number of passages Acosta compares indigenous practices explicitly to those of Muslims and Moriscos. For example, when describing the Andeans' ritual killing of animals, he writes that "the method of slaughtering any livestock, large or small, which the Indians used in accordance with their ancient ceremony, is the same one that the Muslims have, which they call *alquible*, which is to hold the animal above the right arm and turn its eyes toward the sun, saying different words, depending on the type of animal that is being slaughtered."[39] The Andeans, Acosta writes, "fasted from morning until the star appeared, and then they filled themselves and did the zahor in the manner of Muslims."[40] Regarding ritual baths, Acosta notes that "these baths were also used by [the Andeans] when they confessed with a ceremony that resembles closely the one that the Muslims use, which they call the *guadoi* and the Indians call *opacuna*."[41]

The connections that Acosta drew between Andean and Morisco practices would have resonated with contemporary readers. Acosta's *Historia*, a text that through its ethnological approach to evangelization shares elements of its structure and objectives with Santa María's briefer *Tratado*, illustrates how Spanish missionaries were organizing their knowledge about the "new" peoples and practices they encountered. Acosta's work moves beyond Santa María's comparison of indigenous peoples and alárabes: he developed the parallel further to associate specific Andean practices with those of Muslims recognizable to theologians in Spain. Although highlighting these similarities, neither Acosta nor Santa María advocated enslaving Amerindians.

As Acosta discussed indigenous genealogies, he made distinctions between the groups he deemed more "civilized," such as the Aztecs or the Incas, and the seminomadic Chichimeca. In doing so, Acosta referred to an issue that also emerges in Santa María's treatise, namely the obstacles to civility presented by a nomadic lifestyle. Santa María presented a similar image of the shifting alliances of the Chichimeca: "Even among those who share the same language and ethnic unit [*parcialidad*], when it comes to sharing the spoils of a robbery or game after a hunt that they had gone on together they fight and move apart from each other, because they are not saddened to leave their homes, towns, or cultivated lands, because they do not have them. They prefer to live alone independently, like animals or birds of prey, than to join together to better sustain themselves and find their food, and therefore they would never join together were it not for the necessity of war that compels them to live together."[42] Their lack of civil society could be corrected, Santa María argued, only by ending Spanish slaving raids and by increasing the "security of the roads. . . . It would be sufficient to punish the principal and guiltiest persons, and regulate the rest [of the Chichimeca] to remove all the difficulties that might cause them to rebel."[43] Santa María's missionary impulse led him to advocate "settling them on the flatlands [as opposed to rugged terrain that was associated with the uncivilized], indoctrinating them in the law of God and good customs, and giving them all the possible means to accomplish this."[44] Santa María's plans were detailed. He held that the Chichimeca should be taught not only to cultivate the land but also to master the "mechanical trades as potters, carpenters, and masons, and that the women should be taught to make bread or tortillas, and to spin and weave."[45]

Santa María's presence in the missions was closely linked to the silk-raising project proposed by Gonzalo de las Casas, a relationship that displays further the complex competing interests over local land and resources among Spaniards that exacerbated tensions with native communities. Sericulture was introduced in Mexico during the 1540s as a missionary enterprise. First the Dominicans, and later the Augustinians and Franciscans, planted mulberry trees and taught indigenous peoples how to raise silkworms.[46] Mexican Bishop Friar Juan de Zumárraga advocated in his 1537 report to the Spanish Crown that married Moriscos be transported from the Alpujarras region to New Spain to teach the Amerindians "the best methods of sericulture" that were known in the silk-producing region of Granada.[47] Zumárraga hoped that by learning to raise silkworms indigenous peoples would settle in communities, thereby reducing their poverty and becoming more amenable to evangelization. However, his efforts to encourage Granadan Morisco emigration to New Spain were ultimately unsuccessful due to the royal prohibitions.

Nonetheless silk-raising techniques from Granada were carried to New Spain and other parts of the Americas. By the time Gonzalo de Las Casas composed his treatise on sericulture, the *Arte Nuevo Para Criar Seda* (1581), and Santa María accompanied him to the northern frontier, silk raising had become a small industry in Mexico. The results were not always what Zumárraga had envisioned, as indigenous communities found themselves laboring under the constraints of the encomienda or repartimiento labor drafts, rather than for their own profit and sustenance under the supervision of the various religious orders.[48] In the dedication of the first edition of the *Arte Nuevo Para Criar Seda*, Gonzalo de las Casas, who had spent time in both Granada and Mexico, wrote to a patron:

> I learned of your interest in raising silk which is used so much in this Kingdom of Granada, and that while living in Mexico I had written this book, in the manner that would benefit the Indians of New Spain . . . I would like it to be of material so generous that it conforms with your grace's quality, and moreover that it does not cease to be noble, because although raising it is servile work, the use of it belongs to the nobility, and it has never been used by anyone but generous people, and in the most noble uses of the land; and even if it were not thus, it would be enough to expound upon the theory and practice of it so many benefits, and charity to that province, and other peoples.[49]

Many supporters of the nascent silk industry in New Spain argued that cultivating silkworms would be beneficial to the Amerindians. This is likewise consistent with Santa María's notion that by engaging in productive activities, the Chichimeca would live peacefully and thus more easily be converted to Catholicism.

A counterargument to the positions of Gonzalo de Las Casas and Santa María is clearly articulated in the report of Pedro de Ahumada Sámano, the governor of the Marquesado del Valle and a wealthy mine owner. In 1560 he led a campaign to "pacify" the Guachichiles and Zacatecos who were attacking travelers along the road between Mexico City and Zacatecas, burning estates and disrupting access to the rich silver mines.[50] The Audiencia of Nueva Galicia had commissioned Ahumada Sámano to lead the suppression of these raids. In 1562 he produced an account or *Relación* of the enterprise for Viceroy Luis de Velasco and Philip II in which he deemed the soldiers' repressive actions against the rebellious Chichimeca to have been in "just war," and he also advocated their enslavement. Ahumada Sámano dismissed the Chichimeca as "warring Indians . . . [who] walk naked as savages and who have neither law nor houses, nor trade, nor do they work the land or have any other work than hunting."[51] When describing the Zacatecos, Ahumada Sámano stated that "they moved about as alárabes following the war and the hunt."[52] He then depicted the Guachichiles as "being like alárabes and savages without having a fixed place."[53] Ahumada Sámano's ensuing condemnation of them was forceful: "It would be in the service of God and your majesty and for the security of the roads and of that land and of that entire kingdom that we should wage war on them and punish them so that they remain afraid because it would follow . . . to assure the roads as your majesty is obligated to do for the discharge of your royal conscience . . . because they are indomitable and proud peoples . . . and it is thus expedient to first wage just war upon them."[54] Ahumada Sámano's bellicose characterizations of the Guachichiles and Zacatecos show how practices of warfare became important criteria in the early modern Iberian world for assessing whether a group could be justifiably enslaved. By using the term alárabe in his account, Ahumada Sámano was invoking a cultural category familiar to Spanish military, juridical, and theological writers.

The Spanish soldier and historian Luis del Mármol Carvajal traveled throughout North Africa during the sixteenth century and was also involved in suppressing the rebellion of the Granadan Moriscos.

His *Descripción general de África* (1573) contains passages describing the "life and customs of the alárabes, and their way and order of fighting."[55] Mármol Carvajal distinguishes between the various groups of alárabes inhabiting the different regions of North Africa. Those of Berbería possessed greater riches and finer tents and horses, while those of the desert between Berbería and Egypt "are a poor and miserable people because the land where they move is sterile and harsh, and although they have sheep and camels there is so little grass that they gain little from their livestock."[56] For Mármol Carvajal, the alárabes living along the coast comprised "the greatest robbers of the earth, and whichever strangers fall into their hands they rob and capture them, and they sell them to the Christians, so that no Muslim dares to pass through their land, either alone or accompanied."[57] Mármol Carvajal's description of the alárabes' practices of warfare is equally detailed. He stated that the "caudillos de Alárabes" of Fez and Tlemcen carried firearms to "frighten the other alárabes who are like them, because these people generally are frightened of gunfire, and say that it is a treacherous weapon that kills men before they can demonstrate their valor."[58]

Some sixteenth-century writers in Spanish America cited Luis del Mármol Carvajal's work in their attempts to make sense of indigenous practices. Alonso de Zorita, a native of Granada and judge in the Audiencia of Mexico under Viceroy Luis de Velasco, wrote the *Relación de la Nueva España*.[59] In his *Relación*, Zorita drew a parallel between the markets in Mexico City and those of Fez, as depicted by Mármol Carvajal. Zorita wrote about the judges at the marketplace in Tenochtitlán who tried cases brought by the merchants and vendors: "In some ways it seems like this is comparable to what Luis del Marmor [*sic*] says about the city of Fez and its government in the fourth book of the *Descripçion de Africa*."[60] Zorita also corresponded with Gonzalo de las Casas in both Granada and Mexico, and he cited him in his *Catálogo de los autores que han escrito historias de Yndias o tratado algo de ellas* preceding the *Relación*. A number of works drawing from Spanish experiences in North Africa, stories of the Reconquista, and chivalric romances circulated in the Americas during the sixteenth and seventeenth centuries and influenced perceptions of customs, conquest, and colonization.[61]

The same emphasis on customs of warfare present in Mármol Carvajal's work is evident in both Santa María's and Ahumada Sámano's treatises on the Chichimeca. Both follow a similar format, first distinguishing among the various peoples comprising the Chichimeca, and then turning to a more generalized discussion of their cultural practices that range from religiosity to patterns of warfare.[62] For example, Ahumada Sámano noted that the Guachichiles and Zacatecos were "all so brave and bellicose and experienced in archery as soon as they know how to walk . . . until they kill a rabbit or hare with the bow which they do at the age of five or six."[63] Spanish authorities were also concerned with indigenous customs of taking captives during warfare, as expressed in a royal *Instrucción* issued in 1530 to the Audiencia of Mexico.[64] In it Charles V ordered the members of the Audiencia to "inform themselves about it in detail" because "the Indians have among themselves the law and custom of taking slaves, both in wars that they wage among themselves and in the thefts that they carry out."[65] Customary practice informed discussions about what constituted "just war" during both the Guerra de Granada and the Guerra Chichimeca. During the repression of the Morisco uprising in the Alpujarras between 1568 and 1572, jurists debated the manner used in enslaving prisoners of war. In campaigns led by Don Juan of Austria to suppress this rebellion, soldiers captured large numbers of Moriscos as rebels, in spite of their baptism and status as "new Christians," and often regardless of whether they were involved with the fighting.[66] Baptism likewise provided little protection to the Zacatecos who Ahumada Sámano argued "should receive punishment because they go inland [to make trouble] and return freely, some of them having accepted baptism and others who remain in their status as infidels."[67]

Morisco testimonies following the Alpujarras rebellion emphasized the widespread looting and enslavement carried out by Spanish troops, highlighting their "*codicia*," or greed.[68] In 1572 Philip II issued a royal decree in which he attempted to impose order on the rampant enslaving perpetrated by the soldiers suppressing the uprising. The king ordered that Moriscos captured during the rebellion who were above ten and a half years of age in the case of boys and nine and a half in the case of girls could be "sold or used as slaves who were and are justly and legitimately taken."[69] Philip II specifically prohibited the enslavement of younger children and Moriscos from towns not involved in the rebellion, a decision that was backed by "persons of letters and of conscience, who have consulted with us for certain just causes and considerations that were presented."[70]

Similar to the issue of Amerindian slavery, the legal position of the Granadan Moriscos following the Alpujarras rebellion continued to

be redefined. Debates in the Morisco context focused on the legitimacy of enslaving already baptized new Christians. In this way, the
convocation of meetings of jurists and theologians to discuss issues
of enslavement and "just war" had implications on both sides of the
Atlantic, not only in the realm of policy but also in conjunction with
the practices of warfare occurring "on the ground." In his treatise on
the Chichimeca, Santa María acknowledged the role that the experience of warfare played in shaping these debates, and he cited precedents from Iberia and the Mediterranean world: "This is according to
custom in taking captives which is done between Muslims and Christians, and it will be as in other cases in which they are in the power
of the enemy."[71] The transatlantic dimension is especially notice-
able in an undated judicial opinion (parecer) about whether Moriscos captured during the Alpujarras rebellion should be enslaved.[72]
The author supported his argument for their enslavement by making
reference to a decision by Charles V who for "New Spain ordered
something similar in a similar case as there are reliable witnesses in
this city who affirm it and among them one who was a judge of the
Chancery at that time, and one cannot think the decision was reached
without great agreement."[73] The decision to which the author refers is
likely the one expressed in the royal instruction issued by Charles V in
1523 that Amerindians could be enslaved only if they were the aggres-
sors and after the Spaniards made "the necessary *requerimientos* so
that they can come under our obedience."[74] However, Charles V soon
revoked this order in a Real Provisión in 1526 following a flurry of
reports from those opposed to Amerindian enslavement.[75]

In a second work, the *Historia del Rebelión y Castigo de los
Moriscos del Reino de Granada* (1600), Mármol Carvajal described
Spanish authorities' attempts to suppress and punish the Granadan
Moriscos.[76] Besides having traveled and lived in North Africa during twenty-two years, Mármol Carvajal had overseen the financial
accounts of the army of Don Juan of Austria during the Alpujarras
uprising. From his discussion of the debates concerning the enslavement of Moriscos following the rebellion, it becomes clear that their
status as baptized Christians was significant. Mármol Carvajal stated
that "there were doubts from the beginning of this war as to whether
the rebels, men and women and children captured in it, should become
slaves; and the Council has not finished deliberating the matter until
these days, because there was no lack of opinions by letrados and
theologians who argued that they should not be enslaved; because

although Spanish law permits enemies captured in war to be enslaved, this is not the case among Christians; and because the Moriscos were Christians, at least in name, it was not just that they be made captives."[77] Mármol Carvajal noted that Philip II withheld judgment temporarily and ordered the Consejo Real to continue examining the legitimacy of enslaving Moriscos. The king contacted the Royal Audiencia of Granada to advise him on the matter as well. Following further debate the Council

> resolved that [the Moriscos] could and should become slaves, in conformity with a council held in the city of Toledo against the Jews who rebelled at another time, and for having called upon Muhammad and declared themselves Muslims. This ruling was approved by some of the theologians, and His Majesty ordered that the decree be carried out and enforced against the Moriscos, in the same way that it had been carried out against the Jews, with the pious temperance that he wished to use as a prince who was considerate and just: "that boys younger than ten years of age, and girls who are not yet eleven, could not be enslaved, but rather that they should be given in trust to be raised and instructed in matters of the faith."[78]

Mármol Carvajal's account of this legal decision reflects the debates concerning the justifiability of enslaving new Christians. This argument was also being debated both locally in the Americas and at court concerning the Amerindians, although Crown policy toward indigenous peoples opposed their enslavement officially with the promulgation of the New Laws in 1542. Significantly, Mármol Carvajal noted how the events in the Alpujarras were perceived by the Spaniards suppressing the rebellion, as "they declared that the war was against enemies of the faith and rebels against His Majesty; and that it had to be carried out by fire and by sword."[79]

During an earlier 1540s uprising of the Chichimeca in Nueva Galicia, Spaniards used the same phrase, as they advocated war "by fire and by sword" (a fuego y a sangre), seeking to justify the slaughter and "perpetual enslavement" of rebellious Amerindians.[80] When Viceroy Antonio de Mendoza testified before Licentiate Tello de Sandoval in response to charges arising from the cruelties that had been inflicted upon the indigenous population of Mixton during the suppression of the rebellion, he compared the conflict in Nueva Galicia to the actions taken against the Granadan Moriscos. Mendoza stated that he never ordered the Spaniards to kill the Chichimeca. The viceroy claimed that the situation in Mixton had gotten chillingly out of hand as had happened "in the Kingdom of Granada [where] it is customary to cane and stone many of those Muslims who had renounced our holy faith."[81]

These comparisons were not limited to the Chichimeca. A letter from the Audiencia of Santo Domingo to the Council of the Indies on 10 January 1572 requested the Crown to extend privileges to "conquer and take captive the Indians of the nearby islands who are Caribs who go out and infest and might extend themselves to the Caribs of the coast of Tierra Firme. They should be taken captive in the form and with the limitation and order that Your Majesty commanded for the rebellious Muslims of the Kingdom of Granada."[82] In another letter dated 28 January 1568, the city council of San Juan de Puerto Rico advocated the enslavement of Carib women and children, noting that "here the Carib women and boys shoot arrows, and as these Indians are continuously carrying out their military actions on this island like the Turks, and have taken so many captives, this land is in many parts depopulated by them, and in others [the people] are frightened."[83] Earlier in the same document a description of Carib raids emphasizes that the Caribs "have many Spaniards imprisoned as their captives whom they use as Muslims use Christians."[84]

The Araucanos on the Chilean frontier were characterized in similar ways. The bishop of La Imperial, Friar Reginaldo de Lizárraga, wrote in 1599 of the Araucanos in damning terms in a treatise examining whether the war being waged on them was justified and whether they could be enslaved. Lizárraga argued that they should be considered legally as Christians who became rebels, because "there is no doubt that they have completely apostatized of the faith, becoming infidels like their ancestors. Not only is he an apostate who leaves the faith, but also the one who, having been a Christian, becomes a Muslim or a Turk, as well as he who completely leaves it [the faith] and returns to the customs of his elders."[85] Lizárraga then referred to the Granadan Moriscos, who were declared apostates following the Alpujarras rebellion. Concerning the Araucanian "innocents," he recommended that officials could "justly order that they serve those who took them in war, or that they do with them what his majesty ordered against the innocent Muslims of Granada."[86]

In 1614 the Maestre de Campo Alonso González de Nagera wrote a lengthy and scathing work in which he condemned the "indios de Chile." Finished just after the expulsion of the Moriscos from Spain, González de Nagera drew heavily on references to Turks, Muslims, and Moriscos in his work. He wrote that the indigenous slaves among the Spaniards were waiting to be freed by the "warlike Indians" for their "redemption and our total ruin. Just as in Europe the Moriscos of Spain solicited those nations who were ill friends of hers for the same ends."[87] González de Nagera added that it was nonetheless better that the Amerindians be enslaved and live among Christians as opposed to what befell the Moriscos following their expulsion to North Africa where living "among those of their sect [gave them] the opportunity to confirm themselves more in it. . . . It is better that they live in other parts as slaves of Christians than in their land as captives of the Devil."[88] Even the mountainous natural landscape provided a point of comparison between Moriscos and Araucanos. González de Nagera wrote, "In our time we have seen the care that the Moriscos put in the war of Granada just by the strength of the Sierra Nevada and Alpujarras. Because it seems to me that there are enough reasons and examples to taste the war that the Indians of Chile wage upon the Spaniards with the strength of their land, I will end this point with an argument . . . that never will that Kingdom be . . . securely pacified, so long as it is inhabited by Indians who say as proof of their intention that even the last old woman who remains of them, will wage war on us."[89] Like other blanket terms for complex societies such as Chichimeca or alárabe, these descriptions of Caribs and Araucanos carried juridical implications. The recommendations proposed by González de Nagera and others drew from experiences with Moriscos in Spain in which the authors implicitly grouped Araucanos and Moriscos together as rebels. These documents set the enslavement of indigenous peoples within the broader juridical framework and customary practices applied to Muslim-Christian relations since the period of so-called Reconquest. These in turn were being continuously transformed and redefined during the course of new situations such as the rebellion of the Granadan Moriscos and the Guerra Chichimeca. In the Spanish Americas, cases of Muslims and Moriscos provided familiar reference points in treatises concerning the enslavement of the Chichimeca, the Araucanos, the Caribs, and the Chiriguanos.

* * *

Local interactions between Amerindians and Spaniards created a space in which references to Moriscos and Muslims also circulated. Not only public performances and visual representations but also direct experiences with the Guerra Chichimeca conveyed peninsular attitudes toward non-Christians and new Christians to the residents of New Spain. That the indigenous peoples reported seeing ships of "Turks and Moors" skirting the coastline of Nueva Galicia is significant because although the Audiencia conducted an extensive investigation of the matter, local authorities could find no further evidence of the presence of Muslims in Nueva Galicia. While many of the witnesses of varying backgrounds who testified confirmed the existence of the ships, they were unsure of whether they belonged to the French, the English, or the Ottoman fleets. A number of the indigenous witnesses testified that they knew nothing of the matter, although according to a letter by Francisco de Monroy who owned a nearby estancia, "the entire town of Purificación, women and children, are fleeing along the road to Autlan because the Moors made landfall in the Purificación port of Vote."[90] Their disembarkation was discounted by Pero Sánchez Yzquierdo, a Castilian tailor and owner of a cacao farm, who claimed it to be "a joke" (burla), although he did hear it said publicly that the ships belonged to the "Turks or Moors or the French."[91] A year later, in a letter to Philip II dated 24 March 1574 Viceroy Martín Enríquez concluded dismissively that not ships but whales were to blame for the mysterious sightings, and he lamented the upheaval that the situation had caused among both Indians and Spaniards.[92] Whether real or imagined, rumors of "moros en la costa" connected worlds in which Spanish and indigenous litigants, soldiers, artisans, and writers struggled to interpret their changing circumstances.

In the early modern Spanish world, generic categorizations of complex societies such as Chichimeca or alárabe carried with them juridical implications. Precedents from Muslim-Christian relations on the Iberian Peninsula, such as taking captives, influenced Spanish patterns of warfare in the Americas, in spite of official restrictions, and provided a vocabulary for those who wished to advocate extreme measures against peoples they deemed rebellious. These terms were unstable, as they continued to be contested across the Spanish Empire. Heated debates raged about whether to enslave the already baptized Moriscos following the Alpujarras uprising, whose detractors argued that they were really Muslims and apostates, or whether the Chichimeca, by resisting Spanish encroachment, could be labeled as rebels whose robberies and murders along the roads to the silver mines at Zacatecas justified, for some, their suppression and enslavement.

Beyond direct and explicit comparisons, descriptions of indigenous customs and practices of warfare in the Americas, the language used at times paralleled contemporary Spanish accounts of North Africans, Muslims, Turks, and Moriscos. In their accounts, Spanish soldiers carefully observed and recorded indigenous practices taking captives, as some argued that Amerindians could be enslaved if their societies permitted it, or that they could trade with local groups for slaves. Characterizations of customary practices became crucial for arguments concerning juridical identities on both sides of the Atlantic, and they continued to be rearticulated during the course of new interactions. An examination of indigenous responses to and transformations of these symbols is equally important for understanding how, as Lauren Benton notes, "conquered people [were] . . . incorporated in the imposed legal order."[93] As can be glimpsed in the ships sailing the coast of Nueva Galicia, indigenous peoples became increasingly active participants in the debate and quickly began to use Spanish institutions and symbols to their own ends. The assumptions made by each group as they interacted with one another are critical to understanding the changing nature of everyday negotiations in the early modern Iberian world.

Epilogue

Far from being insignificant, discourses about Muslims and Moriscos came to form a part of the vocabulary of belonging and exclusion in sixteenth- and seventeenth-century Spanish America. As individuals negotiated their place in colonial society, they grappled with changing and sometimes overlapping categories of peoples, and with racialized, religious, and national identifications. The very practice of creating and defining empire constructed a sense of belonging to a Spanish "nation" that was different from previous centuries. From the conquest of Granada, to incursions in North Africa, to conquests in the Americas and the Philippines, early modern Spaniards had to present themselves before an international audience as having a legitimate claim to overseas trade routes and territories. Through interactions with peoples at the heart of the territories they were claiming—Muslims and Moriscos inhabited the Iberian Peninsula and were by no means foreign, to the vast numbers of indigenous inhabitants of the Americas who were legally vassals of the Spanish Crown—Spanish administrators proposing policies were forced to define and debate both inclusion and difference. This was further complicated by the growing distinctions between creoles and peninsulares, often possessing distinct regional identities, in attempts to define Spanishness. Theologians, jurists, and colonial officials developed and refined legal categories of peoples by focusing on descriptions of their customs, practices, and histories in order to propose and defend imperial policies. In doing so, they rewrote their own histories and debated categories of peoples who would come to define Spanishness—Romans, Goths, and Christians, to the exclusion of Muslims and Moriscos.

Considering Muslim and Morisco presence, real and imagined, in Spanish America is therefore crucial to understanding how empire functioned at the local level. The existence of Morisco emigrants in Spanish America provided a series of questions and uncertainties as to Spain's legitimate title and disrupted discourses about nation and Iberian identity as its implications expanded to include overseas territories. As Arjun Appadurai has argued, small numbers of peoples can inspire anxieties in the ways nation states define themselves.[1] While Appadurai focuses on twentieth- and twenty-first-century globalization and nation-states, many of his arguments are suggestive for the period under study. Although there are important differences, by considering emerging sixteenth-century empires, it becomes possible to unsettle our understanding of nation-states as monolithic or organic even today. They are made up of individuals with diverse programs and agendas whose conflicting motives allow for fluidity and flexibility in how institutions are defined and operate. Early modern Spanish authorities were concerned with numbers, counting peoples and natural resources, as seen in the *Relaciones Geográficas* and various censuses of the indigenous populations in order to organize their labor in the *mita* or repartimiento systems. Some commentators during this period began to display what Appadurai terms "predatory identities," which advocated a unified sense of national identity to the exclusion of others, specifically Moriscos who embodied the Iberian Peninsula's Muslim past, and emphasized the purity of the body politic.[2] Morisco presence in the Americas further destabilized discourses about nation and identity.

These forbidden crossings, whether of geographic or conceptual boundaries, left an imprint on colonial society. As negotiated in daily practice, attitudes toward Muslims and Moriscos spanned the Spanish world and influenced the creation of legislation that was one of many ways of governing local relationships. The ideals held by Spanish jurists and theologians at court and implemented by some missionaries and local officials were soon tested by the vast expanse of space and jurisdiction. Ineffectively regulated spaces continued to haunt authorities, and they attempted periodically to assert control over specific areas, in response to a particular denunciation or a local conflict. Individuals were aware of these larger obsessions and used them to their advantage to gain status in colonial society or challenge a rival. The very diffuse nature of colonial authority led to a proliferation of lawsuits and documentation in which more crossings were continuously being suggested and rendered plausible.

As the edges of the Spanish Empire expanded, Spaniards came into simultaneous contact with different peoples. Because of the papal donation, this meant for the Americas the formulation of policies at an administrative level aimed at bringing indigenous peoples under Catholicism and introducing early modern Spanish ideas about civility that were rooted in assumptions about customary practices as well as the administrative legacies of Rome. The first groups of missionaries and secular authorities voiced ideals about proper settlement and activities conducive to religiosity that involved the spatial separation of Spaniards and indigenous peoples into two republics. These programs continued throughout the sixteenth and seventeenth centuries with friars like Guillermo de Santa María who advocated that seminomadic groups be congregated into small settlements and learn trades such as weaving or silk raising. Africans and Spaniards who were not considered "good Christians" were banned at various times from entering indigenous settlements, and new Christians, whose devotions remained suspect, were prohibited from emigrating to the Americas.

Moriscos who emigrated to the Americas encountered similar suspicions to those they faced in Spain, fueled further by the intensity of local disputes. Many of the polemical issues separating Moriscos and old Christians concerning the Trinity or the virginity of Mary crossed the Atlantic and were invoked in everyday conflicts. Historical memory of the Reconquista persisted and was inscribed in detailed genealogies that attested to the purity of blood, heroic works, and exemplary Christianity of an applicant to a prestigious office. In this context, accentuated by the oft-cited importance of setting a good example to the newly converted, an individual's behavior during Mass, religious processions, or even on the sickbed acquired religiously charged overtones. As interior piety was rendered "public and notorious" through court testimonies, communal memory of individual and familial religiosity persisted. The Inquisition formalized denunciations and, following lengthy trials, purported to reconcile those who had strayed from the Catholic fold by removing the excommunication incurred by heresy. However, penitenced individuals and their families were subsequently excluded from holding offices and encomiendas, and they were subject to exile to Spain. Other tribunals also served this purpose, and at times several venues were sought to try the same denunciation. Ecclesiastical courts tried cases of insults in which individuals were called publicly Muslims or Jews and had to formally attempt to retain their status as old Christians. Denunciations that someone was a descendant of Muslims or Moriscos also appeared before the New World audiencias and at the court of the Casa de Contratación in Seville.

Beyond contests over status and honor, everyday interactions between Africans, Spaniards, and indigenous peoples also produced concerns that individuals were Muslims or Moriscos. In exchanges of remedies and in relationships between healers, practitioners of love magic, divination, and their clients, the practitioner's religiosity could assume importance. Belief in the effectiveness of a particular remedy was tied conceptually to the religiosity of the person performing the cure. In a multiconfessional world that drew upon practices from Europe and the Mediterranean, North and sub-Saharan Africa, and the Americas, the performance of cures using Christian or Muslim symbols and the overlap of these remedies in an already tense environment could result in the equivalent of malpractice suits.[3] Ecclesiastical officials were especially concerned about the exchange of remedies as they attempted to direct cures according to ones sanctioned within Catholicism and performed by well-trained priests. As in the case of Francisco López de Aponte, the very mention of ideas associated with Islam could incur a severe response from authorities.

While they tried to prevent ideas about Islam from circulating, through daily conversations touching upon religiosity, or through the use of remedies attributed to Muslims and Moriscos, Spanish authorities brought them up in other contexts. At times inquisitors warned that too much discussion of Islam on the part of ecclesiastical officials could result in its adoption and practice, and they cited subtle venues for its transmission: the public reading of edicts of faith, as well as sermons and religious images that dwelled on Santiago or the battle of Lepanto. They provided a vocabulary that could even reach indigenous peoples, as in the claims of sighting ships of "Turks or Muslims" sailing off the Pacific coast of Nueva Galicia.

The edges of empire provided the liminal spaces in which fears about the entrance of Muslims and Moriscos gained much currency. As the Spanish Crown kept sending silver to finance campaigns against the Ottomans in the Mediterranean, authorities obsessed over the expanding northern frontier of New Spain, the ships arriving with Muslim slaves from the Philippines, and the extensive southern borderlands approaching Brazil. In contrast to Spanish policies toward emigration to the Western Hemisphere, exile was a popular means of punishment chosen by Portuguese judicial and church authorities, including inquisitors.[4] This policy of deportment, different from Spanish imperatives to send only individuals lacking the "taint" of heresy to the Americas, had implications for the passage of new Christians, primarily conversos, from Brazil into the Spanish colonies. For example, inquisitors increasingly complained of a growing converso population in the viceroyalty of Peru. If they attempted the voyage, the Portuguese faced numerous difficulties in traveling from Brazil to Lima. Due to the Amazonian terrain, individuals would have had to journey either along the northern coast through Panama, or south toward Buenos Aires and the pampas, where they could then follow routes to Salta, Jujuy, Santa Cruz de la Sierra, and Potosí. Because of the inquisitorial tribunal in Cartagena de Indias, created in response to increasing fears of converso passage, the southern route was considered an easier one.[5] In 1602, Philip III addressed a letter to both the Audiencia and the bishop of Charcas stating that "many Portuguese who are not secure in the things of our holy Catholic faith have entered by way of the Río de la Plata, and in other ports of the Indies there are many persons of this quality. Because these are things which would be worthwhile to investigate so that no error or evil sect is sown among the Indians who are lacking firmness and instruction in the things of our holy faith . . . [I order that you] cleanse the land of this people."[6] Evidence from the Portuguese Inquisition suggests some converts from Islam were sent as degradados to Brazil.[7] The Philippines offers another point of passage, and of contrasting stages, as authorities debated the status of indigenous peoples there as well, some of whom were converting to Islam with conquests during the sixteenth century.

The various categories applied to suspected Moriscos—"lineage," "nation," "casta," and "raza"—reveal the ways early modern Spaniards conceived of Moriscos, at both a juridical level and in everyday interactions. Drawn from notions of horse breeding, raza began to be applied to individuals possessing Jewish or Muslim blood (*mala raza*). In documents proving purity of blood for inquisitorial offices, individuals claimed to be "without race," implying they had no Muslim or Jewish ancestry.[8] Taken together, these terms shed light on the ways Spaniards in the sixteenth and seventeenth centuries were increasingly categorizing others in racializing ways, in attempting to settle disputes and create official policies concerning membership in the Spanish nation, emigration, and enslavement. Some authors crafted genealogical arguments invoking humoral theory and blood purity in order to justify the exclusion of Moriscos from the body politic as Spaniards were debating how to define their nation in light of competition from other emerging European powers. These authors applied arguments about lineage and descent from Muslims and their reputed biblical ancestors to qualities like loyalty to the nation and trustworthiness in business relationships.

The fluidity in practice with which individuals could transform their public status and redefine themselves as they moved from one community to another, whether on the Iberian Peninsula, in the Mediterranean, or in the Americas, produced a response on the part of some Spanish authorities that hardened attitudes and attempts to control and define them. The sheer diversity of images applied to Moriscos and an inability to label them physically unless circumcision could be proven in court meant that Moriscos had to contend with a range of accusations that varied according to who was leveling them and could include assumptions about phenotype and genealogy. Individuals labeled Moriscos brought cases to court both in Spain and Spanish America, in which they laid claims to status as old Christians, nobles, or encomenderos, or being among the earliest voluntary converts on the Peninsula who were exempt from the expulsion decrees. Some witnesses applied physical characteristics to Moriscos—darker complexion or circumcision, in addition to their arguments about lineage—but in practice suspected Moriscos were impossible to pin down. Complaints voiced by some accusers about the "scandalous," "public," and "notorious" nature of a suspected Morisco's conduct can be contrasted with individuals who acquired a public reputation for piety, even if they did not possess the requisite purity of blood. Some jurists and theologians responded to this liminality by producing increasingly racialized writings about the Moriscos, labeling them a pestilence that threatened the body politic and linking their genealogies to sons of Ishmael who by blood would never be assimilated into the Spanish nation. In everyday interactions, insults were hurled at individuals perceived to be Moriscos, using terminology linked to animals, to discourses about lineage and breeding, such as "dog."

In Spanish America, these insults had further ramifications when connected to Spanish ideologies of empire. The Spanish Empire, acknowledged by papal bulls, was necessarily a Catholic one. The presence of Moriscos and their descendants would undermine missionary activities and delegitimize Spanish claims and title to lands in the Western Hemisphere. When faced with similarly racializing discourses from Protestant European rivals labeling Spain a Moorish nation, some Spanish writers responded by rewriting their histories and emphasizing ancient Christian genealogies and descent from the Goths rather than intermixture with Muslims. Obsessive preoccupation with lineage and genealogy, and a belief in some quarters of its ability to "stain" family lines, provided a powerful discourse that attempted to restrict anyone perceived as a religious "other." The conflicting discourses applied to Moriscos both in treatises and on the streets suggest new approaches to studying empire in the early modern Iberian world: by examining the tension between specific court cases that highlight the instability of identities, and the imperative of Spanish authorities to assert their control over bodies and devise policies despite the fluidity of social categories, in often contested and debated ways.

Al-Andalus: Iberia under Muslim rule

Alárabe: Arab

Alcalde: Magistrate of a town

Alcalde mayor: Chief magistrate, or mayor of a town

Algarravia: Arabic

Alguacil: Constable

Aljama: Muslim or Jewish communities within Christian towns

Aljamiado: The literature produced by the Moriscos, using the Spanish language, some Arabic words and phrases, and written in the Arabic script

Alumbrado: Early modern Spanish Christian mystic who rejected as unnecessary for salvation many of the Catholic sacraments, hence considered a heretic

Amancebado: Cohabiting, one having sexual relations without being married

Audiencia: Royal court of justice

Baraka: Blessing; also the supernatural abilities thought to be possessed by holy men and women

Beata / Beato: Holy layperson

Berberisco: North African, someone from Berbería or the Barbary Coast

Buñolero: Maker of buñuelos or buns

Calidad: Status; social standing

Calificador: Assessor or censor examining evidence of heresy

Carta de poder: Power of attorney

Carta executoria: Title of nobility

Casta: Refers to either ancestry or mixed race in Spanish America

Cédula: Royal decree

Chicha: Fermented alcoholic beverage made from maize and consumed in the Andes

Comisario: Local clergyman representing the Inquisition

Composición: Payment allowing descendants of those convicted by the Inquisition to restore their social standing

Conversos: Converts from Judaism to Christianity

Corregidor: Governor

Curandero: Folk healer

Dhimma: Protected status conferred on religious minorities under Muslim or Christian rule, in exchange for paying a tax

Doctrina: Mission parish

Encomienda: Grant of indigenous tributaries / labor grant bestowed by the Crown on conquerors

Ensalmo: Spell, charm

Entrada: Initial campaign

Esclavas blancas: White slaves, a term often applied to Morisca or North African slaves

Estancia: Farm

Fadas: Morisco naming ceremonies

Fakihs / alfaquíes: Muslim religious and scholarly elites

Gitano: Gypsy

Godos: Goths, Visigoths

Guadoc: Ritual ablutions performed by devout Muslims

Hábil: Someone deemed capable of holding office, occupying a post, or pursuing a profession based on abilities or lineage

Habilitación: Procedure by which someone considered inhábil was restored their status or made hábil

Hajj: Pilgrimage to Mecca

Hechicería: Witchcraft or magical practice

Hidalguía: Noble status (hidalgo: member of the minor nobility)

Información: Document providing information or testimony, often about a person's lineage

Islamismo: According to inquisitors, Islamizing or new converts lapsing into practicing Islam

Juegos de cañas: Jousting games

Junta: Meeting

Labrador: Small farmer, land owner

Ladino: Someone conversant in Spanish language, cultural norms, and institutions

Leila: Granadan Morisco song

Letrado: Lettered, educated in the law

Levantisco: Word used to refer to anyone from the Levant or eastern Mediterranean, areas that were part of the Ottoman Empire

Ligar / Ligado / Ligadura: A man who is "tied" or rendered impotent as a result of witchcraft

Limpieza de Sangre: Purity of blood

Linajudo: Genealogist searching for converso or Morisco ancestry

Memorial: Account

Méritos y servicios: Report of services to the Spanish Crown

Moro: Moor / Muslim

Moros y cristianos: "Moors and Christians" celebratory dances or festivals

Mudéjar: Muslim living under Christian rule in medieval Iberia

Naguatatos: Nahuatl-speaking interpreters

Natural: Native of the land or country; term that also referred to indigenous peoples

Naturaleza: Nativeness, generally implying privileged status

Nómina: Small pieces of paper used in magic

Nuevamente convertido: New convert

Parecer: Judicial opinion

Perro: Dog, often used as a slur or insult

Persona de razón: Person who possesses reason

Principales: Leaders of indigenous communities

Pulque: Fermented alcoholic beverage made from maguey or agave

Pulquería: Where pulque is sold

Probanza: Legal proof or evidence

Quemado: Individual executed by being burnt at the stake

Reconciliado: Someone sentenced by the Inquisition to be reconciled into the Catholic fold after appearance in an auto-da-fé and public punishment

Reconquista: The so-called Reconquest of Muslim territories on the Iberian Peninsula by Christian armies

Relación: Account

Residencia: Inspection at the end of a colonial administrator's term of office to review his actions and decisions

Saludador: Folk healer who used the breath to cure

Sanbenito: Penitential garb worn by individuals sentenced by the Inquisition

Shahada: Profession of faith in Islam

Shari'a: Islamic law

Taqiyya: The practice of observing the imposed religion in public while staying true to Islam in one's heart

Toca: Head covering associated with Moorish dress

Tratado: Treatise

Traza: Grid pattern that surrounded the central plaza, a model that provided the idealized plan for Spanish towns and cities

Vecino: Legal resident

Visita: Tour of inspection

Zahorí: Diviner

Zakah: Almsgiving, one of the five Pillars of Islam

Zala: The Salat, or prayer, carried out by Muslims five times daily

Zambras: Granadan Morisco dances

INTRODUCTION

1. For a more contemporary analysis of the impact of small numbers, see Appadurai, *Fear of Small Numbers.*

2. A number of recent works have explored issues of identity and the creation of new colonial categories. For example, see Fisher and O'Hara, *Imperial Subjects*; Martínez, *Genealogical Fictions*; Katzew and Deans-Smith, *Race and Classification*; Rappaport, *Disappearing Mestizo*; Schwaller, "Defining Difference."

3. Rappaport, *Disappearing Mestizo*; Restall, *Black Middle*; Owensby, *Empire of Law*; Yannakakis, *Art of Being In-Between.* Studies focused on the eighteenth century include Herzog, *Defining Nations*; Twinam, *Public Lives*; Wilson, *Island Race.*

4. Adorno and Pautz, *Álvar Núñez Cabeza de Vaca*, vol. 2, pp. 407 and 415. Cabeza de Vaca describes Estevanico as "negro alárabe, natural de Azamor," on p. 416.

5. Adorno and Pautz, *Álvar Núñez Cabeza de Vaca*, vol. 2, p. 421.

6. Until recently, many historians have tended to define Morisco from the perspective of Spanish ecclesiastical authorities, as Spanish converts from Islam whose religious affiliation and broader religiosity remained suspect. This is true to some extent, but it does not capture the nuances and variations among those falling under this category, as well as the legal relationships implicated within it that individuals could manipulate, and which was separate from religious beliefs and practices, if defined in part by their presence. Previous studies have tended to view the Moriscos as either good Muslims who maintained their Islamic practices under the veneer of Christian actions, in line with Spanish authorities' fears. See Harvey, *Muslims in Spain*; Epalza, *Los moriscos.* Other scholars have considered the Moriscos to have been good Christians who were caught in widespread suspicions about their religious identity. See García Arenal, *Inquisición y moriscos*; Tueller, *Good and Faithful Christians.*

7. Bennett, *History Matters*, pp. 117–19. As Judith Bennett has pointed out in her analysis of sexuality during the medieval period, "lesbian" turns up a very limited number of cases and escapes easy definition especially when applied to women living during the Middle Ages. Instead, she uses the

concept "lesbian-like" as an analytical tool to describe a range of practices, attitudes, and relationships that do not merely privilege sexual behavior or focus on specific types of people.

8. In the period under study, ideas about difference were fluid. Nonetheless, it is possible to identify attitudes resembling racism or "socioracial" classification in the sixteenth and seventeenth centuries, in which lineage and religious identity played an important role. Irene Silverblatt has referred to this as "race thinking," and Joanne Rappaport has analyzed the numerous and malleable descriptors such as *raza, casta,* and *calidad,* used to describe mestizos and others in the colonial records. See Silverblatt, *Modern Inquisitions;* Rappaport, *Disappearing Mestizo.*

9. Tueller, *Good and Faithful Christians.*

10. I generally translate "moro" as Muslim throughout the book because that is the term Spaniards used to refer to Muslims in a variety of places, from the Mediterranean to the Philippines. However, it was not a neutral term and could be used in a derogatory sense, as in the cases of insults that appear in later chapters. "Moor" was used more in the English context and has its own set of connotations.

11. Focusing on New Spain, Mercedes García-Arenal first proposed that Morisco histories be examined in a transatlantic context in "Moriscos e indios"; García-Arenal, "El problema morisco." Other studies have analyzed the ideological impact of peninsular relationships between Muslims and Christians on conquests in the Americas. For example, see Garrido Aranda, *Moriscos e indios;* Weckmann, *La herencia medieval;* and Taboada, *La sombra del Islam.* Shorter suggestive studies include Garrido Aranda, "El Morisco y la Inquisición Novohispana," pp. 501–33; Cardaillac, "Le problème morisque en Amérique," pp. 283–303; López Baralt and Caamaño, "Un Morisco Puertorriqueño," pp. 93–109; Lunde, "Muslim History of the New World"; Qamber, *Inquisition Proceedings;* Wheat, "Mediterranean Slavery"; Sagarzazu, *La conquista furtiva.*

12. On conversos, see Gojman Goldberg, *Los conversos en la Nueva España;* Bernardini and Fiering, *Jews and the Expansion of Europe;* Wachtel, *La Foi du souvenir;* Bokser Liwerant and Gojman de Backal, *Encuentro y Alteridad;* Domínguez Ortiz, *Los judeoconversos;* Studnicki-Gizbert, *Nation Upon the Sea.* On Spanish emigrants maintaining transatlantic ties to family and community, see Altman, *Emigrants and Society.* On the Morisco exiles following their expulsion from Spain in 1609–14, see Epalza, *Los moriscos.*

13. Gojman Goldberg, *Los conversos,* pp. 64–65.

14. Like Morisco, the category converso was also becoming racialized. See Nirenberg, "Was There Race Before Modernity?" Also see Hering-Torres, Martínez, and Nirenberg, *Race and Blood;* Pike, *Linajudos and Conversos;* Martínez, *Genealogical Fictions.*

CHAPTER 1

1. AGN, Inq. vol. 151, exp. 5.

2. Schwartz, *All Can Be Saved;* Cook, "Navigating Identities."

3. Catlos, *Victors and the Vanquished*; Constable, *Trade and Traders*.

4. Burns and Chevedden, *Negotiating Cultures*, p. 217.

5. Catlos charts this transformation of Islamic society to mudéjar society, as Iberian Muslims participated in the Aragonese Crown's emerging "Occidental" institutions; see his *Victors and the Vanquished*, p. 390. Mudéjar refers to Muslims living under Christian rule.

6. Catlos, *Victors and the Vanquished*, p. 391.

7. Ibid., p. 392.

8. Miller, *Guardians of Islam*, pp. 47–49.

9. Kagan, *Clio and the Crown*, pp. 46–56.

10. Quoted in García-Arenal, *Los moriscos*, p. 21.

11. Ibid., p. 21.

12. Ibid., p. 24.

13. Ibid., p. 25.

14. Ladero Quesada, *Granada después de la conquista*. Also see Epalza, *Los moriscos*; Rummel, *Jiménez de Cisneros*, pp. 32–35; Coleman, *Creating Christian Granada*.

15. Domínguez Ortiz and Vincent, *Historia de los moriscos*, p. 19.

16. Ibid., pp. 17–23; Cardaillac, *Moriscos y cristianos*, p. 108; Epalza, *Los moriscos*, p. 58.

17. The literature on this subject is extensive. Over the past two decades, historians have debated the degree to which Moriscos remained faithful Muslims, or were assimilated into the Catholic population. Among proponents of Morisco resistance are Epalza, *Los moriscos*; Harvey, *Muslims in Spain*; Perry, *Handless Maiden*. Historians who emphasize the variation in religiosity across Spain, and for the assimilation of some of the Morisco population, include García-Arenal, *Inquisición y moriscos*; Tueller, *Good and Faithful Christians*.

18. Miller, *Guardians of Islam*.

19. Tueller, *Good and Faithful Christians*.

20. Domínguez Ortiz and Vincent, *Historia de los moriscos*, p. 100.

21. Ibid., p. 65.

22. Barrios Aguilera, "Religiosidad y vida cotidiana," pp. 357–433, in Barrios Aguilera and Peinado Santaella, *Historia del reino de Granada*, p. 360. For an exhaustive analysis of religious practices associated with Moriscos, using aljamiado manuscripts and inquisitorial sources, see Longás, *Vida religiosa*.

23. Barrios Aguilera, "Religiosidad y vida cotidiana," p. 416.

24. Barrios Aguilera, *Granada morisca*, pp. 229–30. Aljamiado refers to the literature produced by the Moriscos during the sixteenth and seventeenth centuries, using the Spanish language, some Arabic words and phrases, and written in the Arabic script.

25. Barrios Aguilera, *Granada morisca*, p. 230.

26. Redondo, "El primer plan sistemático," pp. 113–15.

27. Ibid., pp. 115–16.

28. Ibid., p. 120.

29. Gallego Burín and Gámir Sandoval, *Los Moriscos del reino de Granada*, p. 73.

30. See Barletta's "Introduction," pp. 3–4.

31. Domínguez Ortiz and Vincent, *Historia de los moriscos*, pp. 32–33; Barletta, "Introduction," pp. 20–22.

32. Francisco Núñez Muley, *Memorial*, published in Gallego Burín and Gámir Sandoval, *Los Moriscos del reino de Granada*, p. xl.

33. Quoted in Cardaillac, *Moriscos y cristianos*, p. 208. "En nombre del Padre, y del Hijo, y del Espíritu Sancto, un Dios, Amen."

34. References to the "law of the Moors" (*ley de los moros*) or the "law of Muhammad" (*ley de Mahoma*) existed both in the official discourse of church authorities and at the broader local or popular level. The use of "law" in this case is nearly synonymous with "religion," and recognizes the connected religious and legal systems used in medieval Iberia among Christians, Muslims, and Jews within their communities. See Schwartz, *All Can Be Saved*, pp. 51–52. The phrase "law of the Moors" could also have racializing connotations. In other instances, the label "sect" (as in *secta de Mahoma*) was used to discredit Islam as a religion.

35. The bibliography on the Spanish Inquisition is extensive. Works include Kamen, *Spanish Inquisition*; Starr-LeBeau, *In the Shadow of the Virgin*.

36. On the case of the North African slave Cristóbal de la Cruz, see Cook, "Navigating Identities."

37. Perry, *Handless Maiden*; Perry, "Behind the Veil," pp. 39–41. According to Perry, Morisco women played a dominant role in preserving Muslim traditions, as preparing food, observing holidays, and teaching children the Arabic dialect and prayers could all take place at home.

38. AHN, Inq. Toledo, leg. 196, exp. 23.

39. Diouf, *Servants of Allah*, p. 49.

40. Ibid., p. 2. Diouf's work focuses on enslaved African Muslims in the British, French, and Portuguese Americas.

41. Cardaillac, *Moriscos y cristianos*, p. 34.

42. Ibid., p. 113.

43. The list of points against the Moriscos from the *Ut supra* is published in Cardaillac, *Moriscos y cristianos*, pp. 111–12.

44. AHN, Inq. Toledo, leg. 191, exp. 24.

45. Ibid.

46. Ibid.

47. Pérez García and Fernández Chaves, "La infancia morisca," p. 168. A royal order (*pragmática*) dated 1572 and proclaimed in 1573 ordered that Morisco children be placed under the "administration" of old Christians if they were younger than ten and a half in the case of boys and nine and a half in the case of girls. This was to last until they turned twenty, although some were unlawfully kept as slaves by these old Christian families. For more on the role Morisco women played in educating their children see Perry, *Handless Maiden*.

48. AHN, Inq Toledo, leg. 192, exp. 16.

49. AGI, Contratacion 5400, N. 45, 20r. "christianos nuebos libres de naçion Berberiscos." The license stipulated that the Conde de Chinchón had to bring them back to Spain upon his return.

50. AHN, Inq. Toledo, leg. 192, exp. 16. Collective prayer is especially encouraged for Muslims on Fridays. Although Elena could neither pray openly nor go to a mosque, she might have chosen to wear a clean shirt to observe this day secretly.

51. AHN, Inq. Toledo, leg. 192, exp. 16.

52. AHN, Inq. Toledo, leg. 191, exp. 12.

53. AGN, Inq. vol. 151, exp. 5, ff. 3r–3v.

54. Cardaillac, *Moriscos y cristianos*, p. 25. Some Morisco children brought denunciations upon their parents. He cites one case involving Morisco children in Cuenca who made fun of an old Christian woman praying before a cross. In another case, a Morisco father lamented seeing his little sons "misled among the Christians" (*errados entre christianos*) and vowed to teach them Islam when they got older.

55. AHN, Inq. Toledo, leg. 191, exp. 12.

56. Ibid.

57. AHN, Inq. Toledo, leg. 194, exp. 7.

58. AHN, Inq. Toledo, leg. 193, exp. 15.

59. AHN, Inq. Toledo, leg. 191, exp. 12.

60. Diouf, "Servants of Allah," p. 49.

61. Ibid.

62. Martín Casares, "De la Esclavitud," p. 198.

63. AHN, Inq. Toledo, leg. 195, exp. 13.

64. Ibid.

65. AHN, Inq. Toledo, leg. 195, exp. 14.

66. AHN, Inq. Toledo, leg. 192, exp. 16.

67. Harvey, *Muslims in Spain*, p. 291.

68. Domínguez Ortiz and Vincent, *Historia de los moriscos*, pp. 167–72. One memorial from Valencia Archbishop Ribera dated January 1602 recommended that Moriscos not subject to a lord (*sueltos*) be exiled if they were not sent to the galleys or to the American mines.

69. Childers, "Manzanares, 1600."

70. Domínguez Ortiz and Vincent, *Historia de los moriscos*, pp. 162–63.

71. Haliczer, "Moriscos," p. 272.

72. Michel Boeglin estimates that by 1580, Moriscos made up 6 to 8 percent of Seville's total population of roughly one hundred thousand, a factor that increased anxieties as many of those Moriscos were new to the city, resettled from Granada or moved from the countryside seeking employment in the major port city. See "Between Rumor and Resistance," pp. 211–42, in Ingram, *Conversos and Moriscos*, p. 218.

73. Boeglin, "Between Rumor and Resistance," pp. 220–25.

74. Ibid., pp. 232–33.

75. Haliczer, "Moriscos," p. 270.

76. Benjamin Ehlers analyzes Ribera's shifting attitude toward the Moriscos in *Between Christians and Moriscos*.

77. Quoted in Ehlers, *Between Christians and Moriscos*, pp. 130–34. This image of wizened trees contrasts sharply with the notion that neophytes were "new plants," a characterization that emerges in some

missionaries' writings about new converts among both Moriscos and Amerindians.

78. Ehlers, *Between Christians and Moriscos*, p. 129.

79. Magnier, *Pedro de Valencia*, p. 30.

80. Ibid., p. 31.

81. Ibid., pp. 393–97.

82. Aznar Cardona, *Expulsion justificada*, Primera Parte, 1v.

83. Ibid., Primera Parte, 49r "medico celestia" and 4r "pestilencial secta Mahometana."

84. Ibid., Segunda Parte, 2r.

85. Ibid., Segunda Parte, 4r.

86. Valencia, *Tratado acerca*, p. 77.

87. Aznar Cardona, *Expulsion*, Segunda Parte, 22r. Benjamin Braude identifies a similar dynamic in retellings of biblical stories about Ham as applied to Africans following the voyages of Atlantic exploration in "Sons of Noah." The reference to Muhammad as descendant of Ishmael is also not taken from the Bible, but it is present in many accounts by Arab scholars whom Aznar Cardona may have been familiar with.

88. Valencia, *Tratado*, p. 78. Joseph Ziegler identifies a shift in the sixteenth century where complexion "established itself as a collective category" applied to Africans and Amerindians from an "invisible, internal blend of fluids in one's body to something identifiable on the skin," in "Physiognomy," pp. 181–99, in Eliav-Feldon, Isaac, and Ziegler, *Origins of Racism*, p. 199. Also see Daston and Vidal, *Moral Authority of Nature*. On the meanings of "complexion," also see Hering Torres, "Color, pureza, raza," pp. 451–70.

89. Valencia, *Tratado*, p. 138. He cites Seneca and Straban's writings on Roman incorporations of other peoples, including *hiberos* and *españoles*, into their empire.

90. Valencia, *Tratado*, p. 139.

91. Ibid., p. 140.

92. Domínguez Ortiz and Vincent, *Historia de los moriscos*, p. 179.

93. Printed in García-Arenal, *Los moriscos*, p. 252.

94. Ibid, pp. 254–55. " . . . de tiempo atras considerable . . . "

95. Domínguez Ortiz and Vincent, *Historia de los moriscos*, p. 187.

96. Ibid.

97. Ibid., p. 188.

98. Ibid., p. 183.

99. Ibid., p. 181.

100. Perry, *Handless Maiden*, pp. 158–60.

101. Ibid., p. 161.

102. Ibid., p. 166.

103. AHN, Inq. libro 1009, 360r.

104. AHN, Inq. libro 1009, 360r.

105. AHN, Inq. libro 1010, 49v.

106. AHN, Inq. libro 1010, 49v.

107. AHN, Inq. libro 1010, 332r.

CHAPTER 2

1. Quoted in Varela, *Cristóbal Colón*, pp. 43–44.
2. Russell-Wood, *Portuguese Empire*.
3. Thornton, *Africa and Africans*, pp. 24–36.
4. Alvarado Planas, "La polémica," p. 220.
5. Muldoon, *Americas in the Spanish World Order*, p. 22.
6. This led some, like Bartolomé de Las Casas, to question the extent of Spanish dominion because indigenous peoples did not consent explicitly to Spanish rule. Claims to dominion were upheld by jurists and theologians such as Solórzano and Juan Ginés de Sepúlveda. See Alvarado Planas, "La polémica," pp. 222–23.
7. Through their royal chroniclers, Ferdinand and Isabel shaped official histories in ways that presented themselves as possessing a "divine mandate to unite Hispania" and carried this program overseas to convert or subjugate non-Christians. See Kagan, *Clio and the Crown*, pp. 46–56.
8. See Hanke, *Spanish Struggle for Justice*. On the Requerimiento, see Seed, *Ceremonies of Possession*.
9. See Alvarado Planas, "La polémica"; Muldoon, *Americas in the Spanish World Order*; Adorno, *Polemics of Possession*; Hanke, *All Mankind Is One*; Pagden, *Fall of Natural Man*. On the Canary Islands, see Fernández-Armesto, *Canary Islands After the Conquest*, pp. 126–27.
10. Las Casas, *Brevísima relación*.
11. Poole, *Juan de Ovando*, p. 107.
12. Ibid., p. 111.
13. Ibid., pp. 112–13.
14. In 1567 Philip II appointed Juan de Ovando to inspect and reform the Council of the Indies, and in 1568 he created the Junta Magna to revise colonial policies. See Poole, *Juan de Ovando*, pp. 114–15.
15. Muldoon, *Americas in the Spanish World Order*, p. 97. Muldoon notes that this conflict extended from the medieval period, as rulers attempted to define the jurisdictional boundaries between ecclesiastical and temporal authority, with the investiture controversy in the eleventh and twelfth centuries.
16. Muldoon, *Americas in the Spanish World Order*, pp. 97–98.
17. Ibid., p. 113.
18. Alvarado Planas, "La polémica," pp. 227–29.
19. Muldoon, *Americas in the Spanish World Order*, pp. 96–97. Solórzano develops this idea in *De Indianum Jure*.
20. Ibid., pp. 171–72. On English and Dutch privateering, see Lane, *Pillaging the Empire*.
21. Pigafetta, *Magellan's Voyage*, p. 165.
22. Altman, *War for Mexico's West*, p. 162.
23. Metcalf, *Go-Betweens*, p. 20.
24. Ibid., p. 25.
25. Ibid., pp. 30–34.
26. Adorno and Pautz, *Álvar Núñez Cabeza de Vaca*, vol. 2, pp. 414–18.

27. Ibid., vol. 1, pp. 246–47. Cabeza de Vaca calls this trade language Primahaitu on p. 250.

28. Ibid., vol. 2, p. 421.

29. Ibid., vol. 2, p. 422.

30. Quoted in Ibid., vol. 2, p. 421.

31. Adorno and Pautz translate alárabe as Arabic-speaking. While this is correct, I would like to suggest further implications to the use of the term that varied depending on who was using it. Cabeza de Vaca emphasized that Estevanico was a Christian precisely because of the term's associations with Islam, and he needed to stress Estevanico's status as a pious convert whose presence in the Americas could be justified and whose position as interpreter could be deemed reliable. See Adorno and Pautz, *Álvar Núñez Cabeza de Vaca*, vol. 2, pp. 416–17 for their discussion of alárabe. For uses of the term, see Carvajal, *Descripción General de Africa*.

32. Adorno and Pautz, *Álvar Núñez Cabeza de Vaca*, vol. 2, p. 420. I have used Adorno and Pautz's translation of "asaeteado como un San Sebastian en servicio de Su Magestad," in Dorantes de Carranza, *Sumaria Relación*, p. 266.

33. I am indebted to Ida Altman for her generosity in sharing these references. For more context on these cases, see Altman, *War for Mexico's West*.

34. By the seventeenth century, members of the native elite who claimed noble status filled this role as cultural brokers between their communities and Spanish authorities. They were also often mistrusted by both as *indios ladinos* whose "cross-cultural and linguistic skills were considered dangerous." See Yannakakis, *Art of Being In-Between*, pp. 36–37.

35. Altman, *War for Mexico's West*, p. 51.

36. Aiton, *Antonio de Mendoza*, pp. 3–10. On the Mendoza family, see Nader, *Power and Gender*.

37. Tello, *Libro segundo*, pp. 57–58.

38. Ibid., p. 11.

39. Ibid., p. 125.

40. Ibid., p. 84.

41. Magnier, *Pedro de Valencia*, pp. 99–104.

42. Altman, *War for Mexico's West*, pp. 124–25.

43. On the Guerra Chichimeca, see Powell, *Soldiers, Indians*.

44. Altman, *War for Mexico's West*, pp. 215–21.

45. Ibid., p. 162.

46. AGI, Justicia 260.

47. AGI, Justicia 260, 175r. "haze mas vida de moro que de cristiano," variations of which appear in the charges against Triana and Romero and Ortiz de Zúñiga.

48. AGI, Justicia 260, 22r.

49. AGI, Justicia 260, 23r.

50. Taylor, *Drinking, Homicide*; Garofalo, "Conjuring with Coca."

51. AGI, Justicia 260, 21v.

52. Ibid.

53. Ibid.

54. AGI, Justicia 260, 22r.

55. Ibid.

56. Martínez, "Space, Order," pp. 13–16. On the concept of *policía* and desire to congregate indigenous peoples into towns, also see Kagan, *Urban Images*, pp. 26–39.

57. On reducciones in Peru, see Mumford, *Vertical Empire*; Scott, *Contested Territory*, pp. 69–70; Cook with Cook, *People of the Volcano*; Mac-Cormack, *Religion in the Andes*, pp. 140–41; Stern, *Peru's Indian Peoples*.

58. Martínez, "Space, Order," p. 31. Joanne Rappaport documents this process for Nueva Granada in *Disappearing Mestizo*.

59. Martínez, "Space, Order," p. 17. Sabine MacCormack provides an excellent study of Roman influences on colonial Peruvian urban spatial and civic organization in *On the Wings of Time*, pp. 101–36.

60. Altman, *War for Mexico's West*, p. 61.

61. Ibid., p. 69.

62. Metcalf, *Go-Betweens*, pp. 30–32.

63. Ibid., pp. 2–3. She uses Georg Simmel's distinction between arbitrator and mediator, someone who "guides the process of coming to terms," a more neutral role. The arbitrator can become the tertius gaudens, the "third who rejoices," or the "egoistic exploiter of the situation." Interpreters in this sense could be feared for their potential to influence outcomes to their advantage and harm others in the process. Also see Simmel, *Sociology of Georg Simmel*. Also see Yannakakis, *Art of Being In-Between*.

64. AGI, Justicia 260, 21v.

65. AGI, Justicia 260, 175v.

66. AGI, Justicia 260, 21v–22r.

67. AGI, Justicia 260, 22r.

68. AGI, Justicia 260, 22v.

69. AGI, Contratacion 5390, N.8.

70. Ibid.

71. AGI, Indiferente 1956, L.2, f. 93r–93v.

72. AGI, Indiferente 418, L.3, f. 319v. On Morisca slaves, see Qamber, *Inquisition Proceedings*.

73. AGI, Santo Domingo 868, L. 1, f. 73v–74r.

74. Ibid.

75. Lockhart, *Spanish Peru*; Cáceres Enríquez, "La Mujer Morisca," pp. 567–68.

76. Lockhart, *Spanish Peru*, p. 197.

77. Rappaport, *Disappearing Mestizo*.

78. AGI, Justicia 343, N. 4, 13r–v.

79. AGI, Justicia 343, N. 4, 31v. Information concerning Juana Morisca's carta de libertad is on 20v–22r.

80. AGI, Justicia 343, N. 4, 34v.

81. AGI, Justicia 343, N. 4, sf. On 28 April 1543 Antonio Pérez testified on behalf of Zevallos that Juana and her daughter were worth more than six hundred pesos of gold because their father Luis Suárez "es honbre honrrado y rrico." Debra Blumenthal notes similar patterns and assumptions in paternity

suits filed by enslaved women in fifteenth-century Valencia, in which they petitioned for their child's freedom in *Enemies and Familiars*, pp. 173–76.

82. AGI, Justicia 343, N. 4, sf. Interrogatorio of Luys Suárez presented on 30 April 1543: " . . . a visto en el Peru vender otras moriscas esclavas tan hermosas e aun mas que la dha Juana en menos."

83. For the early years of the Aliaga family in Peru, see Lockhart, *Men of Cajamarca*, 258–62.

84. AGI, Justicia 343, N. 4, sf.

85. Ibid.

86. Ibid. Dated Aranda del Duero, 24 September 1547 and signed by Licenciado Velázquez, Licenciado Salmerón and Dr. Hernán Pérez.

87. Lockhart, *Spanish Peru*, p. 99.

88. On Havana, see de la Fuente, *Havana and the Atlantic*, p. 81.

89. Ibid., p. 102.

90. Ibid., pp. 103–5.

91. Ibid., p. 106.

92. Sluiter, "Dutch-Spanish Rivalry," pp. 185–86; Andrews, *Spanish Caribbean*, p. 203.

93. Borah, *Silk Raising*, p. 9.

94. Feliciano Chaves, Mudejarismo in its Colonial Context.

CHAPTER 3

1. AGN, Inq. vol. 82, 217r. The term *quemado* referred to an individual remitted by the Inquisition to secular authorities and burned at the stake.

2. See Anzoátegui, *El poder*; Owensby, *Empire of Law*; Mörner, *Region and State*; Yannakakis, *Art of Being In-Between*; Rappaport, *Disappearing Mestizo*.

3. Cook, "Muslims and the Chichimeca."

4. Concerning the early conflicts over encomiendas, see Lavallé, *Las promesas ambiguas*, pp. 26–30.

5. *Cedulario Indiano Recopilado por Diego de Encinas*, vol. 1, p. 455.

6. AGI, Indiferente 1961, L. 1, f. 38v.

7. AGI, Indiferente 419, L. 5, f. 250r.

8. Jacobs, *Los movimientos migratorios*, pp. 28 and 46. The *composición* was a payment established by King Ferdinand in 1508 that allowed descendants of those convicted by the Inquisition to restore their social standing. Ferdinand's general license to Castilian converso communities remained valid until 1518. Under Philip II the composición was discontinued. Alicia Gojman Goldberg also notes the decrees were not enforced systematically until later; see *Los conversos en la Nueva España*, pp. 65 and 70–71.

9. *Cedulario Indiano Recopilado por Diego de Encinas*, vol. 1, pp. 452–53.

10. Ibid., vol. 1, p. 452.

11. Ibid., vol. 1, p. 453.

12. A prominent member of the Morisco nobility, Don Alonso de Granada Venegas certainly had the confidence to request in 1608 that the

Crown support his son, Leandro de Granada, who was educated at Salamanca, in pursuing an ecclesiastical post in the Americas. The king ordered that Granada Venegas's request be forwarded to the Council of the Indies for further review. AGI, Quito 27, N. 30. On the Granada Venegas family, see García-Arenal and Rodríguez Mediano, *Un Oriente español*.

13. Tueller, *Good and Faithful Christians*, p. 24; Perry, *Handless Maiden*, p. 93. Between 1530 and 1539, the Granadan Moriscos were especially active negotiating a respite from inquisitorial scrutiny. See Vincent, *Minorías y marginados*, p. 120.

14. Perry, *Handless Maiden*, p. 92; Vincent, *Minorías y marginados*, p. 119.

15. Harris, *From Muslim to Christian Granada*, p. 23.

16. Tueller, *Good and Faithful Christians*, p. 24; de Borja Medina, "La compañía de Jesús."

17. Martínez, *Genealogical Fictions*, see especially pp. 42–60.

18. Hess, "An Ottoman Fifth Column"; Perry, *Handless Maiden*, p. 93.

19. Ehlers, *Between Christians and Moriscos*, p. 20.

20. Perry, *Handless Maiden*, p. 94.

21. Tueller, *Good and Faithful Christians*, pp. 27–28.

22. AGI, Indiferente 424, L. 22, 240r.

23. Jacobs argues that 1552 presented a turning point in enforcement of religious restrictions in *Los movimientos migratorios*, p. 33. These decrees can be found in *Cedulario Indiano Recopilado por Diego de Encinas*, vol. 1, p. 455.

24. AGI, Indiferente 427, L. 30, 96r.

25. AGI, Indiferente 427, L. 30, 96r–v.

26. *Cedulario Indiano Recopilado por Diego de Encinas*, vol. 1, p. 453.

27. Jacobs, *Los movimientos migratorios*, p. 29.

28. The third tribunal was established in Cartagena de Indias in 1610. For New Spain, see Alberro, *Inquisition et société au Mexique*. For Peru, see Castañeda Delgado and Hernández Aparicio, *La Inquisición de Lima*.

29. Greenleaf, *Mexican Inquisition*; see also Clendinnen, *Ambivalent Conquests*.

30. *Cedulario Indiano Recopilado por Diego de Encinas*, vol. 1, p. 46.

31. Ibid.

32. Ibid., vol. 1, p. 47.

33. Ibid.

34. Studnicki-Gizbert, *Nation Upon the Ocean Sea*, p. 69.

35. On the idea of the corpus mysticum, see primarily Kantorowicz, *King's Two Bodies*. For the Spanish American context, see Cañeque, *King's Living Image*, p. 20.

36. Cañeque, *King's Living Image*, pp. 20–21.

37. Ibid., p. 21.

38. Quoted in Magnier, *Pedro de Valencia*, pp. 396–97. From Aznar Cardona's *Expulsion ivstificada*.

39. AHN, Inq. libro 1033, 318v and 409r–v. Signed by the notary Pedro González on 1 March 1575 after being read aloud by the priest (*cura*) in

Cuzco, Luis de Ribera, on 30 January. The edict was read again on 26 January 1578 by the bishop in Cuzco's *iglesia mayor*.

40. AGN, Inq. vol. 89, 57v–58r. On Spanish authorities' attempts to restrict the religious practices of some Moriscos, see Cardaillac, *Moriscos y cristianos*; Ehlers, *Between Christians and Moriscos*; Perry, *Handless Maiden*.

41. AHN, Inq. libro 1047, f. 544r.

42. AHN, Inq. libro 1033, 25v.

43. Jacobs provides a brief discussion of clandestine emigration in *Los movimientos migratorios*, pp. 103–4.

44. AGN, Inq. vol. 82, 218r. His parents' names were Pedro Hernández and María de Céspedes.

45. AGN, Inq. vol. 82, 218v. Hornachos had a large Morisco population during the sixteenth century that has been well studied. See González Rodríguez, *Hornachos, enclave morisco*; and Harvey, *Muslims in Spain*.

46. AGN, Inq. vol. 82, 219r.

47. AGN, Inq. vol. 82, 220r.

48. AGN, Inq. vol. 82, 220v.

49. AGN, Inq. vol. 82, 229v. "quietos e pacificos de buen vivir e fama."

50. AGN, Inq. vol. 82, 219v.

51. See Jacobs, "Legal and Illegal Emigration," pp. 59–84; Martínez, *Pasajeros de Indias*.

52. *Cedulario Indiano Recopilado por Diego de Encinas*, vol. 1, p. 442.

53. Ibid., vol. 1, pp. 444–46.

54. Ibid., vol. 1, pp. 443–44.

55. AGI, Justicia 509, N.1.

56. AHN, Inq. leg. 2943, exp. 55. On the Inquisition in the Canary Islands, see Fajardo Spínola, *Las Víctimas del Santo Oficio*.

57. AHN, Inq. leg. 2943, exp. 55, 1v.

58. AGN, Inq. vol. 82, 237r.

59. AGI, Patronato 292, N. 3, R. 134, f. 1r–v.

60. AGI, Patronato 292, N. 3, R. 133, f. 2v.

61. AGI, Patronato 292, N. 3, R. 133, f. 4r.

62. AGI, Justicia 856, N. 7, R. 1, 10. The witness is Alonso García, a calcetero living in Seville.

63. AGI, Justicia 856, N. 7, R. 1, 7.

64. AGI, Justicia 856, N. 7, R. 1, 44.

65. AGI, Justicia 856, N. 7, R. 1, 58. "la raiz de una poblacion es los labradores."

66. AGI, Justicia 856, N. 7, R. 1, 56. "porque yo nonbre personas abiles y no de los proybidos." In this instance, *habil* refers to an individual's capacity to hold prestigious offices or be qualified to carry out certain actions including emigration to the Americas. The implication is that the individual possesses limpieza de sangre, whereas the designation *inhabil* could refer to someone lacking blood purity, or whose ancestors had been convicted by the Inquisition.

67. AGI, Justicia 856, N. 7, R. 1, 56–57.

68. De la Fuente, *Havana and the Atlantic*, p. 86. Desertion rates could reach approximately 20 percent of a ship's crew during the first years of the seventeenth century.

69. AGI, Contratacion 143B, N. 23, 2r. "por ser morisco y de los prohibidos a passar a las yndias."

70. AGI, Contratacion 143B, N. 23, 5r.

71. AGI, Contratacion 143B, N. 23, 4v.

72. AGI, Contratacion 143B, N. 23, 6r.

73. Martz, *Network of Converso Families*. On a similar dynamic among Morisco families claiming elite status, see García-Arenal, "El entorno de los Plomos," pp. 51–78.

74. *Cedulario Indiano Recopilado por Diego de Encinas*, vol. 4, p. 383.

75. Ibid.

76. AGI, Contratacion 143B, N. 23, 7r.

77. AGI, Contratacion 143B, N. 23, 8v. The *carta de poder* is dated Gibraltar 3 July 1595.

78. AGI, Contratacion 143B, N. 23, 11v.

79. AGI, Contratacion 143B, N. 23, 13v.

80. AGI, Contratacion 143B, N. 23, 15r.

81. AGI, Contratacion 143B, N. 23, 22r–23r.

82. For various ways these spaces have been imagined, see Kennedy and Daniels, *Negotiated Empires*; White, *Middle Ground*; Weber, *Spanish Frontier*; and Weber, *Bárbaros*.

83. AGI, Santo Domingo 155, R.6, N.35, 1r.

84. Ibid.

85. AGI, Mexico 23, N. 79, capitulo 13 of letter dated 4 August 1597.

86. AGI, Mexico 23, N. 79, capitulo 14 of letter dated 4 August 1597.

87. Parry, "Audiencia of New Galicia," p. 267.

88. AGI, Guadalajara 51, 42r.

89. Ibid. It was eventually transferred to the city of Guadalajara in 1560.

90. AGI, Guadalajara 51, 42v. "como moros sin rei."

91. AGN, Inq. vol. 90, f. 31r.

92. Ibid.

93. AGI, Guadalajara 51, 438v.

94. AHN, Inq. libro 1047, 380v.

95. AHN, Inq. libro 1047, 380v–381r.

96. Ibid.

97. AGN, Inq. vol. 220, exp. 6.

98. AGI, Guadalajara 51, 471r.

99. AHN, Inq. libro 1034, 152v–153r. A *letrado* was someone who was university educated.

100. AHN, Inq. libro 1008, 35r.

101. AHN, Inq. libro 1008, 61r.

102. AGN, Inq. vol. 82, 182r.

103. AGN, Inq. vol. 82, 157r.

104. Ibid.

105. AGI, Guadalajara 55, 1v.

106. Ibid. Letter dated Zacatecas 16 July 1584.
107. AGN, Inq. vol. 141, f. 9r.
108. AGN, Inq. vol. 292, f. 5r. "extirpar vicios de la repu[bli]ca."
109. AGN, Inq. vol. 292, f. 5r.

CHAPTER 4

1. Haliczer, "Moriscos," p. 272.
2. AGN, Inq. vol. 151, exp. 5, f. 3r. Her case is first discussed in Chapter 1.
3. Aranda Doncel, "Las prácticas musulmanas," p. 12.
4. Cardaillac provides a useful discussion of taqiyya in *Moriscos y cristianos*, pp. 85–98.
5. A copy of the fatwa dated 3 May 1563 is published in Longás, *La Vida Religiosa*, p. 305.
6. Longás, *La Vida Religiosa*, p. 305.
7. Cardaillac, *Moriscos y cristianos*, pp. 147–48; García-Arenal, *Inquisición y moriscos*, pp. 46–47.
8. AGN, Inq. vol. 151, exp. 5, ff. 3v–4r.
9. AGN, Inq. vol. 151, exp. 5, ff. 8v–9r. I have not found references to "Halamay" in other inquisitorial documents or secondary sources on the subject. In many trials, Moriscos were accused of saying Alhanduliley (praise God) or Bismillah (in the Name of God), which precedes the shahada, or profession of faith in Islam. It is also not impossible that the scribe garbled Ruiz's words when recording her statement.
10. AGN, Inq. vol. 151, exp. 5, f. 9r.
11. Cardaillac, *Moriscos y cristianos*, pp. 211–13. These statements are taken from inquisitorial records of Granadan Moriscos, examined by Cardaillac, as well as a polemical text in aljamiado by Muhammad al-Qaysī. Entitled "Deskonkordamiyento de los Kiristiyanos," this manuscript attempted to show the disagreement among Christians and their subsequent separation into sects as each tried to falsify the divine word to suit their purposes. According to Cardaillac this image of Christian disunity was not infrequent in the aljamiado polemical literature (p. 153).
12. Cardaillac has characterized these conversations as an ongoing polemic between Moriscos and old Christians in *Moriscos y cristianos*, pp. 237–49.
13. Cardaillac, *Moriscos y cristianos*, p. 276.
14. Ibid., p. 213.
15. Ibid.
16. AGN, Inq. vol. 151, exp. 5, f. 9r.
17. AGN, Inq. vol. 151, exp. 5, f. 8v.
18. AGN, Inq. vol. 151, exp. 5, f. 21r.
19. Ibid.
20. Bennassar and Bennassar, *Los cristianos de Alá*; Graizbord, *Souls in Dispute*.
21. Another compelling example is that of Cristóbal de la Cruz in Cook, "Navigating Identities." For an analysis of claims that "all can be saved" in their own law or religion, see Schwartz, *All Can Be Saved*.

22. AGN, Inq. vol. 276, f. 194r.

23. Ibid.

24. AGN, Inq. vol. 276, f. 195r.

25. AGN, Inq. vol. 276, f. 195v. " . . . y que savia muy bien lo que se dezia que no era el ningun barbaro y cavallo . . . "

26. The *Viage de Hierusalem* was written by Francisco Guerrero, the racionero and maestro de capilla of the Cathedral of Seville, and published in 1593 in Valencia. This edition is available online at http://parnaseo.uv.es/Lemir/Textos/Viaje/index.htm.

27. AGN, Inq. vol. 276, f. 199r.

28. AGN, Inq. vol. 276, f. 200r.

29. This work has been transcribed and published as *El Manuscrito Misceláneo 774 de la Biblioteca Nacional de París*.

30. *El Manuscrito Misceláneo 774*, p. 200.

31. Ibid., p. 201. "Demanda, i serte á dada/ tu demanda, rruwega, i será oída tu rrogarýa."

32. Ibid., p. 212. "ves al-ffuwego i saka d-él kiyen tiyene en xu / koraçón peso de una darra (átomo) de kere/ençiya . . . a kiyen dišo una vegada: / la ilaha illa Allah Muhammad rraçulu / Allah (no hay dios sino Dios, Mahoma es su enviado) de koraçón."

33. Ibid., pp. 212–13. "serán taraýdos a una ffuwente / ke está a la puwerta del aljannat (paraíso), ke se / llama La Ffuwente de la Vida; serán bañados / en ella; saldarán d-ella komo la luna llena / la noche de katorçe; sakarán eskiribto / sobre xus ferentes ke dirán 'éstos / son los ke ahurró (liberó) Allah del ffuwego de jahannam (el infierno).'"

34. AGN, Inq. vol. 302, f. 104r. " . . . el dho Di[eg]o dijo en boz clara y distincta . . . bien aya el paraiso de Mahoma y los que en el crehen e io creo en el . . . " They were all in the service of Simón Hernández, *armador de pesquería*. *Calificadores* were theologians appointed by the Inquisition to censor books and heretical statements (*proposiciones*).

35. AGN, Inq. vol. 302, f. 104r.

36. AGN, Inq. vol. 127, f. 404r. According to Luis García Ballester, algarabia refers to the dialect of Arabic spoken in Valencia. García Ballester, "Inquisition and Minority Medical Practitioners," p. 176.

37. AGN, Inq. vol. 127, f. 410v.

38. Ibid. "tierra de moros."

39. AGN, Inq. vol. 127, f. 413v.

40. Ibid.

41. Bennassar and Bennassar, *Los cristianos de Alá*.

42. AGN, Inq. vol. 486, f. 473r.

43. Ibid.

44. AGN, Inq. vol. 486, f. 473v.

45. Ibid.

46. AGN, Inq. vol. 486, f. 475v.

47. AGN, Inq. vol. 486, f. 473v. "digo que como son muchos y biven entre indios y otra gte. miserable todo qto. quieren tiraniçan y todo lo traen tan confundido que libertades y vicios con n[ombr]e de virtud igualeçen."

48. AGN, Inq. vol. 486, f. 473v–474r.
49. AGN, Inq. vol. 486, f. 474r.
50. Cardaillac, *Moriscos y cristianos.*
51. Barrios Aguilera and Sánchez Ramos, *Martirios y mentalidad martirial*, p. 116.
52. Selections from the *Actas de Ugíjar* are reproduced in Barrios Aguilera and Sánchez Ramos, *Martirios y mentalidad martirial*. Request that Escolano investigate the Alpujarras martyrs, made by Don Antonio de Torres, beneficiado of the church of Santa María Magdalena, p. 216.
53. Barrios Aguilera and Sánchez Ramos, *Martirios y mentalidad martirial*, p. 306.
54. Ibid., p. 153.
55. Ibid., pp. 163–64.
56. AGN, Inq. vol. 151, exp. 5, f. 5r.
57. Ibid.
58. AGN, Inq. vol. 151, exp. 5, f. 23r.
59. AGN, Inq. vol. 58, f. 87v. "la ley q quisiese." *Levantisco* was the word used to refer to anyone from the Levant or eastern Mediterranean, areas that were part of the Ottoman Empire.
60. AGN, Inq. vol. 58, f. 85v. "q amainase por la nueva religion."
61. AGN, Inq. vol. 58, ff. 87v–88r.
62. AGN, Inq. vol. 58, f. 88r.
63. Ibid. "el dho yndio dezia q tenia sospecha q un morisco q venia con los dhos françeses lo avia hecho . . . " This is still Maçuca's testimony.
64. AGN, Inq. vol. 58, f. 153v.
65. AGN, Inq. vol. 58, f. 89v.
66. AGN, Inq. vol. 58, f. 151v. The witness is referred to in this case as an "indio ladino" from Guatemala who was baptized there and confirmed in "these provinces," presumably the Yucatan. However, his testimony is copied alongside that of Francisco Pat from the case of Pierre Sanfroy, one of the French pirates, in AGN, Inq. vol. 50, f. 225v. Here his name appears as Pedro Suchil, from San Salvador, Guatemala.
67. AGN, Inq. vol. 58, f. 151v.
68. Epalza, *Los moriscos.*
69. Cardaillac, *Moriscos y cristianos*, pp. 133–40.
70. Ibid., pp. 120–21.
71. Ibid., p. 122. He cites these manuscripts as MSS 9067 and MSS 9655 of the Biblioteca Nacional in Madrid. For a discussion of Valera and his work, see Kinder, "Religious Literature."
72. AGN, Inq. vol. 16, f. 317r.
73. AGN, Inq. vol. 16, f. 317v.
74. Ibid.
75. AGN, Inq. vol. 16, f. 318v–319r.
76. AGN, Inq. vol. 16, f. 319r.
77. AGN, Inq. vol. 16, f. 319v.
78. AGN, Inq. vol. 16, f. 320r. By jubilees, Beltrán may have been referring to the indulgences granted during the year of the Jubilee, declared

periodically by the popes. Paul III declared a Jubilee in 1550, which was opened by Julius III.

79. AGN, Inq. vol. 16, f. 320v.

80. Ibid.

81. AGN, Inq. vol. 16, f. 324r.

82. AGN, Inq. vol. 151, exp. 5, f. 26v–27r.

83. AGN, Inq. vol. 151, exp. 5, f. 29r.

84. AHN, Inq. libro 1064, f. 213v.

85. On emigrants maintaining ties to their home communities in Spain, see Altman, *Emigrants and Society.*

86. AGN, Inq. vol. 315, f. 351v.

87. AGN, Inq. vol. 315, f. 354r.

88. AGN, Inq. vol. 315, f. 355v.

89. AGN, Inq. vol. 315, f. 355r.

90. AGN, Inq. vol. 315, f. 355v. "perro moro y que se lo provaria."

91. Ibid.

92. AGN, Inq. vol. 315, f. 357r. " . . . loado sea jesuxpo que es señal que alçen del trabajo y a esto dixo el dho Pedro Hernandez estos perros no conocen a jesuxpo diziendolo por los indios y que a oydo dezir que le llamaron morisco y no se acuerda quien."

93. AGN, Inq. vol. 292, f. 194r. " . . . era mal cristiano y entendian que era morisco por que en el color la muestra, y en su trato porque a sido bunolero oficio que lo usan de ordinario moriscos en España . . . " In the 1589 census of Moriscos in Seville, buñolero was listed as one of the more common professions. See Boeglin, *Entre la Cruz y el Corán,* p. 160.

94. Hering Torres, "Color, pureza, raza."

95. See Fuchs, *Exotic Nation,* pp. 76–77; Harvey, *Muslims in Spain,* p. 252.

96. AGN, Inq. vol. 292, f. 199v.

97. AGN, Inq. vol. 292, f. 194r.

98. AGN, Inq. vol. 292, f. 194v.

99. AGN, Inq. vol. 292, f. 198v.

100. Ibid.

101. AGN, Inq. vol. 292, ff. 198v–199r.

102. Haliczer, "Moriscos."

103. AGN, Inq. vol. 292, f. 199r. "perro moro retajado de Greçia."

104. AGN, Inq. vol. 292, f. 199r.

105. AGN, Inq. vol. 292, f. 199v. " . . . y que en su cassa anda con un calçon de manta corto abierto y una camissa de lo mysmo y una toaza çuçia rebuelta en la caveça a usança y traxe de morisco . . . "

106. Fuchs, *Exotic Nation*; Feliciano Chaves, "Mudejarismo in its Colonial Context."

107. AGN, Inq. vol. 292, f. 202r.

108. Ibid.

109. AGN, Inq. vol. 292, f. 202r–v.

110. AGN, Inq. vol. 292, f. 204r.

111. According to the casta categories that were beginning to be invoked during this period, being the daughter of a Spaniard and a mulata would

have made her a morisca. This casta category would have been based on descent, and not on being a convert from Islam. It is interesting that neither of the two witnesses who mention her call her a morisca.

112. AGN, Inq. vol. 292, ff. 204r–v.

113. Ibid.

114. AGN, Inq. vol. 292, ff. 204v–205r.

115. AHN, Inq. leg. 2075, exp. 7, f. 102r. "decendiente de los moros de Tunez."

116. AHN, Inq. leg. 2075, exp. 7, f. 102r.

117. Tueller, *Good and Faithful Christians*, pp. 130–31. Also see Valencia, *Tratado*, p. 131. As an insult, "dog" also began to be applied to indigenous peoples, and according to Garcilaso de la Vega in his *Comentarios Reales*, the word "cholo" meant "gazcones" or "dogs" in the language of the windward Caribbean islands, that Sebastián de Covarrubias notes in his *Tesoro de la lengua castellana* as pertaining to once-noble dogs whose line was "lost and bastardized." Cited in Burns, "Unfixing Race," p. 194 and p. 369 fn. 28. Cholo refers not to "castizo" dogs but rather the "muy bellacos gazcones."

CHAPTER 5

1. On the *Tribunal de Protomedicato*, or royal governing board for medical licensing, see Bowers, *Plague and Public Health*, pp. 91–93; Campos Díez, *El Real Tribunal*.

2. Ciruelo, *Reprouacion de las supersticiones y hechizerias*, vol. 1.

3. Ibid., p. 140.

4. Ibid.

5. Ibid., p. 81.

6. Relación sumaria del auto particular de fee que el Tribunal del Santo Oficio de la Inquisición de los Reynos y Provincias de la Nueva España celebró en la muy noble y leal Ciudad de México a . . . 1659. Imprenta del Secreto del Santo Oficio "Por la viuda de Bernardo Calderón, Calle de San Agustín." Held in a collection of Relaciones of *autos–da–fé* at the Newberry Library: Ayer 655.52. I5 1646.

7. Relación sumaria, 11v.

8. Relación sumaria, 1r.

9. AHN, Inq. leg. 1733, exp. 11, 3r. " . . . diçe ser Moro blanco de los empeñados, q los havia empeñado un Rey." This may have been a reference to Alfonso X "the Wise" who was known to have suffered from a debilitating eye ailment throughout his life. See Kinkade, "Alfonso X, Cantiga 235."

10. AHN, Inq. leg. 1733, exp. 11, 3v. Buitron described the wax tablets as being "como agnus," referring to the agnus dei that began to proliferate during this period for healing and devotional practices. In Spain, women wore them for protection during childbirth, and most inventories of women's possessions in Triana by the late sixteenth century listed at least one agnus dei (Alexandra Parma Cook, personal communication). On uses of the agnus dei, also see Gentilcore, *From Bishop to Witch*. "Saludador," along with "curandero" and

"sanador" are terms that designate someone who was a healer. According to Covarrubias Orozco, *Tesoro de la Lengua Castellana o Española [1611]*, saludador has the additional connotation of someone who cures with the breath.

11. AHN, Inq. leg. 1733, exp. 11, 3v.

12. AHN, Inq. leg. 1733, exp. 11, f. 4v.

13. García Ballester, *Los moriscos y la medicina*, p. 100. He notes that the declaration of the University of Paris in 1398 put forth this idea, which was echoed in the pronouncements of a priest in Zaragoza in 1492 and of the bishop of Simancas in 1552. He also notes that F. Torreblanca in his *Epitome Delictorum sive de Magia* argues that a demonic pact exists where "nothing is used, natural nor supernatural, other than mere words recited or whispered, a touch, a breath or a simple dress that has no virtue in and of itself."

14. Doutté, *Magie et religion*, pp. 104 and 441.

15. Mami, "Los milagros del profeta Mahoma," p. 462. "El que con sólo tocar su mano a una pierna quebrada quedó sana, y el que con sólo la saliva de su boca escupió en sus ojos de un ziego le bolbió la bista." The original manuscript is held at the Biblioteca Nacional in Madrid, MSS 9067, f. 10r. I have used Ridha Mami's transcription of this text. Camilo Álvarez de Morales also discusses Muhammad's use of saliva in his cures in "Elementos mágicos y religiosos en la medicina andalusí," p. 37.

16. García Ballester, *Los moriscos y la medicina*, pp. 60–66. García Ballester mentions not only aljamiado manuscripts, but also Dioscorides's *Materia medica* as being in the possession of some of the Moriscos he studies, and influencing their practice, p. 66.

17. García Ballester, *Los moriscos y la medicina*, pp. 57–64. The limpieza de sangre statutes barred Moriscos from holding honorable professions and from attending most Spanish universities, although the University of Valencia was more open to allowing Moriscos to study medicine.

18. García Ballester, *Los moriscos y la medicina*, pp. 57–64.

19. Ibid., pp. 51–54.

20. A portion of this document from the Actas de las Cortes de Castilla, dated 13 September 1607, is printed in García-Arenal, *Los moriscos*, pp. 220–21.

21. Ibid., p. 220.

22. García Ballester, "Medicine in a Multicultural Society," p. 160. Also see López-Baralt, "El conjuro mágico," pp. 431–43.

23. García Ballester, *Los moriscos y la medicina*, pp. 73–74.

24. Ibid., pp. 58 and 101.

25. García Ballester, "Inquisition and Minority Medical Practitioners," p. 169. Also see Gallego Burín and Gámir Sandoval, *Los Moriscos del reino de Granada*.

26. Gallego Burín and Gámir Sandoval, *Los Moriscos del reino de Granada*, p. 119. "supersticiones de nóminas, adivinaciones, saludadores, ensalmadores, santigüeras y oraciones de ciegos." Here they quote directly from the *Constituciones sinodales* (Granada 1573).

27. Gallego Burín and Gámir Sandoval, *Los Moriscos del reino de Granada*, p. 119.

28. For discussions of Morisco magic, see Cardaillac-Hermosilla, *La magie en Espagne* and *Los nombres del diablo*; Labarta, *Libro de dichos maravillosos*. For discussions of magical practices in Europe, see Gentilcore, *From Bishop to Witch*; Kieckhefer, "Specific Rationality of Medieval Magic"; Kieckhefer, *Forbidden Rites*; Ruggiero, *Binding Passions*.

29. Shah, *Oriental Magic*; Doutté, *Magie et religion*.

30. Cardaillac-Hermosilla, *La magie en Espagne*, p. 178.

31. Ze'evi, *Producing Desire*, p. 101.

32. Ibid., p. 103. The *Oneirocritica* was composed during the second century AD. The translator into Arabic of this dream manual changed passages to make it suitable for monotheist Christian, Muslim, and Jewish readers. Thus references to Greek gods shifted to include Allah and the angels, and Muslim ceremonies replaced pagan ones. On this, see Mavroudi, *Byzantine Book on Dream Interpretation*; Sirriyeh, *Sufi Visionary*, pp. 70–71; Lamoreaux, *Early Muslim Tradition of Dream Interpretation*.

33. Kieckhefer, *Magic in the Middle Ages*.

34. AHN, Inq. leg. 1733, exp. 11, f. 9v.

35. AHN, Inq. leg. 1733, exp. 11, f. 4v. Taken from the testimony of Augustina Buitrón Muxica. Pulido confirms this on 9v although because she was blind she only heard López de Aponte unfold the paper and the other women describe what was on it.

36. AHN, Inq. leg. 1733, exp. 11, f. 10v. Francisco Hernández describes the wide range of uses the plant *tecomahaca*, native to Michoacán and the Mixteca in New Spain, had for curing a variety of ailments from menstrual problems to sciatica. Dragon's blood was a red resin from the dragon tree, also used in medicine. See Varey, *Mexican Treasury*, pp. 120–21.

37. AHN, Inq. leg. 1733, exp. 11, f. 10v.

38. AHN, Inq. leg. 1733, exp. 11, f. 25r.

39. AHN, Inq. leg. 1733, exp. 11, f. 5r.

40. AHN, Inq. leg. 1733, exp. 11, f. 5r. " . . . le dixo q tenia muy grandes patas para ello y no fuesse q ambos se fuessen al infierno."

41. AHN, Inq. leg. 1733, exp. 11, f. 5r.

42. AHN, Inq. leg. 1733, exp. 11, ff. 5r–v.

43. Andezian, "Maghreb," p. 97. Andezian cautions that the French word "saint" homogenizes the range of social actors who fall under this category.

44. Ibid. The concept of *baraka* has been translated as blessing and grace. For discussions of the term, see Le Gall, *Culture of Sufism*; Naamouni, *Le Culte de Bouya Omar*; Sirriyeh, *Sufi Visionary of Ottoman Damascus*. Renée Claisse-Dauchy notes the difficulty of defining *baraka* and describes it as a combination of benediction, protection and luck. See Claisse-Dauchy, *Médecine traditionnelle du Maghreb*.

45. Andezian, "Maghreb," p. 99.

46. Ibid., pp. 102–5.

47. Ze'evi, *Producing Desire*, p. 80. Tarīqa, meaning path, also connotes brotherhood. For a discussion of Sufi healers and the use of medical ideas based on the Qur'ān and hadīth, see Ze'evi, *Producing Desire*, p. 18. Also see Karamustafa, *God's Unruly Friends*.

48. Harris, *From Muslim to Christian Granada*, p. 115.
49. Ibid., p. 117.
50. Ibid., p. 114.
51. Gentilcore, *Healers and Healing*, p. 157.
52. Gentilcore argues that the church considered living saints to be "something of a battleground: where the eager faithful saw visions, ecstasies and healing wonders, the Church saw the possibility of diabolical trickery . . . " (*Healers and Healing*, p. 158).
53. Schutte, *Aspiring Saints*, p. 155.
54. Ibid., p. 223. Demeanor, attire, and the objects used in their cures could all raise questions for inquisitors about an individual's sanctity.
55. AHN, Inq. leg. 1733, exp. 11, f. 11r.
56. Ibid.
57. Ibid.
58. AHN, Inq. leg. 1733, exp. 11, f. 5r.
59. Epalza, *Jesús entre judíos*, pp. 174–75.
60. Ibid., pp. 173–74.
61. Ibid., pp. 176 and 182.
62. Ibid., p. 179.
63. Münzer, *Viaje por España y Portugal*, p. 127. "Un anciano me mostró un rosario hecho de huesos de dátiles, diciendo que era de la palmera de la que comió María, cuando su huida a Egipto. Lo besaba diciendo que era muy útil para las embarazadas, conforme él lo había experimentado."
64. Münzer, *Viaje por España y Portugal*, p. 127.
65. Labarta, *Libro de dichos maravillosos*, p. 126. The *Libro de dichos maravillosos*, or Book of Marvelous Sayings, was a Morisco miscellany copied by a scribe named Muhammad in the Aragonese town of Almonacid de la Sierra, sometime between the late-sixteenth and early-seventeenth centuries. It provides information about local Morisco religiosity, divination, talismans and legends.
66. Gentilcore, *Medical Charlatanism*.
67. Ibid., p. 295.
68. The literature on captivity in Ottoman lands is extensive. For the western Mediterranean, see Bennassar and Bennassar, *Los cristianos de Alá*; Braudel, *Mediterranean and the Mediterranean World*; Hess, *Forgotten Frontier*. For Britain, see Mattar, *Turks, Moors and Englishmen*; Vitkus, *Turning Turk*.
69. Gentilcore, *Medical Charlatanism*, pp. 295–96. Gentilcore notes some inconsistencies with Franchi's claim, specifically that the sultan in question, given the dates, would have been Mehmed IV, and while there were Italians practicing in the sultan's court, no one fitting his description was active at the time of his father's reputed career.
70. Gentilcore, *Medical Charlatanism*, p. 297. Also see Çirakman, *From the "Terror of the World."*
71. Gentilcore, *Medical Charlatanism*, p. 298.
72. AHN, Inq. leg. 1733, exp. 11, ff. 12v and 14r. "grandiss[i]mo embustero."

73. AHN, Inq. leg. 1733, exp. 11, f. 14r. "q era moro o turco de naçion por q hablava muy çerrado."

74. AHN, Inq. leg. 1733, exp. 11, f. 21r. "en romançe mal dicho."

75. AHN, Inq. leg. 1733, exp. 11, f. 27r. López de Aponte testified that he was approximately forty-two years old.

76. AHN, Inq. leg. 1733, exp. 11, ff. 19v–20r.

77. AHN, Inq. leg. 1733, exp. 11, f. 36r. "español fino y no estrangero ni moro blanco."

78. López de Aponte was accused not only of carrying out illicit healing practices and disregarding the virginity of Mary, but also of acting as a zahorí, or diviner, a practice that contemporaries associated with Moriscos. Rangel accused López de Aponte of telling her he was a zahorí and that he knew what was in her heart by the grace that God had given him. Another witness, the weaver Benito de Rojas, testified how he and his wife sought López de Aponte's help when their young nephew disappeared.

79. AHN, Inq. leg. 1733, exp. 11, f. 22r.

80. AHN, Inq. leg. 1733, exp. 11, f. 23v.

CHAPTER 6

1. Adorno and Pautz, *Álvar Núñez Cabeza de Vaca*, vol. 1, p. 273. I have used the translation provided by Rolena Adorno and Patrick Charles Pautz in this bilingual edition.

2. Ibid., vol. 1, p. 275.

3. On African practices in Brazil, see Sweet, *Recreating Africa*. On indigenous and African practices in Spanish America, see Aguirre Beltrán, *Medicina y magia*; Bristol, *Christians, Blasphemers*; Few, *Women Who Live Evil Lives*; Lewis, *Hall of Mirrors*; Mills, *Idolatry and Its Enemies*, see especially chap. 4. On repression of indigenous ritual practices in Mexico, see Ruiz de Alarcón, *Treatise on the Heathen Superstitions*.

4. Behar, "Sexual Witchcraft," p. 183.

5. Ibid., p. 192. Also see Sánchez Ortega, "Sorcery and Eroticism."

6. See especially Geertz, "Anthropology of Religion and Magic, I." In her critique of Keith Thomas's *Religion and the Decline of Magic*, Hildred Geertz notes the clear distinction Thomas draws between religion as comprising a clearly defined belief system, and magic as "incoherent, and primarily oriented toward providing practical solutions to immediate problems" (p. 72). According to Geertz, Thomas has used the categories of his seventeenth-century subjects in understanding magic as separate from religion, thereby "he takes part in the very cultural process that he is studying" (p. 77). This is of concern to historians of the process labeled magic, since much of the documentation is from inquisitorial and ecclesiastical sources that condemn the practices under study. Other historians and scholars of religion have since provided new frameworks for analyzing the place of "magical" practices within local societies. On early medieval Christian sanctionings of "magic," see Flint, *Rise of Magic*.

7. Richard Kieckhefer favors the term "unofficial ritual" in "Specific Rationality of Medieval Magic," p. 833.

8. Jonathan Z. Smith cautions that "magic" is a category empty of meaning due to the varied ways in which it has been used. He advocates using more specific terminology for the practices under question, such as healing and divination. See his chapter "Trading Places," pp. 215–29 in Smith, *Relating Religion*, pp. 218–19.

9. For discussions of the terms, see Behar, "Sexual Witchcraft"; Cardaillac-Hermosilla, *La magie en Espagne*, p. 94; Cardaillac-Hermosilla, *Los nombres del diablo*, p. 8; and Lewis, *Hall of Mirrors*, p. 185, fn. 1.

10. Covarrubias Orozco, *Tesoro*, p. 1032.

11. Ibid.

12. Ibid., p. 1226.

13. Ciruelo, *Reprouacion*, p. 40.

14. Ibid., p. 42.

15. Ibid., p. 34. " . . . que estas hechizerias y supersticiones se deuen mucho castigar por los prelados y juezes y echarlas de la tierra de los christianos: como cosas muy malas y ponçonosas: y muy prejudiciales a la honrra de dios . . . "

16. Del Río, *Investigations into Magic*, p. 27. I have relied here on P. G. Maxwell-Stuart's translation.

17. Ibid., pp. 27–28.

18. Ibid., p. 28.

19. Ibid. Maxwell-Stuart translates *daemones* as evil spirits instead of demons to note the nuances and broader range of the Latin term.

20. Del Río, *Investigations into Magic*, p. 105.

21. Ibid.

22. Ibid., pp. 106–7. On the play, see Ruiz de Alarcón, *Quien Mal Anda*; and Ángel Martínez Blasco's preliminary study.

23. See Fuchs, *Exotic Nation*.

24. On Mediterranean corsairs, see Bono, *Corsari nel Mediterraneo*.

25. AGN, Inq. vol. 471, exp. 31, ff. 89r–89v.

26. AGN, Inq. vol. 471, exp. 31, f. 89v.

27. Ibid.

28. AGN, Inq. vol. 471, exp. 31, ff. 89v–90r.

29. Álvarez de Morales, "Elementos mágicos y religiosos," pp. 36–37.

30. García Ballester, "Medicine in a Multicultural Society," p. 174. Also see García Ballester, *Los moriscos y la medicina*, pp. 47–136.

31. Cardaillac Hermosilla, *Los nombres del diablo*, p. 106.

32. Labarta, *Libro de dichos maravillosos*, p. 0.32.

33. Cardaillac-Hermosilla, *Los nombres del diablo*, p. 111.

34. Ibid., p. 98.

35. Ibid., p. 100.

36. Labarta, *Libro de dichos maravillosos*, p. 0.35. These phrases in Arabic mean "in the name of God, the Compassionate, the Merciful," "God is great," and "oh, God," respectively. Suras are chapters from the Qur'an.

37. Labarta, *Libro de dichos maravillosos*, pp. 0.34–0.35.

38. AHN, Inq. leg. 1829, exp. 1L, f. 43r. A quartilla refers to a piece of paper the size of the fourth part of a folio.

39. Ibid.

40. Ibid.
41. AHN, Inq. leg. 1829, exp. 1L, 43r–43v.
42. AHN, Inq. leg. 1829, exp. 1L, f. 43v.
43. AHN, Inq. leg. 1829, exp. 1L, f. 44r.
44. AHN, Inq. leg. 2075, exp. 7, f. 23r.
45. AHN, Inq. leg. 2075, exp. 7, f. 23v.
46. AHN, Inq. leg. 2075, exp. 7, f. 24v.
47. Ibid.
48. Printed in García Ballester, *Los moriscos y la medicina*, p. 80. He takes this citation from Ribera, *Disertaciones y opúsculos*.
49. García Ballester, *Los moriscos y la medicina*, p. 74.
50. AHN, Inq. leg. 2075, exp. 9, f. 17v.
51. Ibid. This case is listed in the account of the auto–da–fé in Seville of 1592.
52. AGN, Inq. vol. 471, exp. 113, f. 375r.
53. Ibid.
54. AGN, Inq. vol. 471, exp. 113, f. 375v.
55. AGN, Inq. vol. 471, exp. 113, f. 376r.
56. Ibid.
57. AGN, Inq. vol. 486, f. 201r. " . . . que bende polvos para atraer mugeres que se los enbio el gran Turco."
58. Ibid.
59. Cardaillac-Hermosilla, *La magie en Espagne*, pp. 97–116. For López de Aponte's case, see AHN, Inq. leg. 1733, exp. 11.
60. Cardaillac-Hermosilla, *La magie en Espagne*, pp. 60–63; Cardaillac-Hermosilla, *Los nombres del diablo*, pp. 91–119; Albarracín Navarro and Martínez Ruiz, *Medicina, farmacopea y magia*, pp. 19–20. For the sacralization of words in Morisco magical practices, see Labarta's introduction to the *Libro de dichos maravillosos*, p. 0.21.
61. AGN, Inq. vol. 220, exp. 41, f. 125r.
62. AGN, Inq. vol. 220, exp. 35, f. 113r. " . . . ciertas palabras en lengua mora . . . "
63. Morga, *Sucesos de las Islas Filipinas*, f. 139v.
64. Ibid., f. 146r. Ghazi can refer to mercenary fighters and were used by the Ottomans to expand their territories.
65. Morga, *Sucesos de las Islas Filipinas*, f. 122v. " . . . los Moros se revelavan contra los Españoles . . . "
66. Ibid., f. 122r. " . . . que como gente Mahometana, y de suyo faciles y de poca constancia, inquietos y hechos a desasosiegos y guerras; cada ora, y por diversas partes, las movian y se alçavan. . . ."
67. Ibid., f. 122r.
68. AGN, Inq. vol. 308, f. 143v. " . . . en esta tierra ay munchos chinos que quando fueron conquistados eran ya grandes y como seguian en su tierra la secta de Mahoma estan sircunsidados y aun algunos que lo estan despues de bautisados." On slaves from the Philipinnes in New Spain, see Seijas, *Asian Slaves in Colonial Mexico*.
69. AGN, Inq. vol. 308, f. 143v.

70. AGN, Inq. vol. 486, f. 294r.

71. Ibid.

72. Ibid.

73. AGN, Inq. vol. 486, f. 294v.

74. For a discussion of the *aiguillette* in early modern Europe, see Ruggiero, *Binding Passions*.

75. AGN, Inq. vol. 486, f. 294v. " . . . y esta le dixo que ella las diria por que en España se las avia enseñado una morisca con unos palmos que tambien le enseño para saber donde estava su galan." The palmos most likely refers to the *conjuro de palmos* for love magic, that is described in Cirac Estopañán, *Los procesos de hechicerías*, p. 125.

76. AGN, Inq. vol. 486, f. 292r.

77. AGN, Inq. vol. 322, f. 227r.

78. Ibid.

79. Ibid.

80. AGN, Inq. vol. 322, ff. 227r–v.

81. AGN, Inq. vol. 322, f. 227v.

82. Ibid.

83. AGN, Inq. vol. 322, f. 228r.

84. Ibid.

85. Ibid.

86. Cardaillac-Hermosilla, *La magie en Espagne*, pp. 92–93 and 172.

87. Bristol, *Christians, Blasphemers*, pp. 129–30.

88. AGN, Inq. vol. 38, f. 52r.

89. AGN, Inq. vol. 38, f. 88v. Marta and two others were sentenced to two hundred lashes. The midwife Ysabel de Morales, "la morilla partera," accused of curing the evil eye with her breath (*bostezos*) and rosemary incense (*sahumerios*) was ordered to be confined in a monastery for religious instruction. There is no indication that she was a Morisca, as the designation "morilla" most likely refers to her being the wife of a man named Alonso Morillo. However the cures she performed bear striking resemblance to those appearing in the aljamiado miscellanies.

90. AGN, Inq. vol. 38, f. 78v.

91. AGN, Inq. vol. 38, f. 79r.

92. Bristol, *Christians, Blasphemers*, pp. 156–64.

93. Gentilcore provides an excellent discussion of the sacramentalia offered by the church in order to heal the sick or exorcise plagues in chapter 4 of *From Bishop to Witch*.

94. García-Ballester, *Los moriscos y la medicina*, p. 97. He notes that the sickbed provided one of the sites at which old Christians and Moriscos came to define themselves.

95. AGN, Inq. vol. 303, f. 357r.

96. Ibid.

97. Ibid.

98. Ibid.

99. Don Francisco Núñez Muley's family also claimed descent from Granadan and Moroccan nobility, using the surname "de Fez" and the

Moroccan term of respect Muley/maula alongside the Spanish "Don." His nephew stated in a document, "[Soy] de linaje de los reyes de Fez y Marruecos . . . soy del linaje de los reyes." Quoted in Núñez Muley, *Memorandum*, p. 9.

100. AGN, Inq. vol. 303, f. 357v.

101. AGN, Inq. vol. 303, f. 359v. The term bocado refers to a life-threatening stomach illness that was believed to be caused by witchcraft.

102. AGN, Inq. vol. 303, f. 359v.

103. Claisse-Dauchy, *Médecine traditionnelle du Maghreb*, p. 53. She translates Tukal as "ce qui est donné à manger."

104. Moroccan fqihs would have filled similar social roles to the Morisco alfaquíes, as religious specialists who might have also performed cures.

105. Claisse-Dauchy discusses how practitioners, in classifying the curative properties of plants, consulted treatises on classical Arab medicine that were influenced by the writings of Galen, Hippocrates, Aristotle, and Dioscorides. Religious meanings became attached to plants as well, ascribing "virtues" to them that linked them to the spiritual world. Fqihs made small bags full of papers and leaves that bore Qur'anic verses associated with the names of plants. (p. 76 and p. 95) Interestingly, if the bundles were transported across the sea, they had to be baked inside bread, so the djinns in the sea water didn't kill them. (p. 109)

106. Cardaillac-Hermosilla, *La magie en Espagne*, p. 186.

107. Cardaillac-Hermosilla, *Los nombres del diablo*, p. 90.

108. AGN, Inq. vol. 303, f. 360r.

109. Ibid.

110. AGN, Inq. vol. 38, f. 93r.

111. AGN, Inq. vol. 38, f. 102v.

112. Ysabel de Morales's nickname is ambiguous. *Morilla partera* can be translated literally as "little Moorish midwife," but was also mentioned in the inquisitorial records as referring specifically to her husband's last name, Morales. *Morilla* therefore may have been an affectionate nickname, "little Morales."

113. Albarracín Navarro and Martínez Ruiz, *Medicina, farmacopea y magia*.

114. García Ballester, *Los moriscos y la medicina*, p. 127.

CHAPTER 7

1. See the introduction to Pedro Mexía de Ovando's *La Ovandina*, published in the series *Colección de libros y documentos referentes a la historia de América*. The only known copy of the original edition is held at the Real Academia de la Historia in Madrid. This was the copy sent by inquisitors in Lima to the Supreme Council of the Inquisition in Madrid for scrutiny, while the case was being reviewed. The remaining copies were ordered to be destroyed by the Inquisition of Lima.

2. AHN, Inq. leg. 4466, exp. 10.

3. Archivo Arzobispal de Lima (hereafter AAL), Causas Criminales, leg. 10, exp. 4, 4r. I would like to thank Peter Gose for making me aware of these sources.

4. AAL, Causas Criminales, leg. 10, exp. 4, 5v.

5. AAL, Causas Criminales, leg. 10, exp. 4, 5r. "hijodalgo notorio de executoria."

6. One of the witnesses is Juan Gómez Castellanos, who described the event on 7v–8r, and the other is Diego Guerra on 10v.

7. AAL, Causas Criminales, leg. 10, exp. 4, 11r.

8. AAL, Causas Criminales, leg. 10, exp. 4, 14r.

9. See Pike, *Linajudos and conversos in Seville*; also see, Sicroff, *Los estatutos de limpieza de sangre*.

10. Ann Twinam identifies a separation between public and private actions, and an individual's place within their community. During the eighteenth century, private practices or lineage did not always result in an individual's exclusion from "status in the public world of laws, reputation, and honor." Individuals could manipulate their status to a certain degree because the Crown was able to issue dispensations allowing someone without the required purity of blood to gain access to restricted occupations or positions. See Twinam, "Negotiation of Honor," p. 78. Also see Martínez, *Genealogical Fictions* and Rappaport, *Disappearing Mestizo*.

11. Sicroff, *Los estatutos de limpieza de sangre*, p. 302.

12. Pike, *Linajudos and Conversos in Seville*.

13. Sicroff, *Los estatutos de limpieza de sangre*, pp. 255–56.

14. Ibid., p. 245. Barbara Fuchs analyzes how Spain was also portrayed as a "Moorish nation" in *Exotic Nation*.

15. Sicroff, *Los estatutos de limpieza de sangre*, p. 278. Sicroff notes that in his *Defensa de los estatutos*, Friar Gerónimo de la Cruz wrote that Moriscos were so careful to intermarry, practice Islam and speak Arabic that, unlike the conversos, "en la expulsión huvo pocas dudas sobre lo que se avia de hazer de los hijos nacidos de mezcla de Moros y Christianos."

16. Sicroff, *Los estatutos de limpieza de sangre*, p. 237. Sicroff dates Salucio's *Discurso* to 1599, based on its mention of Philip II's attempts to reform the estatutos in the last years of his reign.

17. Sicroff, *Los estatutos de limpieza de sangre*, p. 230. "justamente se rezelaban que no eran christianos de veras, sino antes enemigos del nombre de Christo, al modo que ahora nos rezelamos de los moriscos."

18. Sicroff, *Los estatutos de limpieza de sangre*, p. 233.

19. Ibid., p. 230.

20. Tueller, *Good and Faithful Christians*, p. 21. Tueller contrasts these local, contemporary notions of what it meant to be a "good Christian" with the Tridentine ideal that a good Catholic "must not only know the doctrine, but also live and work out his own salvation through the Church's sacraments."

21. Tueller, *Good and Faithful Christians*, p. 59. Here Tueller refers to Diego Venegas who presented his petition on 31 January 1610.

22. Tueller, *Good and Faithful Christians*, p. 57.

23. Ibid., p. 85.

24. Ibid., p. 172.

25. Ibid., p. 160. According to Tueller, this letter was anonymous.

26. Ibid., p. 67.

27. Ibid., p. 170.

28. Ibid., p. 223.

29. Newberry, Ayer Ms. 1130, f. 1r. "la maior honrra que yo tengo y el maior blason de mi linpieça."

30. Ibid.

31. Newberry, Ayer Ms. 1130, ff. 17r–27r is a copy of the case heard by López de Mesa. It includes testimonies by Enríquez and Quintanilla that are almost identical to those that surface in Zavala's investigation. The most salient difference is that before Zavala, witnesses testify that Yrayzoz called Martínez a mestizo, whereas before López de Mesa, witnesses used the term coyote, which was also a casta category that implied indigenous descent, but more distant than mestizo. Other witnesses summoned by López de Mesa, who lived in the area, stated that they were not present during the conflict, so could not provide testimony.

32. Newberry, Ayer Ms. 1130, f. 17r.

33. Newberry, Ayer Ms. 1130, f. 5r. This is part of Friar Diego de San Joseph's testimony on 18 September 1629.

34. Newberry, Ayer Ms. 1130, f. 5r. "muy onrrados amigos."

35. Newberry, Ayer Ms. 1130, f. 6v.

36. Ibid.

37. Newberry, Ayer Ms. 1130, f. 11v.

38. Newberry, Ayer Ms. 1130, f. 10r.

39. Ibid.

40. Ibid.

41. Newberry, Ayer Ms. 1130, f. 16v.

42. Newberry, Ayer Ms. 1130, f. 16r. "me trato mal de palabra llamandome publicam[en]te de picaro, mestiço, y desvergonzado, en lo qual me agravio notablem[en]te por estar en aquella villa en buena y honrrada reputacion y ser como soy limpio de toda raza y hespañol de todas quatro abolengos." Here raza is used to refer to lineage, to not having Muslim or Jewish ancestors, rather than nineteenth- and twentieth-century understandings of "race."

43. Newberry, Ayer Ms. 1130, f. 16r.

44. Ibid.

45. Ibid.

46. Newberry, Ayer Ms. 1130, f. 16v.

47. Lavallé, *Las promesas ambiguas*, pp. 30–37.

48. I explore Diego Romero's case in depth in Cook, "'Moro de linaje y nación.'"

49. See Pike, *Linajudos and Conversos in Seville*.

50. Ignacio Avellaneda, *Conquerors of the New Kingdom*, p. 3. Avellaneda highlights six main expeditions, led by Gonzalo Jiménez de Quesada, Nikolaus Federmann, Sebastián de Belalcázar, Jerónimo Lebrón, Lope Montalvo de Lugo, and Alonso Luis de Lugo.

51. Francis, *Invading Colombia*, p. 7. Three-quarters of the eight hundred men who initially made up the expedition perished. The median age at death of the survivors was over sixty years.

52. Avellaneda, *Conquerors of the New Kingdom*, p. 78.

53. Lavallé, *Las promesas ambiguas*, pp. 30–37.

54. Avellaneda, *Conquerors of the New Kingdom*, p. 104.

55. Ibid., p. 119.

56. Ibid., p. 120.

57. Porro Gutiérrez, *Venero de Leiva*, pp. 12–13; Avellaneda, *Conquerors of the New Kingdom*, p. 121. Members of Alonso Luis de Lugo's expedition appear to have accepted the designation of "second conquerors;" see Avellaneda, *Conquerors of the New Kingdom*, p. 141. This also affected Romero, who claimed in his méritos y servicios to having obtained the encomiendas of Boza and Marcheta from Hernán Pérez, only to lose them in the redistribution of Luis de Lugo. See AGI, Patronato 154, N. 3, R. 1.

58. AGI, Justicia 509, N. 1, 2r. Letter to the Royal Council of the Indies in 1568.

59. Murdo J. MacLeod discusses the genre of méritos y servicios in "Self-Promotion."

60. AGI, Justicia 509, N. 1, 3r. "era y es xpiano biejo y de limpia generacion."

61. Avellaneda discusses Romero's méritos y servicios, dated 1561, in *Conquerors of the New Kingdom*, pp. 145–50. Avellaneda uses it in his discussion of signs of *hidalguía*, but does not mention that it surfaced in the context of the heated disputes over Romero's encomienda, in which Romero's status as an old Christian was at stake.

62. Avellaneda, *Conquerors of the New Kingdom*, p. 106.

63. Sanchiz Ochoa, "La conquista como plataforma de ascenso social," p. 85.

64. Avellaneda, *Conquerors of the New Kingdom*, p. 142.

65. Ibid., p. 143.

66. Sanchiz Ochoa, "La conquista como plataforma de ascenso social," p. 83.

67. Ibid., p. 82.

68. Avellaneda, *Conquerors of the New Kingdom*, pp. 119–22.

69. AGI, Patronato 154, N.3, R.1.

70. Ibid. " . . . muy adereçada y bien tratada como qualquier buen hijodalgo." On the association between nobility and military service, that included providing arms and horses, see Sanchiz Ochoa, "La conquista como plataforma de ascenso social," p. 88.

71. AGI, Justicia 509, N.1, 11r.

72. AGI, Justicia 509, N. 1, 15r.

73. AGI, Justicia 509, N. 1, 15v. "moro de linage y nacion."

74. AGI, Justicia 509, N. 1, f. 11r. " . . . en cassa del dho contador andar en abito de hombre de bien . . . "

75. AGI, Justicia 509, N. 1, f. 11v. The military governor of the Canary Islands was Pedro Fernández de Lugo who, in 1535, headed an expedition to the New Kingdom of Granada, stopping in Santa Marta. Gonzalo Jiménez de Quesada formed part of this expedition and is credited with leading subsequent expeditions to establish a Spanish settlement at Santa Fe and conquer parts of New Granada.

76. AGI, Justicia 509, N. 1, f. 11v.

77. AGI, Justicia 509, N. 1, ff. 28r–31v.

78. AGI, Justicia 509, N. 1, ff. 30v and 38v.

79. AGI, Justicia 509, N. 1, f. 80r.

80. AGI, Justicia 509, N. 1, f. 82r.

81. AGI, Justicia 509, N. 1, f. 84v.

82. AGI, Justicia 509, N. 1, ff. 90v–91r.

83. AGI, Justicia 509, N. 1, f. 94r.

84. Silverblatt, *Modern Inquisitions*, p. 6.

85. AHN, Inq. leg. 1640 exp. 3, n. 12, 17r. This document is the "Provy[si] on de la resolucion de la visita de la Inqui[sici]on del Peru q hizo el doctor Prado."

86. AHN, Inq. libro 1035, 34v.

87. AHN, Inq. libro 1035, 48v.

88. AHN, Inq. libro 1035, 34v.

89. AHN, Inq. leg. 2944, exp. 131, s/f.

90. Ibid.

91. Ibid.

92. AHN, Inq. libro 1035, 36r–v.

93. AHN, Inq. libro 1035, 36v.

94. AHN, Inq. leg. 1641, exp. 1, 141r–v.

95. AHN, Inq. leg. 1641, exp. 1, 321r. "muy allegado."

96. AHN, Inq. leg. 1641, exp. 3, 23v. Gutiérrez de Ulloa's response, presented to Ruiz de Prado in Lima, is dated 11 March 1591.

97. AHN, Inq. leg. 1641, exp. 3, 24r.

98. AHN, Inq. leg. 1641, exp. 3, 56v.

99. Altman, *Emigrants and Society*; Studnicki, *Nation Upon the Ocean Sea*.

100. AHN, Inq. leg. 1641, exp. 3, 611r.

101. AHN, Inq. leg. 1641, exp. 3, 615r.

102. On Morisca slaves marrying Spaniards, see Lockhart, *Spanish Peru*.

103. Quoted in Sicroff, *Los estatutos de limpieza de sangre*, p. 312.

104. AHN, Inq. leg. 4466, exp. 10. " . . . si toda ella es ynvencion/sacada de tu archibon/mezclando hidalgos de barro/cubriendolos con çamarro/y haciendolos del tuson." This reference is to the Spanish Order of the Golden Fleece. See Irigoyen-García, *Spanish Arcadia*.

105. AHN, Inq. leg. 4466, exp. 10. "No sabes que Oquendo dijo/ deste Piru las verdades/ y que en buenas puridades/ donde Pero Sanchez hizo/ y tu si por remedalles/ haces aquesos exçesos/ nobles de a çinq[en]ta pesos/ podremos muy bien llamarles."

106. Lavallé considers this to be an expression of protocreole nationalism; see *Las promesas ambiguas*.

107. Quoted in Lasarte, *Lima satirizada*, pp. 184–85.

108. AHN, Inq. leg. 4466, exp. 10, 6r.

109. AHN, Inq. leg. 4466, exp. 10, 5v.

110. AHN, Inq. leg. 4466, exp. 10, 5r.

111. AHN, Inq. leg. 4466, exp. 10, 2r.

112. AHN, Inq. leg. 4466, exp. 10, 2v.

113. Ibid.

114. BNE, Mss. 3249.

115. García-Arenal, "El entorno de los Plomos," p. 56. Linda Martz provides an excellent study of the challenges faced by converso families who attempted to incorporate themselves into the elite in Toledo. See *Network of Converso Families*.

116. Harris, *From Muslim to Christian Granada*, p. 47.

117. García-Arenal, "El entorno de los Plomos," p. 60. On Granada elites and their relationship to the city's past, see also Harris, *From Muslim to Christian Granada*, pp. 33–36.

118. García-Arenal, "El entorno de los Plomos," p. 61.

119. Coleman, *Creating Christian Granada*, pp. 41–43.

120. García-Arenal, "El entorno de los Plomos," pp. 69–70. Enrique Soria Mesa has studied this attempt by the Granada Venegas family. See his "Una versión genealógica," pp. 213–21. The *Origen de la Casa de Granada* also presents the actions that Don Pedro de Granada, also named before his conversion to Catholicism Cidi Yahya Alnayar and his son Don Alonso Venegas or Ali Omar ben Nazar. Cidi Yahya Alnayar aided the Crown in the fall of Baza as well as in defeating his brother-in-law, the king Zagal.

121. Soria Mesa, "Una versión genealógica," p. 216.

122. Ibid., p. 220.

123. García-Arenal, "El entorno de los Plomos," p. 70. Harris provides a detailed analysis of the urban patriciate's patronage of local writers and printers in *From Muslim to Christian Granada*, pp. 47–51.

124. García-Arenal, "El entorno de los Plomos," p. 73.

125. Cummins, "We Are the Other," pp. 208–9.

126. Ibid., p. 217.

CHAPTER 8

1. AHN, Diversos Colecciones, 25, N.12, 1r.

2. See Parker, *Grand Strategy of Philip II*. Irene Silverblatt explores the connection between extirpation of idolatry investigations and inquisitorial trials in *Modern Inquisitions*.

3. AGI, Justicia 1041, N.2, 1v.

4. AGI, Justicia 1041, N.2, 1v–2r.

5. AGI, Justicia 1041, N.2, 2v.

6. AGI, Justicia 1041, N.2, 6r.

7. AGI, Justicia 1041, N.2, 6r–v.

8. AGI, Justicia 1041, N.2, 7v.

9. See Haliczer, "Moriscos," and Hess, *Forgotten Frontier*.

10. De Benavente Motolinía, *Historia de los indios*. William B. Taylor analyzes the significance of the image of Santiago for the indigenous population of Mexico in "Santiago's Horse," pp. 153–89. On the moros y cristianos dances, see Harris, *Aztecs, Moors*; Bataillon, "Por un inventario," pp. 193–202.

11. Taboada, *La Sombra del Islam*.

12. Díaz del Castillo, *Historia verdadera*, p. 171.

13. See Wright, *Conquistadores Otomíes*; and a chronicle of the Guerra Chichimeca written by an indigenous participant, Francisco de Sandoval Acacictli, *Conquista y pacificación*.

14. Burkhart, *Slippery Earth*, p. 60.

15. Taylor, "Santiago's Horse," pp. 155–59; Harris, *Aztecs, Moors*, pp. 148–49.

16. BNE, Mss. 3044, "Relación de las fiestas q se hicieron en la ciudad del Cuzco por la nueva de la batalla naval," 111r.

17. BNE, Mss. 3044, 111r.

18. BNE, Mss. 3044, 111v.

19. BNE, Mss. 3044, 112r.

20. BNE, Mss. 3044, 113r.

21. Cummins, "Indulgent Image," p. 223. For a study of the Bull of the Santa Cruzada, see Goñi Gaztambide, *Historia de la Bula*.

22. Cummins, "Indulgent Image," pp. 224–25.

23. Juan Martínez de Ormachea printed his sermon in Lima in 1600. For a study of this sermon, see Itier, "Un sermón desconocido."

24. Alberto Carrillo Cázares develops this idea in *El debate sobre la Guerra Chichimeca*.

25. Ibid., pp. 33–34.

26. On representations of Ottomans, see Bisaha, *Creating East and West*; Meserve, *Empires of Islam*. Also see Pagden, *Fall of Natural Man*.

27. Carrillo Cázares, *El debate sobre la Guerra Chichimeca*, pp. 226–27.

28. The issue of indigenous peoples as protected vassals of the Crown is discussed by García Añoveros, *El pensamiento y los argumentos sobre la esclavitud*, pp. 213–14. The papal bull is cited in Carrillo Cázares, *El debate sobre la Guerra Chichimeca*, pp. 44–45.

29. Carrillo Cázares, *El debate sobre la Guerra Chichimeca*, p. 207.

30. Behar, "Visions of a Guachichil Witch," p. 116.

31. Carrillo Cázares, *El debate sobre la Guerra Chichimeca*, p. 220.

32. Ibid., pp. 236 and 283.

33. While the *Catálogo del Fondo Manuscrito Americano de la Real Biblioteca del Escorial* attributes this treatise to Gonzalo de Las Casas, a recent reading by Carrillo Cázares, upon comparing it to a copy at the Bibliothèque Nationale de Paris, has allowed him to attribute this work to Santa María and date it to 1575. See Campos y Fernández de Sevilla, *Catálogo del Fondo Manuscrito Americano*, pp. 328–33; Carrillo Cázares, *El debate sobre la Guerra Chichimeca*, p. 236.

34. Carrillo Cázares, *El debate sobre la Guerra Chichimeca*, p. 272.

35. *Tratado de los chichimecas de nueva España* (Biblioteca de El Escorial, MS K. III, 8), p. 392.

36. Covarrubias Orozco, *Tesoro*, p. 39.

37. Mármol Carvajal, *Descripción general de África*.

38. See Grafton, "José de Acosta," pp. 166–88; Lupher, *Romans in a New World*; Hartog, *Mirror of Herodotus*.

39. Acosta, *Historia natural y moral de las Indias*, p. 349. The reference to the alquible concerns the direction, toward Mecca, that Muslims and Moriscos were to turn following the ritual slaughter of an animal. See reference to an inquisitorial trial concerning Antón Polo and Luis Caminero, in Longás, *La Vida Religiosa*, fn. p. 266.

40. Acosta, *Historia*, p. 350. The zahor refers to the meal that is eaten after sunset during Ramadan, once the fast is broken. See Longás, *La Vida Religiosa*, pp. 223–26.

41. Acosta, *Historia*, p. 365.

42. *Tratado de los chichimecas de nueva España* (Biblioteca de El Escorial, MS K. III, 8), pp. 392–93.

43. Ibid., p. 417.

44. Ibid.

45. Ibid., p. 418.

46. Borah, *Silk Raising*, p. 46.

47. Ibid., p. 9.

48. Ibid., p. 52.

49. De Las Casas, *Arte Nuevo*, p. xliv.

50. Román Gutiérrez, *Sociedad y evangelización*, p. 382; and Carrillo Cázares, *El debate sobre la Guerra Chichimeca*, pp. 218–21.

51. AGI, Patronato 182, R.5, 1v.

52. AGI, Patronato 182, R.5, 2r. " . . . andaban echos Alarves siguiendo la guerra e caça . . . "

53. Ibid. " . . . andan como alarbes y salvajes sin tener lugar cierto . . . "

54. AGI, Patronato 182, R.5, 3r.

55. Mármol Carvajal, *Descripción general de África*, p. 411.

56. Ibid., p. 42r.

57. Ibid., p. 42v.

58. Ibid., p. 43r.

59. For more on Zorita, see the introductory article by Ahrndt, "Alonso de Zorita," pp. 17–53.

60. Alonso de Zorita, *Relación de la Nueva España*, p. 198.

61. On the books read by emigrants to Spanish America, see Leonard, *Books of the Brave*.

62. *Tratado de los chichimecas de nueva España* (Biblioteca de El Escorial, MS K. III, 8), pp. 395–97.

63. AGI, Patronato 182, R.5, 1v.

64. "De la instruction de la audiencia de Mexico doze de Iunio año de treynta que manda provean lo que convenga cerca de la costumbre que tienen los Indios de hazerse esclavos los unos a los otros," from *Cedulario Indiano Recopilado por Diego de Encinas*, vol. 4, p. 364.

65. *Cedulario Indiano Recopilado por Diego de Encinas*, vol. 4, p. 364.

66. The enslavement of Moriscos in Granada is discussed by Martín Casares, *La esclavitud en la Granada*; and Domínguez Ortiz and Vincent, *Historia de los moriscos*.

67. AGI, Patronato 182, R.5, 3r.

68. Manuel Barrios Aguilera discusses the Alpujarras rebellion and Morisco responses in *Granada Morisca*, p. 349.

69. Philip II's *Pragmática y Declaración sobre los Moriscos que fueron tomados por esclavos de edad de diez años y medio, y de las esclavas de nueue* [sic] *medio, del Reyno de Granada* is printed in Bauer Landauer, *Papeles de Mi Archivo*, p. 139.

70. Landauer, *Papeles de Mi Archivo*, p. 138.

71. *Tratado de los chichimecas de nueva España* (Biblioteca de El Escorial, MS K. III, 8), p. 417.

72. Archivo de la Catedral de Granada (ACG), Libro de Varios # 3, ff. 520r–520v.

73. ACG, Libro de Varios #3, f. 520r.

74. *Cedulario Indiano Recopilado por Diego de Encinas,* vol. IV, p. 361. On the *Requerimiento* as a legal protocol for conquest, see Seed, *Ceremonies of Possession.*

75. "De la instruction que el Emperador Don Carlos de gloriosa memoria dio al Marques del Valle en [26 junio 1523] . . . y se dio a Diego Velazquez año de diez y ocho para nuevos descubrimientos que manda pudiesse hazer guerra a los Indios, y poner los que tomaren por esclavos (1523)" and "Provision que manda que los Indios naturales de la nueva Espana no puedan ser esclavos ni herrados (1526)," pp. 361–62, in *Cedulario Indiano Recopilado por Diego de Encinas,* vol. IV.

76. Mármol Carvajal, *Historia del Rebelión y Castigo*, p. 8.

77. Ibid., p. 153.

78. Ibid.

79. Ibid.

80. Carrillo Cázares, *El debate sobre la Guerra Chichimeca*, p. 45.

81. Ibid., p. 46. The "Descargos del Virrey Don Antonio de Mendoza" during the visita of Licentiate Tello de Sandoval is cited in Pérez Bustamante, *Don Antonio de Mendoza*, pp. 162–63.

82. AGI, Santo Domingo 50, R.9, N.26, p. 2v.

83. AGI, Justicia 980, N.1, p. 60v.

84. AGI, Justicia 980, N.1, p. 6r. " . . . de los quales se sirben como moros hazen de los cristianos . . . "

85. BNE, Mss. 2010, 179v–180r.

86. BNE, Mss. 2010, 181r.

87. BNE, Mss. 10.646, 158r.

88. BNE, Mss. 10.646, 190v.

89. BNE, Mss. 10.646, 57r–v.

90. AGI, Justicia 1041, N.2, 57v.

91. AGI, Justicia 1041, N.2, 120r.

92. AGI, Mexico 19, N.28, p. 3v.

93. Benton, *Law and Colonial Cultures*, p. 81.

EPILOGUE

1. Appadurai, *Fear of Small Numbers.*

2. Appadurai defines predatory identities as "those identities whose social construction and mobilization require the extinction of other, proximate social categories, defined as threats to the very existence of some group, defined as a we" (see *Fear of Small Numbers*, p. 51). On the dynamics of Spain being understood or labeled in the sixteenth century as a "Moorish nation," see Fuchs, *Exotic Nation*.

3. On this issue, see Pomata, *Contracting a Cure*.

4. Coates, *Convicts and Orphans*; Pieroni, "Outcasts from the Kingdom," pp. 242–51.

5. Domínguez Ortiz, *Los judeoconversos en España y América*, pp. 136–37.

6. Ibid., p. 138. The original document is reproduced in Lewin, *El judío en la época colonial*.

7. Evidence from the Arquivo Nacional da Torre do Tombo in Lisbon suggests a few Moriscos were denounced for suspected continued practice of Islam in Brazil. One such case appears in the published *Primeira Visitação do Santo Ofício ás Partes do Brasil: Denunciações e Confissões de Pernambuco 1593–1595* (Recife: FUNDARPE, 1984), pp. 131–33. Finally, Brazilian slaves were not subject to the same restrictions as in Spain's territories, and Muslim Wolof slaves (Gelofes) were brought into Brazil until the nineteenth century. On this, see Reis, *Slave Rebellion in Brazil*.

8. For a comprehensive discussion of the relationship between "raza" and "casta," see Martínez, *Genealogical Fictions*; and Martínez, "Language, Genealogy," pp. 25–42. Also see Burns, "Unfixing Race."

BIBLIOGRAPHY

ARCHIVES

Archivo Arzobispal de Lima, Peru (AAL)
Archivo de la Catedral de Granada, Granada, Spain (ACG)
Archivo Histórico Nacional, Madrid, Spain (AHN)
Archivo General de Indias, Seville, Spain (AGI)
Archivo General de la Nación, Mexico City, Mexico (AGN)
Biblioteca de El Escorial, Spain
Biblioteca Nacional de España, Madrid, Spain (BNE)
Biblioteca Nacional del Peru, Lima, Peru
Henry E. Huntington Library, San Marino, CA
The John Carter Brown Library, Providence, RI
Newberry Library, Chicago, IL
Real Academia de la Historia, Madrid, Spain

PUBLISHED PRIMARY SOURCES

Acosta, José de. *Historia natural y moral de las Indias.* Madrid: Historia 16—Información y Revistas, S.A., 1987.

Adorno, Rolena, and Patrick Charles Pautz, eds. *Álvar Núñez Cabeza de Vaca: His Account, His Life, and the Expedition of Pánfilo de Narváez.* Lincoln: University of Nebraska Press, 1999.

Albarracín Navarro, Joaquina, and Juan Martínez Ruiz. *Medicina, farmacopea y magia en el 'Misceláneo de Salomón.'* Granada: Universidad de Granada, 1987.

Aznar Cardona, Pedro. *Expulsion justificada de los Moriscos españoles.* Huesca: Pedro Cabarte, 1612.

Bauer Landauer, Ignacio. *Papeles de Mi Archivo: Relaciones y Manuscritos (Moriscos).* Madrid: Editorial Ibero-Africano-Americano, 1923.

Cedulario Indiano Recopilado por Diego de Encinas, Oficial Mayor de la Escribanía de Cámara del Consejo Supremo y Real de las Indias. Madrid: Ediciones Cultura Hispánica, 1945–46.

Ciruelo, Pedro. *Reprouacion de las supersticiones y hechizerias.* Vol. 1. Valencia: Ediciones Albatros Hispanofila, 1978.

Colección de libros y documentos referentes a la historia de América. XVII. Madrid: Imprenta Clásica Española, 1915.

Covarrubias Orozco, Sebastián de. *Tesoro de la Lengua Castellana o Española [1611].* Madrid: Editorial Castalia, 1994.

Del Río, Martín. *Investigations into Magic.* Ed. and trans. P. G. Maxwell-Stuart. New York: Manchester University Press, 2000.

Díaz del Castillo, Bernal. *Historia verdadera de la conquista de la Nueva España.* Madrid: n.p., 1632.

Dorantes de Carranza, Baltasar. *Sumaria Relación de las Cosas de la Nueva España.* Mexico City: Imprenta del Museo Nacional, 1902.

El Manuscrito Misceláneo 774 de la Biblioteca Nacional de París (Leyendas, itinerarios de viajes, profecías sobre la destrucción de España y otros relatos moriscos). Ed. Mercedes Sánchez Álvarez. Madrid: Editorial Gredos, S.A., 1982.

García-Arenal, Mercedes. *Los Moriscos.* Granada: Universidad de Granada, 1996.

Labarta, Ana. *Libro de Dichos Maravillosos: (Misceláneo Morisco de Magia y Adivinación).* Madrid: CSIC, 1993.

Las Casas, Bartolomé de. *Brevísima relación de la destrucción de las Indias.* Madrid: Catedra, 2006.

Las Casas, Gonzalo de. *Arte Nuevo Para Criar Seda [1581].* Granada: Universidad de Granada, 1996.

Mármol Carvajal, Luis del. *Descripción general de África (1573–1599).* Madrid: Consejo Superior de Investigaciones Científicas, 1953.

———. *Historia del Rebelión y Castigo de los Moriscos del Reino de Granada.* Málaga: Editorial Arguval, 1991.

Morga, Antonio de. *Sucesos de las Islas Filipinas.* Mexico: En casa de Geronymo Balli, 1609.

Motolinía, Fray Toribio de Benavente. *Historia de los indios de la Nueva España [1541].* Madrid: Alianza Editorial, 1988.

Münzer, Jerónimo. *Viaje por España y Portugal (1494–1495).* Madrid: Ediciones Polifemo, 1991.

Núñez Muley, Francisco. *A Memorandum for the President of the Royal Audiencia and Chancery Court of the City and Kingdom of Granada.* Ed. Vincent Barletta. Chicago: University of Chicago Press, 2007.

Pigafetta, Antonio. *Magellan's Voyage: A Narrative Account of the First Circumnavigation.* New York: Dover Publications, 1994.

Primeira Visitação do Santo Ofício ás Partes do Brasil: Denunciações e Confissões de Pernambuco 1593–1595. Recife: FUNDARPE, 1984.

Ruiz de Alarcón, Hernando. *Treatise on the Heathen Superstitions That Today Live Among the Indians Native to This New Spain, 1629.* Norman: University of Oklahoma Press, 1984.

Ruiz de Alarcón, Juan. *Quien Mal Anda En Mal Acaba.* Kassel: Edition Reichenberger, 1993.

Sandoval Acacictli, Francisco de. *Conquista y pacificación de los indios chichimecas.* Mexico: El Colegio de Jalisco, 1996.

Tello, Antonio. *Libro segundo de la cronica miscelanea en que se trata de la conquista espiritual y temporal de la Santa Provincia de Xalisco.* Guadalajara: Impr. de "La República Literaria" de C. L. de Guevara, 1891.

Valencia, Pedro de. *Tratado acerca de los moriscos de España.* Málaga: Editorial Algazara, 1997.

Varela, Consuelo, ed. *Cristóbal Colón: Los cuatro viajes. Testamento.* Madrid: Alianza Editorial, 1992.

Varey, Simon, ed. *The Mexican Treasury: The Writings of Dr. Francisco Hernández.* Stanford, CA: Stanford University Press, 2000.

Zorita, Alonso de. *Relación de la Nueva España.* Mexico City: CONACULTA, 1999.

SECONDARY SOURCES

Adorno, Rolena. *The Polemics of Possession in Spanish American Narrative.* New Haven, CT: Yale University Press, 2008.

Aguirre Beltrán, Gonzalo. *Medicina y magia: El proceso de aculturación en la estructura colonial.* Mexico City: Fondo de Cultura Económica, 1992.

Ahrndt, Wiebke. "Alonso de Zorita: Un funcionario colonial de la corona española." In *Relación de la Nueva España,* by Alonso de Zorita, 17–53. Mexico City: CONACULTA, 1999.

Aiton, Arthur Scott. *Antonio de Mendoza: First Viceroy of New Spain.* Durham, NC: Duke University Press, 1927.

Alberro, Solange. "Crypto-Jews and the Mexican Holy Office in the Seventeenth Century." In *The Jews and the Expansion of Europe to the West, 1450–1800,* ed. Paolo Bernardini and Norman Fiering, 172–85. New York: Berghahn Books, 2001.

———. *Inquisition et société au Mexique, 1571–1700.* Mexico City: Centre d'études mexicaines et centraméricaines, 1988.

Altman, Ida. *Emigrants and Society: Extremadura and America in the Six-teenth Century.* Berkeley: University of California Press, 1989.

———. *The War for Mexico's West: Indians and Spaniards in New Galicia, 1524–1550.* Albuquerque: University of New Mexico Press, 2010.

Alvarado Planas, Javier. "La polémica de los justos títulos en la iconografía americana." In *Observation and Communication: The Construction of Realities in the Hispanic World,* ed. Johannes-Michael Scholz and Tamar Herzog, 219–51. Frankfurt: Klostermann, 1997.

Álvarez de Morales, Camilo. "Elementos mágicos y religiosos en la medicina andalusí." *Ilu. Revista de Ciencias de las Religiones,* Anejos, XVI (2006): 23–46.

Andezian, Sossie. "Maghreb." In *La culte des saints dans le monde musul-man,* ed. Henri Chambert-Loir and Claude Guillot, 97–118. Paris: École française d'Extrême-Orient, 1995.

Andrews, Kenneth R. *The Spanish Caribbean, Trade and Plunder, 1530–1630.* New Haven, CT: Yale University Press, 1978.

Appadurai, Arjun. *Fear of Small Numbers: An Essay on the Geography of Anger.* Durham, NC: Duke University Press, 2006.

Aranda Doncel, Juan. "Las prácticas musulmanas de los moriscos andaluces a través de las relaciones de causas del tribunal de la inquisición de Cór-doba." In *Las prácticas musulmanas de los moriscos andaluces (1492–1609),* ed. Abdeljelil Temimi, 11–26. Zaghouan: CEROMDI, 1989.

Avellaneda, José Ignacio. *The Conquerors of the New Kingdom of Granada.* Albuquerque: University of New Mexico Press, 1995.

Barrios Aguilera, Manuel. *Granada Morisca, La Convivencia Negada.* Granada: Editorial Comares, 2002.

———. "Religiosidad y vida cotidiana de los moriscos." In *Historia del Reino de Granada: La época morisca y la repoblación (1502–1630),* ed. Manuel Barrios Aguilera and Rafael G. Peinado Santaella, 357–433. Granada: Universidad de Granada, 2000.

Barrios Aguilera, Manuel, and Valeriano Sánchez Ramos. *Martirios y men-talidad martirial en las Alpujarras (De la rebelión morisca a las Actas de Ugíjar).* Granada: Universidad de Granada, 2001.

Bataillon, Marcel. "Por un inventario de las fiestas de moros y cristianos: Otro toque de atención." In *La colonia: Ensayos peruanistas,* compiled by Dr. Alberto Tauro, 193–202. Lima: Universidad Nacional Mayor San Marcos, 1995.

Behar, Ruth. "Sexual Witchcraft, Colonialism, and Women's Powers: Views from the Mexican Inquisition." In *Sexuality and Marriage in Colonial Latin America,* ed. Asunción Lavrin, 178–206. Lincoln: University of Nebraska Press, 1989.

———. "The Visions of a Guachichil Witch in 1599: A Window on the Subjugation of Mexico's Hunter-Gatherers." *Ethnohistory* 34.2 (spring 1987): 115–38.

Bennassar, Bartolomé, and Lucile Bennassar. *Los cristianos de Alá*. Madrid: Editorial Nerea, S.A., 2001.

Bennett, Judith M. *History Matters: Patriarchy and the Challenge of Feminism*. Philadephia: University of Pennsylvania Press, 2006.

Benton, Lauren A. *Law and Colonial Cultures: Legal Regimes in World History, 1400–1900*. New York: Cambridge University Press, 2002.

Bisaha, Nancy. *Creating East and West: Renaissance Humanists and the Ottoman Turks*. Philadelphia: University of Pennsylvania Press, 2004.

Blumenthal, Debra. *Enemies and Familiars: Slavery and Mastery in Fifteenth-Century Valencia*. Ithaca, NY: Cornell University Press, 2009.

Boeglin, Michel. "Between Rumor and Resistance: The Andalucían Morisco 'Uprising' of 1580." In *The Conversos and Moriscos in Late Medieval Spain and Beyond. Volume One: Departures and Change*, ed. Kevin Ingram, 211–42. Leiden: Brill, 2009.

———. *Entre la cruz y el Corán. Los moriscos en Sevilla (1570–1613)*. Seville: Ayuntamiento de Sevilla, 2010.

Bohm, Günter. "Crypto-Jews and New Christians in Colonial Peru and Chile." In *The Jews and the Expansion of Europe to the West, 1450–1800*, ed. Paolo Bernardini and Norman Fiering, 203–12. New York: Berghahn Books, 2001.

Bokser Liwerant, Judit, and Alicia Gojman de Backal, eds. *Encuentro y alteridad: Vida y cultura judía en América Latina*. Mexico City: Fondo de Cultura Económica, 1999.

Borah, Woodrow. *Silk Raising in Colonial Mexico*. Berkeley: University of California Press, 1943.

Borja Medina, Francisco de. "La compañía de Jesús y la minoría morisca (1545–1614)." *Archivum Historicum Societatis Iesu* 57 (1988): 3–136.

Bowers, Kristy Wilson. *Plague and Public Health in Early Modern Seville*. Rochester, NY: Rochester University Press, 2013.

Braude, Benjamin. "The Sons of Noah and the Construction of Ethnic and Geographical Identities in the Medieval and Early Modern Periods." *The William and Mary Quarterly* 54.1 (January 1997): 103–42.

Braudel, Fernand. *The Mediterranean and the Mediterranean World in the Age of Philip II*. New York: Harper & Row, 1972–73.

Bristol, Joan Cameron. *Christians, Blasphemers, and Witches: Afro-Mexican Ritual Practice in the Seventeenth Century*. Albuquerque: University of New Mexico Press, 2007.

Burkhart, Louise. *The Slippery Earth: Nahua-Christian Moral Dialogue in Sixteenth-Century Mexico*. Tucson: University of Arizona Press, 1989.

Burns, Kathryn. "Unfixing Race." In *Rereading the Black Legend: The Discourses of Religious and Racial Difference in the Renaissance Empires*, ed. Margaret R. Greer, Walter D. Mignolo, and Maureen Quilligan, 188–202. Chicago: University of Chicago Press, 2007.

Cáceres Enríquez, Jaime. "La mujer morisca o esclava blanca en el Peru del siglo XVI." *Sharq al-Andalus, Estudios Árabes: Anales de la Universidad de Alicante* 12 (1995): 565–74.

Campos Díez, María Soledad. *El real tribunal del Protomedicato Castellano (siglos XIV–XIX)*. Cuenca: Ediciones de la Universidad de Castilla-La Mancha, 1999.

Campos y Fernández de Sevilla, F.-Javier. *Catálogo del Fondo Manuscrito Americano de la Real Biblioteca del Escorial*. San Lorenzo de El Escorial: Ediciones Escurialenses, 1993.

Cañeque, Alejandro. *The King's Living Image: The Culture and Politics of Viceregal Power in Colonial Mexico*. New York: Routledge, 2004.

Cardaillac, Louis. *Moriscos y cristianos: Un enfrentamiento polémico (1492–1640)*. Madrid: Fondo de Cultura Económica, 1979.

———. "Le problème morisque en Amérique." In *Mélanges de la Casa Velázquez*, vol. 12, 283–303. Paris: Éditions de Boccard, 1976.

Cardaillac-Hermosilla, Yvette. *La magie en Espagne: Morisques et vieux chrétiens aux XVIe et XVIIe siècles*. Zaghouan: FTERSI, 1996.

———. *Los nombres del diablo. Ensayo sobre la magia, la religión y la vida de los últimos musulmanes de España: Los moriscos*. Granada: Editorial Universidad de Granada, 2005.

Carrillo Cázares, Alberto. *El debate sobre la Guerra Chichimeca, 1531–1585: Derecho y política en la Nueva España*. Zamora: El Colegio de Michoacán, A. C., 2000.

Castañeda Delgado, Paulino, and Pilar Hernández Aparicio. *La Inquisición de Lima*. Madrid: Deimos, 1989.

Catlos, Brian A. *The Victors and the Vanquished: Christians and Muslims of Catalonia and Aragon, 1050–1300*. New York: Cambridge University Press, 2004.

Childers, William. "Manzanares, 1600: Moriscos from Granada Organize a Festival of 'Moors and Christians.'" In *The Conversos and Moriscos in Late Medieval Spain and Beyond. Volume One: Departures and Change*, ed. Kevin Ingram, 287–306. Leiden: Brill, 2009.

Cirac Estopañán, Sebastián. *Los procesos de hechicerías en la Inquisición de Castilla la Nueva (Tribunales de Toledo y Cuenca)*. Madrid: Diana, 1942.

Çirakman, Asli. *From the "Terror of the World" to the "Sick Man of Europe": European Images of Ottoman Empire and Society from the Sixteenth Century to the Nineteenth*. New York: Peter Lang, 2002.

Claisse-Dauchy, Renée. *Médecine traditionnelle du Maghreb: Rituels d'envoûtement et de guérison au Maroc*. Paris: Éditions L'Harmattan, 1996.

Clendinnen, Inga. *Ambivalent Conquests: Maya and Spaniard in Yucatan, 1517–1570*. New York: Cambridge University Press, 1987.

Coates, Timothy J. *Convicts and Orphans: Forced and State-Sponsored Colonizers in the Portuguese Empire, 1550–1755*. Stanford, CA: Stanford University Press, 2001.

Coleman, David. *Creating Christian Granada: Society and Religious Culture in an Old-World Frontier City, 1492–1600*. Ithaca, NY: Cornell University Press, 2003.

Cook, Karoline P. "'Moro de linaje y nación': Religious Identity, Race, and Status in New Granada." In *Race and Blood in the Iberian World*, ed. Max Hering Torres, María Elena Martínez, and David Nirenberg, 81–97. Berlin: LIT VERLAG, 2012.

———. "Muslims and the Chichimeca in New Spain: The Debates over Just War and Slavery." *Anuario de Estudios Americanos* 70.1 (June 2013): 15–38.

———. "Navigating Identities: The Case of a Morisco Slave in Seventeenth-Century New Spain." *The Americas* 65.1 (July 2008): 63–79.

———. "'De los Prohibidos': Muslims and Moriscos in Colonial Spanish America." In *Crescent Over Another Horizon: Islam in Latin America, the Caribbean, and Latino USA*, ed. María del Mar Logroño Narbona, Paulo G. Pinto, and John Tofik Karam, 25–45. Austin: University of Texas Press, 2015.

Cook, Noble David, with Alexandra Parma Cook. *People of the Volcano: Andean Counterpoint in the Colca Valley of Peru*. Durham, NC: Duke University Press, 2007.

Cummins, Thomas B. F. "The Indulgent Image: Prints in the New World." In *Contested Visions in the Spanish Colonial World*, ed. Ilona Katzew, 203–25. New Haven and Los Angeles: Yale University Press and the Los Angeles County Museum of Art, 2011.

———. "We Are the Other: Peruvian Portraits of Colonial *Kurakakuna*." In *Transatlantic Encounters: Europeans and Andeans in the Sixteenth Century*, ed. Kenneth J. Andrien and Rolena Adorno, 203–31. Berkeley: University of California Press, 1991.

Daston, Lorraine, and Fernando Vidal, eds. *The Moral Authority of Nature*. Chicago: University of Chicago Press, 2004.

De la Fuente, Alejandro. *Havana and the Atlantic in the Sixteenth Century*. Chapel Hill: University of North Carolina Press, 2008.

Diouf, Sylviane A. *Servants of Allah: African Muslims Enslaved in the Americas*. New York: New York University Press, 1998.

Domínguez Ortiz, Antonio. *Los judeoconversos en España y América.* Madrid: ISTMO, 1988.

Domínguez Ortiz, Antonio, and Bernard Vincent. *Historia de los moriscos: Vida y tragedia de una minoría.* Madrid: Alianza Editorial, 2003.

Doutté, Edmond. *Magie et religion dans l'Afrique du Nord.* Paris: Maisonneuve, 1984.

Ehlers, Benjamin. *Between Christians and Moriscos: Juan de Ribera and Religious Reform in Valencia, 1568–1614.* Baltimore, MD: Johns Hopkins University Press, 2006.

Eliav-Feldon, Miriam, Benjamin Isaac, and Joseph Ziegler, eds. *The Origins of Racism in the West.* New York: Cambridge University Press, 2009.

Epalza, Míkel de. *Jesús entre judíos, cristianos y musulmanes hispanos (siglos VI–XVII).* Granada: Universidad de Granada, 1999.

———. *Los moriscos antes y después de la expulsión.* Madrid: Editorial MAPFRE, 1992.

Fajardo Spínola, Francisco. *Las Víctimas del Santo Oficio: Tres siglos de actividad de la Inquisición de Canarias.* Las Palmas de Gran Canaria: Fundación de Enseñanza Superior a Distancia, 2003.

Feliciano Chaves, María Judith. Mudejarismo in its Colonial Context: Iberian Cultural Display, Viceregal Luxury Consumption, and the Negotiation of Identities in Sixteenth-Century New Spain. PhD dissertation, University of Pennsylvania, 2004.

Fernández-Armesto, Felipe. *The Canary Islands After the Conquest: The Making of a Colonial Society in the Early Sixteenth Century.* New York: Oxford University Press, 1982.

Few, Martha. *Women Who Live Evil Lives: Gender, Religion, and the Politics of Power in Colonial Guatemala.* Austin: University of Texas Press, 2002.

Fisher, Andrew, and Matthew D. O'Hara, eds. *Imperial Subjects: Race and Identity in Colonial Latin America.* Durham, NC: Duke University Press, 2009.

Flint, Valerie I. J. *The Rise of Magic in Early Medieval Europe.* Princeton, NJ: Princeton University Press, 1991.

Francis, J. Michael. *Invading Colombia: Spanish Accounts of the Gonzalo Jiménez de Quesada Expedition of Conquest.* University Park: Pennsylvania State University Press, 2007.

Fuchs, Barbara. *Exotic Nation: Maurophilia and the Construction of Early Modern Spain.* Philadelphia: University of Pennsylvania Press, 2011.

———. *Mimesis and Empire: The New World, Islam, and European Identities.* New York: Cambridge University Press, 2001.

Gallego Burín, Antonio, and Alfonso Gámir Sandoval. *Los Moriscos del reino de Granada según el sínodo de Guadix de 1554.* Granada: Universidad de Granada, 1996.

García Añoveros, Jesús María. *El pensamiento y los argumentos sobre la esclavitud en Europa en el siglo XVI y su aplicación a los indios americanos y a los negros africanos.* Madrid: Consejo Superior de Investigaciones Científicas, 2000.

García-Arenal, Mercedes. "El entorno de los Plomos: historiografía y linaje." In *Los Plomos del Sacromonte: Invención y tesoro,* ed. Manuel Barrios Aguilera and Mercedes García-Arenal, 51–78. Valencia: Publicacions de la Universitat de València, 2006.

———. *Inquisición y moriscos: Los procesos del tribunal de Cuenca.* Madrid: Siglo Veintiuno Editores, 1978.

———. "Moriscos e indios: Para un estudio comparado de métodos de conquista y evangelización." *Chronica nova* 20 (1992): 153–75.

———. "El problema morisco: Propuestas de discusión." *al-Qantara* 13.1 (1992): 491–503.

———. "Últimos estudios sobre moriscos: Estado de la cuestión." *al-Qantara* 4 (1983): 101–14.

García-Arenal, Mercedes, and Fernando Rodríguez Mediano. *Un Oriente español: Los moriscos y el Sacromonte en tiempos de Contrarreforma.* Madrid: Marcial Pons Historia, 2010.

García Ballester, Luis. "The Inquisition and Minority Medical Practitioners in Counter-Reformation Spain: Judaizing and Morisco Practitioners, 1560–1610." In *Medicine and the Reformation,* ed. Ole Peter Grell and Andrew Cunningham, 156–91. New York: Routledge, 1993.

———. *Los moriscos y la medicina: Un capítulo de la medicina y la ciencia marginadas en la España del siglo XVI.* Barcelona: Labor Universitaria, 1984.

Garofalo, Leo J. "Conjuring with Coca and the Inca: The Andeanization of Lima's Afro-Peruvian Ritual Specialists, 1580–1690." *The Americas* 63.1 (July 2006): 53–80.

Garrido Aranda, Antonio. "El Morisco y la Inquisición Novohispana (Actitudes Antiislamicas en la Sociedad Colonial)." In *Andalucía y América en el siglo XVI: Actas de las II jornadas de Andalucía y América,* 501–33. Seville: Escuela de Estudios Hispano-Americanos, 1983.

———. *Moriscos e indios: precedentes hispánicos de la evangelización en México.* Mexico City: Universidad Nacional Autónoma de México, 1980.

Geertz, Hildred. "An Anthropology of Religion and Magic, I." *Journal of Interdisciplinary History* 6.1 (summer 1975): 71–89.

Gentilcore, David. *From Bishop to Witch: The System of the Sacred in Early Modern Terra d'Otranto.* New York: Manchester University Press, 1992.

———. *Healers and Healing in Early Modern Italy*. New York: St. Martin's Press, 1998.

———. *Medical Charlatanism in Early Modern Italy*. Oxford: Oxford University Press, 2006.

Gojman Goldberg, Alicia. *Los conversos en la Nueva España*. Mexico City: Universidad Nacional Autónoma de México, 1984.

González Rodríguez, Alberto. *Hornachos, enclave morisco: Peculiaridades de una población distinta*. Mérida: Asanblea de Extremadura Publicaciones, 1990.

Goodman, Jennifer R. *Chivalry and Exploration, 1298–1630*. Rochester: Boydell Press, 1998.

Goñi Gaztambide, José. *Historia de la Bula de la Cruzada en España*. Vitoria: Editorial del Seminario, 1958.

Grafton, Anthony. "José de Acosta: Renaissance Historiography and New World Humanity." In *The Renaissance World*, ed. John Jeffries Martin, 166–88. New York: Routledge, 2007.

Graizbord, David. *Souls in Dispute: Converso Identities in Iberia and the Jewish Diaspora, 1580–1700*. Philadelphia: University of Pennsylvania Press, 2003.

Graubart, Karen. "The Creolization of the New World: Local Forms of Identification in Urban Colonial Peru, 1560–1640." *Hispanic American Historical Review* 89.3 (2009): 471–99.

Greenleaf, Richard E. *The Mexican Inquisition of the Sixteenth Century*. Albuquerque: University of New Mexico Press, 1969.

Halevy, Schulamith C., and Nachum Dershowitz. "Prácticas Ocultas de los 'Anusim' del Nuevo Mundo." In *Encuentro y alteridad: Vida y cultura judía en América Latina*, ed. Judit Bokser Liwerant and Alicia Gojman de Backal, 35–46. Mexico City: Fondo de Cultura Económica, 1999.

Haliczer, Stephen. "The Moriscos: Loyal Subjects of His Catholic Majesty Phillip II." In *Christians, Muslims and Jews in Medieval and Early Modern Spain: Interaction and Cultural Change*, ed. Mark D. Meyerson and Edward D. English, 265–73. Notre Dame: University of Notre Dame Press, 1999.

Hanke, Lewis. *All Mankind Is One: A Study of the Disputation Between Bartolomé de las Casas and Juan Ginés de Sepúlveda in 1550 on the Intellectual and Religious Capacity of the American Indians*. DeKalb: Northern Illinois University Press, 1974.

———. *The Spanish Struggle for Justice in the Conquest of America*. Dallas, TX: Southern Methodist University Press, 2002.

Harris, A. Katie. *From Muslim to Christian Granada: Inventing a City's Past in Early Modern Spain*. Baltimore, MD: Johns Hopkins University Press, 2007.

Harris, Max. *Aztecs, Moors, and Christians: Festivals of Reconquest in Mexico and Spain*. Austin: University of Texas Press, 2000.

Hartog, François. *The Mirror of Herodotus: The Representation of the Other in the Writing of History*. Berkeley: University of California Press, 1988.

Harvey, L. P. *Muslims in Spain, 1500–1614*. Chicago: University of Chicago Press, 2005.

Hering Torres, Max, María Elena Martínez, and David Nirenberg, eds. *Race and Blood in the Iberian World*. Berlin: LIT VERLAG, 2012.

Hering Torres, Max S. "Color, pureza, raza: la calidad de los sujetos colonials." In *La Cuestión Colonial*, ed. Heraclio Bonilla, 451–70. Bogotá: Universidad Nacional de Colombia, 2011.

Herzog, Tamar. *Defining Nations: Immigrants and Citizens in Early Modern Spain and Spanish America*. New Haven, CT: Yale University Press, 2003.

Hess, Andrew C. *The Forgotten Frontier: A History of the Sixteenth-Century Ibero-African Frontier*. Chicago: University of Chicago Press, 1978.

———. "An Ottoman Fifth Column in Sixteenth-Century Spain." *American Historical Review* 74 (October 1968): 1–25.

Ingram, Kevin, ed. *The Conversos and Moriscos in Late Medieval Spain and Beyond. Volume One: Departures and Change*. Leiden: Brill, 2009.

Irigoyen-García, Javier. *The Spanish Arcadia: Sheep Herding, Pastoral Discourse, and Ethnicity in Early Modern Spain*. Toronto: University of Toronto Press, 2013.

Itier, César. "Un sermón desconocido en quechua general: La 'plática que se ha de hazer a los indios en la predicación de la Bulla de la Santa Cruzada' (1600)." *Revista andina* 10.1 (1992): 135–46.

Jacobs, Auke P. "Legal and Illegal Emigration from Seville, 1550–1650." In *"To Make America": European Emigration in the Early Modern Period*, ed. Ida Altman and James Horn, 59–84. Berkeley: University of California Press, 1991.

———. *Los movimientos migratorios entre Castilla e Hispanoamérica durante el reinado de Felipe III, 1598–1621*. Amsterdam: Editions Rodopi, B.V., 1995.

Kagan, Richard L. *Clio and the Crown: The Politics of History in Medieval and Early Modern Spain*. Baltimore, MD: Johns Hopkins University Press, 2009.

———. *Urban Images of the Hispanic World, 1493–1793*. New Haven, CT: Yale University Press, 2000.

Kantorowicz, Ernst Hartwig. *The King's Two Bodies: A Study in Medieval Political Theology*. Princeton, NJ: Princeton University Press, 1957.

Karamustafa, Ahmet T. *God's Unruly Friends: Dervish Groups in the Islamic Middle Period, 1200–1550*. London: Oneworld Publications, 2006.

Katzew, Ilona, and Susan Deans-Smith, eds. *Race and Classification: The Case of Mexican America*. Stanford, CA: Stanford University Press, 2009.

Kennedy, Michael V., and Christine Daniels, eds. *Negotiated Empires: Centers and Peripheries in the Americas, 1500–1820*. New York: Taylor & Francis, 2002.

Kieckhefer, Richard. *Forbidden Rites: A Necromancer's Manual of the Fifteenth Century*. Gloucestershire: Sutton Publishing, 1997.

———. *Magic in the Middle Ages*. New York: Cambridge University Press, 1990.

———. "The Specific Rationality of Medieval Magic." *American Historical Review* 99 (1994): 813–36.

Kinder, A. Gordon. "Religious Literature as an Offensive Weapon: Cipriano de Valera's Part in England's War with Spain." *The Sixteenth Century Journal* 19.2 (summer 1988): 223–35.

Ladero Quesada, Miguel Ángel. *Granada después de la conquista: Repobladores y mudéjares*. Granada: Diputación Provincial de Granada, 1993.

Lamoreaux, J. C. *The Early Muslim Tradition of Dream Interpretation*. New York: State University of New York Press, 2002.

Lane, Kris E. *Pillaging the Empire: Piracy in the Americas, 1500–1750*. New York: M. E. Sharpe, 1998.

Lasarte, Pedro. *Lima satirizada (1598–1698): Mateo Rosas de Oquendo y Juan del Valle y Caviedes*. Lima: PUCP, 2006.

Lavallé, Bernard. *Las promesas ambiguas: Ensayos sobre el criollismo colonial en los Andes*. Lima: PUCP, 1993.

Le Gall, Dina. *A Culture of Sufism: Naqshbandīs in the Ottoman World, 1450–1700*. Albany: State University of New York Press, 2005.

Leonard, Irving A. *Books of the Brave: Being an Account of Books and of Men in the Spanish Conquest and Settlement of the Sixteenth-Century New World*. Berkeley: University of California Press, 1992.

Lewin, Boleslao. *El judío en la época colonial. Un aspecto de la historia rioplatense*. Buenos Aires: Colegio Libre de Estudios Superiores, 1939.

Lewis, Laura A. *Hall of Mirrors: Power, Witchcraft, and Caste in Colonial Mexico*. Durham, NC: Duke University Press, 2003.

Lockhart, James. *The Men of Cajamarca: A Social and Biographical Study of the First Conquerors of Peru*. Austin: University of Texas Press, 1972.

———. *Spanish Peru, 1532–1560: A Colonial Society*. Madison: University of Wisconsin Press, 1968.

Longás, Pedro. *La Vida Religiosa de Los Moriscos*. Ed. Darío Cabanelas. Granada: Universidad de Granada, 1990.

López-Baralt, Luce. "El conjuro mágico de Salomón a la Alhabiba." In *Mélanges Louis Cardaillac*, vol. 1, ed. Abdeljelil Temimi, 431–43. Zaghouan: FTERSI, 1995.

López-Baralt, Luce, and Josué Caamaño. "Un Morisco Puertorriqueño, médico y alcalde de San Juan de Puerto Rico, en pleitos con Juan Ponce de León II." In *Morisques, Mediteranée et Manuscrits aljamiados. Actes du Xe Congrès International d'Études Morisques*, ed. Abdeljelil Temimi, 93–109. Zaghouan: FTERSI, 2003.

Lunde, Paul. "A Muslim History of the New World." *Aramco World* 43.3 (1992): 26–31.

Lupher, David A. *Romans in a New World: Classical Models in Sixteenth-Century Spanish America*. Ann Arbor: University of Michigan Press, 2003.

MacCormack, Sabine. *On the Wings of Time: Rome, the Incas, Spain, and Peru*. Princeton, NJ: Princeton University Press, 2007.

———. *Religion in the Andes: Vision and Imagination in Early Colonial Peru*. Princeton, NJ: Princeton University Press, 1991.

MacLeod, Murdo J. "Self-Promotion: The *Relaciones de Méritos y Servicios* and Their Historical and Political Interpretation." *Colonial Latin American Historical Review* (winter 1998): 25–42.

Magnier, Grace. *Pedro de Valencia and the Catholic Apologists of the Expulsion of the Moriscos: Visions of Christianity and Kingship*. Leiden: Brill, 2010.

Mami, Ridha. "Los milagros del profeta Mahoma en algunos manuscritos moriscos." In *Mélanges Louis Cardaillac*, vol. 1, ed. Abdeljelil Temimi, 457–64. Zaghouan: FTERSI, 1995.

Manrique, Nelson. *Llegaron los sarracenos: El universo mental de la conquista de América*. Lima: DESCO, 1993.

Martín Casares, Aurelia. "De la esclavitud a la libertad: las voces de moriscas y moriscos en la Granada del Siglo XVI." *Sharq al-Andalus* 12 (1995): 197–212.

———. *La esclavitud en la Granada del Siglo XVI*. Granada: Universidad de Granada, 2000.

Martínez, José Luis. *Pasajeros de Indias: Viajes transatlánticos en el siglo XVI*. Mexico City: Fondo de Cultura Económica, 1999.

Martínez, María Elena. *Genealogical Fictions: Limpieza de Sangre, Religion, and Gender in Colonial Mexico*. Stanford, CA: Stanford University Press, 2008.

———. "Interrogating Blood Lines: 'Purity of Blood,' the Inquisition, and

Casta Categories." In *Religion in New Spain*, ed. Susan Schroeder and Stafford Poole, 196–217. Albuquerque: University of New Mexico Press, 2007.

———. "The Language, Genealogy, and Classification of 'Race' in Colonial Mexico." In *Race and Classification: The Case of Mexican America*, ed. Ilona Katzew and Susan Deans-Smith, 25–42. Stanford, CA: Stanford University Press, 2009.

———. "Space, Order and Group Identities in a Spanish Colonial Town: Puebla de los Angeles." In *The Collective and the Public in Latin America: Cultural Identities and Political Order*, ed. Luis Roniger and Tamar Herzog, 13–36. Portland: Sussex Academic Press, 2000.

Martz, Linda. *A Network of Converso Families in Early Modern Toledo: Assimilating a Minority*. Ann Arbor: University of Michigan Press, 2003.

Mattar, Nabil. *Turks, Moors and Englishmen in the Age of Discovery*. New York: Columbia University Press, 1999.

Mavroudi, Maria V. *A Byzantine Book on Dream Interpretation: The Oneirocriticon of Achmet and its Arabic Sources*. Leiden: Brill, 2002.

Meserve, Margaret. *Empires of Islam in Renaissance Historical Thought*. Cambridge, MA: Harvard University Press, 2008.

Metcalf, Alida C. *Go-Betweens and the Colonization of Brazil, 1500–1600*. Austin: University of Texas Press, 2005.

Milhou, Alain. *Colón y su mentalidad mesiánica en el ambiente franciscanista español*. Valladolid: Casa-Museo de Colón: Seminario Americanista de la Universidad de Valladolid, 1983.

Miller, Kathryn. *Guardians of Islam: Religious Authority and Muslim Communities of Late Medieval Spain*. New York: Columbia University Press, 2008.

Mills, Kenneth R. *Idolatry and Its Enemies: Colonial Andean Religion and Extirpation, 1640–1750*. Princeton, NJ: Princeton University Press, 1997.

Mörner, Magnus. *Region and State in Latin America's Past*. Baltimore, MD: Johns Hopkins University Press, 1993.

Muldoon, James. *The Americas in the Spanish World Order: The Justification for Conquest in the Seventeenth Century*. Philadelphia: University of Pennsylvania Press, 1994.

Mumford, Jeremy Ravi. *Vertical Empire: The General Resettlement of Indians in the Colonial Andes*. Durham, NC: Duke University Press, 2012.

Naamouni, Khadija. *Le Culte de Bouya Omar*. Casablanca: Éditions EDDIF, 1993.

Nader, Helen, ed. *Power and Gender in Renaissance Spain: Eight Women of the Mendoza Family, 1450–1650*. Urbana: University of Illinois Press, 2004.

Nirenberg, David. "Was There Race Before Modernity? The Example of

'Jewish' Blood in Late Medieval Spain." In *The Origins of Racism in the West*, ed. Miriam Eliav-Feldon, Benjamin Isaac, and Joseph Ziegler, 232–64. New York: Cambridge University Press, 2009.

Núñez Roldán, Francisco, ed. *La infancia en España y Portugal siglos XVI–XIX*. Madrid: Sílex ediciones, S.A., 2011.

Owensby, Brian P. *Empire of Law and Indian Justice in Colonial Mexico*. Stanford, CA: Stanford University Press, 2008.

Pagden, Anthony. *The Fall of Natural Man: The American Indian and the Origins of Comparative Ethnology*. New York: Cambridge University Press, 1986.

Parker, Geoffrey. *The Grand Strategy of Philip II*. New Haven, CT: Yale University Press, 1998.

Parry, J. H. "The Audiencia of New Galicia in the Sixteenth Century." *Cambridge Historical Journal* 6.3 (1940): 263–82.

Pérez García, Rafael M., and Manuel F. Fernández Chaves. "La infancia morisca, entre la educación y la explotación." In *La infancia en España y Portugal siglos XVI–XIX*, ed. Francisco Núñez Roldán, 149–86. Madrid: Sílex ediciones, S.A., 2011.

Pérez Bustamante, Ciriaco. *Don Antonio de Mendoza, primer virrey de la Nueva España (1535–1550)*. Santiago de Compostela: Anales de la Universidad de Santiago, 1928.

Perry, Mary Elizabeth. *The Handless Maiden: Moriscos and the Politics of Religion in Early Modern Spain*. Princeton, NJ: Princeton University Press, 2005.

Phelan, John Leddy. *The Millennial Kingdom of the Franciscans in the New World*. Berkeley: University of California Press, 1970.

Pieroni, Geraldo. "Outcasts from the Kingdom: The Inquisition and the Banishment of New Christians to Brazil." In *The Jews and the Expansion of Europe to the West, 1450–1800*, ed. Paolo Bernardini and Norman Fiering, 242–51. New York: Berghahn Books, 2001.

Pike, Ruth. *Linajudos and Conversos in Seville: Greed and Prejudice in Sixteenth- and Seventeenth-Century Spain*. New York: Peter Lang, 2000.

Pomata, Gianna. *Contracting a Cure: Patients, Healers and the Law in Early Modern Bologna*. Baltimore, MD: Johns Hopkins University Press, 1998.

Poole, Stafford. *Juan de Ovando: Governing the Spanish Empire in the Reign of Philip II*. Norman: University of Oklahoma Press, 2004.

Porro Gutiérrez, Jesús María. *Venero de Leiva: Gobernador y primer presidente de la Audiencia del Nuevo Reino de Granada*. Valladolid: Universidad de Valladolid, 1995.

Powell, Philip Wayne. *Soldiers, Indians, and Silver: The Northward Advance of New Spain, 1550–1600*. Berkeley: University of California Press, 1952.

Qamber, Rukhsana. *Inquisition Proceedings Against Muslims in 16th Century Latin America*. Islamabad: Islamic Research Institute Press, 2007.

———. "Inquisition Proceedings Against Muslims in 16th Century Latin America." *Islamic Studies* 45.1 (spring 1426–27/2006): 21–58.

Rappaport, Joanne. *The Disappearing Mestizo: Configuring Difference in the Colonial New Kingdom of Granada*. Durham, NC: Duke University Press, 2014.

Redondo, Augustín. "El primer plan sistemático de asimilación de los moriscos granadinos: El del doctor Carvajal (1526)." In *Les morisques et leur temps*, ed. Louis Cardaillac, 113–23. Paris: Éditions du CNRS, 1983.

Reis, João José. *Slave Rebellion in Brazil: The Muslim Uprising of 1835 in Bahia*. Baltimore, MD: Johns Hopkins University Press, 1993.

Restall, Matthew. *The Black Middle: Africans, Mayas, and Spaniards in Colonial Yucatan*. Stanford, CA: Stanford University Press, 2009.

Ribera, Julián. *Disertaciones y opúsculos*. Vol. I. Madrid: Impr. de E. Maestre, 1928.

Román Gutiérrez, José Francisco. *Sociedad y evangelización en Nueva Galicia durante el siglo XVI*. Guadalajara: El Colegio de Jalisco, 1993.

Ruggiero, Guido. *Binding Passions: Tales of Magic, Marriage and Power at the End of the Renaissance*. New York: Oxford University Press, 1993.

Rummel, Erika. *Jiménez de Cisneros: On the Threshold of Spain's Golden Age*. Tempe: Arizona State University, 1999.

Russell-Wood, A. J. R. *The Portuguese Empire, 1415–1808: A World on the Move*. Baltimore, MD: Johns Hopkins University Press, 1998.

Sanchiz Ochoa, Pilar. "La conquista como plataforma de ascenso social." In *Proceso histórico al conquistador*, ed. Francisco de Solano, 81–94. Madrid: Alianza, 1988.

Shah, Idries. *Oriental Magic*. London: Octagon Press, 1992.

Schutte, Anne Jacobson. *Aspiring Saints: Pretense of Holiness, Inquisition and Gender in the Republic of Venice, 1618–1750*. Baltimore, MD: Johns Hopkins University Press, 2001.

Schwaller, Robert C. *Defining Difference in Early New Spain*. PhD dissertation, Department of History, Pennsylvania State University, 2010.

Schwartz, Stuart B. *All Can Be Saved: Religious Tolerance and Salvation in the Iberian Atlantic World*. New Haven, CT: Yale University Press, 2008.

Scott, Heidi V. *Contested Territory: Mapping Peru in the Sixteenth and Seventeenth Centuries*. Notre Dame, IL: University of Notre Dame Press, 2009.

Seed, Patricia. *Ceremonies of Possession in Europe's Conquest of the New World, 1492–1640*. New York: Cambridge University Press, 1995.

Seijas, Tatiana. *Asian Slaves in Colonial Mexico: From Chinos to Indians*. New York: Cambridge University Press, 2014.

Sicroff, Albert A. *Los estatutos de limpieza de sangre: controversias entre los siglos XV y XVII*. Madrid: Taurus, 1985.

Silverblatt, Irene. *Modern Inquisitions: Peru and the Colonial Origins of the Civilized World*. Durham, NC: Duke University Press, 2004.

Simmel, Georg. *The Sociology of Georg Simmel*. Trans. Kurt H. Wolff. New York: Free Press, 1950.

Sirriyeh, Elizabeth. *Sufi Visionary of Ottoman Damascus: 'Abd al-Ghanī al-Nābulusī, 1641–1731*. New York: Routledge Curzon, 2004.

Sluiter, Engel. "Dutch-Spanish Rivalry in the Caribbean Area, 1594–1609." *The Hispanic American Historical Review* 28.2 (May 1948): 165–96.

Smith, Jonathan Z. *Relating Religion: Essays in the Study of Religion*. Chicago: University of Chicago Press, 2004.

Soria Mesa, Enrique. "Una versión genealógica del ansia integradora de la élite morisca: El *Origen de la Casa de Granada*." *Sharq al-Andalus* 12 (1995): 213–21.

Stern, Steve. *Peru's Indian Peoples and the Challenge of Spanish Conquest: Huamanga to 1640*. Madison: University of Wisconsin Press, 1993.

Studnicki-Gizbert, Daviken. *A Nation Upon the Sea: Portugal's Atlantic Diaspora and the Crisis of the Spanish Empire, 1492–1640*. New York: Oxford University Press, 2007.

Sweet, James H. *Recreating Africa: Culture, Kinship, and Religion in the African-Portuguese World, 1441–1770*. Chapel Hill: University of North Carolina Press, 2003.

Taboada, Hernán G. H. *La sombra del Islam en la conquista de América*. Mexico City: Fondo de Cultura Económica, 2004.

Tau Anzoátegui, Victor. *El poder de la costumbre: estudios sobre el derecho consuetudinario en América hispana hasta la emancipación*. Buenos Aires: Instituto de Investigaciones de Historia del Derecho, 2001.

Taylor, William B. "Between Global Process and Local Knowledge: An Inquiry into Early Latin American Social History, 1500–1900." In *Reliving the Past: The Worlds of Social History*, ed. Olivier Zunz, 115–89. Chapel Hill: University of North Carolina Press, 1985.

———. *Drinking, Homicide and Rebellion in Colonial Mexican Villages*. Stanford, CA: Stanford University Press, 1979.

———. "Santiago's Horse: Christianity and Colonial Indian Resistance in the Heartland of New Spain." In *Violence, Resistance, and Survival in the Americas: Native Americans and the Legacy of Conquest*, ed. William B. Taylor and Franklin Pease G.Y., 153–89. Washington, DC: Smithsonian Institution Press, 1994.

Thomas, Keith. *Religion and the Decline of Magic*. New York: Scribner, 1971.

Thornton, John. *Africa and Africans in the Making of the Atlantic World, 1400–1800*. New York: Cambridge University Press, 1998.

Tueller, James B. *Good and Faithful Christians: Moriscos and Catholicism in Early Modern Spain*. New Orleans, LA: University Press of the South, 2002.

Twinam, Ann. "The Negotiation of Honor: Elites, Sexuality, and Illegitimacy in Eighteenth-Century Spanish America." In *The Faces of Honor: Sex, Shame and Violence in Colonial Latin America*, ed. Lyman L. Johnson and Sonya Lipsett-Rivera, 68–102. Albuquerque: University of New Mexico Press, 2001.

———. *Public Lives, Private Secrets: Gender, Honor, Sexuality, and Illegitimacy in Colonial Spanish America*. Stanford, CA: Stanford University Press, 1999.

Uchmany, Eva Alexandra. "Identidad y asimilación: Cristianos nuevos y criptojudíos en el imperio español." In *Encuentro y alteridad: Vida y cultura judía en América Latina*, ed. Judit Bokser Liwerant and Alicia Gojman de Backal, 73–84. Mexico City: Fondo de Cultura Económica, 1999.

Vincent, Bernard. *Minorías y marginados en la España del siglo XVI*. Granada: Diputación Provincial de Granada, 1987.

Vinson III, Ben. "Moriscos y lobos en la Nueva España." In *Debates históricos contemporáneos: Africanos y afrodescendientes en México y Centroamérica*, ed. María Elisa Velázquez. Mexico City: Instituto Nacional de Antropología e Historia, 2011.

Vitkus, Daniel. *Turning Turk: English Theater and the Multicultural Mediterranean, 1570–1630*. New York: Palgrave Macmillan, 2003.

Wachtel, Nathan. *La Foi du souvenir: Labyrinthes marranes*. Paris: Éditions du Seuil, 2001.

Weber, David J. *Bárbaros: Spaniards and Their Savages in the Age of Enlightenment*. New Haven, CT: Yale University Press, 2006.

———. *The Spanish Frontier in North America*. New Haven, CT: Yale University Press, 1994.

Wheat, David. "Mediterranean Slavery, New World Transformations: Galley Slaves in the Spanish Caribbean, 1578–1635." *Slavery and Abolition* 31.3 (September 2010): 327–44.

White, Richard. *The Middle Ground: Indians, Empires, and Republics in the Great Lakes Region, 1650–1815*. New York: Cambridge University Press, 1991.

Wilson, Kathleen. *The Island Race: Englishness, Empire and Gender in the Eighteenth Century*. New York: Routledge, 2003.

Wright, David. *Conquistadores otomíes en la Guerra Chichimeca.* Querétaro: Dirección de Patrimonio Cultural, Secretaría de Cultura y Bienestar Social, Gobierno del Estado de Querétaro, 1988.

Yannakakis, Yanna. *The Art of Being In-Between: Native Intermediaries, Indian Identity, and Local Rule in Colonial Oaxaca.* Durham, NC: Duke University Press, 2008.

Zea, Leopoldo. "Sentido y proyección de la cultura latinoamericana y de la árabe." In *Arturo Andrés Roig, filósofo e historiador de las ideas,* ed. Manuel Rodríguez Lapuente and Horacio Cerutti, 335–43. Guadalajara: Universidad de Guadalajara, 1989.

Ze'evi, Dror. *Producing Desire: Changing Sexual Discourse in the Ottoman Middle East, 1500–1900.* Berkeley: University of California Press, 2006.

Ziegler, Joseph. "Physiognomy, Science and Proto-racism 1200–1500." In *The Origins of Racism in the West,* ed. Miriam Eliav-Feldon, Benjamin Isaac, and Joseph Ziegler, 181–99. New York: Cambridge University Press, 2009.

ACKNOWLEDGMENTS

I am indebted to the many people whose generosity and support have been invaluable as I pursued my interest in Moriscos in Spanish America. I have benefited greatly from the mentorship and guidance of Anthony Grafton and Kenneth Mills, who witnessed the beginnings of this project unfold. Richard Kagan at The Johns Hopkins University was also instrumental as I began research, sharing his profound knowledge of Spanish history and the intricacies of working in the Spanish archives. At the USC-Huntington Early Modern Studies Institute, Peter Mancall provided immeasurable support and encouragement.

Research and the time to write would not have been possible without grants from the USC-Huntington Early Modern Studies Institute, an NEH fellowship at the John Carter Brown Library, a Charlotte W. Newcombe Fellowship, the Fulbright Foundation, and the Center for the Study of Religion, the Department of History, and the Program in Latin American Studies at Princeton University. An Andrew W. Mellon Fellowship at the Illinois Program for Research in the Humanities at the University of Illinois at Urbana-Champaign provided critical space and support for completing my manuscript.

Essential to this project were the efforts and expertise of the directors, archivists, and staff at the Huntington Library, the John Carter Brown Library, the Newberry Library, the Archivo General de Indias in Seville, the Archivo Histórico Nacional, the Biblioteca Nacional de España and the Real Academia de la Historia in Madrid, the Biblioteca de El Escorial, the Archivo de la Catedral de Granada, the Archivo General de la Nación in Mexico City, and the Archivo Arzobispal de Lima, the Biblioteca Nacional del Peru, and the Archivo General de la Nación in Lima.

Exchanges of ideas and personal connections forged over coffee or meals following a long day's immersion in archival documents provided much inspiration. From tapas bars in Seville to taquerías in Mexico City to cevicherías in Lima, the support and intellectual sustenance has proved immeasurable. In Mexico City I would like to thank Eréndira Gallo and her mother for their warmth and hospitality, as well as Gabriela Betancourt, Yovana Celaya Nandez, Guadalupe Pinzón Ríos, and Juan Carlos Ruiz Guadalajara. In Lima I extend many thanks to Mariana Mould de Pease for making me feel like part of the family, Miguel Costa, Marco Curatola Petrocci, Eduardo Hurtado, Gisela Hurtado, Sandro Patrucco and his family, Liliana Regalado de Hurtado, Margarita Suárez, and Rafael Varón. In Seville and Madrid I remain forever grateful to the kindness and generosity of Juan Gil, José Hernández Palomo, Nicolás Sánchez Albornoz, and Consuelo Varela.

Conversations over coffee and at various conferences and research institutes also stimulated ideas. Warm thanks to Thomas Abercrombie, Ida Altman, Michelle Armstrong-Partida, Jovita Baber, Emily Berquist, Daniela Bleichmar, Kristen Block, Sherwin Bryant, Antoinette Burton, Jodi Campbell, Jorge Cañizares-Esguerra, Sarah Chambers, Luis Corteguera, Ryan Crewe, Christian Crouch, Clare Crowston, Susan Deans-Smith, María Elena Díaz, Michael Francis, Barbara Fuchs, Karen Graubart, Mayte Green-Mercado, Sara Guengerich, Dianne Harris, Valerie Hoffman, Renzo Honores, Kristin Huffine, Javier Irigoyen-García, Nils Jacobsen, Craig Koslofsky, Karen Kupperman, Kris Lane, Kittiya Lee, Laura León Llerena, Yuen-Gen Liang, W. George Lovell, Jane Mangan, Laura Matthew, Adrian Masters, Silvia Mitchell, Aurora Morcillo, Anna More, Bob Morrissey, Katrina Olds, Lindsay O'Neill, Elizabeth Penry, Michael Perri, Heather Peterson, Juan José Ponce-Vazquez, Allyson Poska, Dana Rabin, Cynthia Radding, Carla Rahn Phillips, Frances Ramos, Leslie Reagan, Michele Reid-Vazquez, Monica Ricketts, Roy Ritchie, Dede Ruggles, Teófilo Ruiz, Elena Schneider, Fritz Schwaller, Stuart Schwartz, Tatiana Seijas, Jyotsna Singh, Maya Soifer, Carol Symes, Victor Uribe-Uran, Nancy van Deusen, Karin Vélez, Marta Vicente, Cécile Vidal, Ben Vinson III, Ken Ward, Molly Warsh, and David Wheat. At Washington State University, Lawrence Hatter, Steve Kale, Jesse Spohnholz, Charles Weller, and Ashley Wright provided insightful feedback. Others who provided me with advice and encouragement in the early stages are no longer with us, but remain *presentes* as sources of inspiration: Sabine MacCormack, Elsa Malvido, María Elena Martínez, Franklin Pease, and Alfonso Quiroz.

Portions of four chapters were published in an earlier form, and I am grateful to the editors for their helpful feedback at the time. Some of the examples in Chapters 1 and 4 appeared in "De los Prohibidos: Muslims and Moriscos in Colonial Spanish America," in *Crescent of Another Horizon: Islam in Latin America, the Caribbean, and Latino U.S.A.*, edited by María del Mar Logroño Narbona, Paulo Gabriel Hilu da Rocha Pinto, and John Tofik Karam (Austin: University of Texas Press, 2015). The section of Chapter 7 about the encomienda dispute involving Diego Romero appeared in "'Moro de linaje y nación': Religious Identity, Race, and Status in New Granada," in *Race and Blood in the Iberian World*, edited by Max Hering Torres, María Elena Martínez, and David Nirenberg (Berlin: LIT VERLAG, 2012), 81–97. Part of Chapter 8 was published as "Muslims and the Chichimeca in New Spain: The Debates over Just War and Slavery," *Anuario de Estudios Americanos* 70.1 (June 2013): 15–38.

Special thanks to Robert Lockhart at the University of Pennsylvania Press and to the two anonymous readers for their incisive comments. I would also like to thank Marilyn Bliss for preparing the index.

Finally, *mil gracias* to my parents for their love and moral support throughout this journey.

www.ingramcontent.com/pod-product-compliance
Lightning Source LLC
Chambersburg PA
CBHW030423100426

42812CB00028B/3073/J